THE BIG LEAP

Sharmila Kantha is the author of two books on Indian business, *Building India with Partnership: The Story of CII 1895–2005* and *India Unlimited: A Corporate Journey*. She has also published fiction and children's picture books. A former bank executive, she is economic consultant to CII.

Praise for the Book

'Perhaps there is no better time to read this book than now, when Indian firms are finding it hard to dominate the market.'

– *Outlook Business*

'This book outlines the remarkable structural changes that Indian companies underwent after economic reforms in 1991. It affirms the multiple positive dimensions of engaging industry as a partner in development.'

– Adi Godrej, Chairman, Godrej Group

'Initiated by CII, the book offers the experiences of diverse companies in building competitiveness and coping with huge changes. It contributes valuable insights to the overall conversation on economic reforms in India.'

– S. Gopalakrishnan, executive vice-chairman, Infosys

'The reform journey has been challenging and exciting, but every step has been worth it – for the nation and for industry.'

– Ajay S. Shriram, chairman and senior managing director, DCM Shriram Consolidated

THE BIG LEAP

HOW INDIAN COMPANIES LEVERAGED REFORMS FOR SUCCESS

An Initiative of

CII
Confederation of Indian Industry

SHARMILA KANTHA

HARPER VANTAGE

First published in hardback in India in 2013 by Harper Vantage
An Imprint of HarperCollins *Publishers* India

First published in paperback in 2014

Building 10, Tower A, 4th Floor, DLF Cyber City, Phase II,
Gurugram Haryana – 122002, India
www.harpercollins.co.in

PISBN: 978-93-5136-823-6
EISBN: 978-93-5116-033-5

2 4 6 8 10 9 7 5 3 1

Typeset in 10.5/14.2 Constantia
by Jojy Philip, New Delhi 110 015

Printed and bound at
MicroPrints India, New Delhi

CONTENTS

Foreword by Adi Godrej vii

Preface by Chandrajit Banerjee x

Introduction: 'Winners and Champions' xvi

1. Border-Dwellers: Godrej Group 1
2. Reinventing Banking: ICICI Bank 25
3. Triple Bottom Line for the Nation: ITC Limited 57
4. Life Sciences to Lifestyles: Jubilant Bhartia Group 83
5. Putting India on Wheels: Maruti Suzuki India Limited 104
6. The Power of Small: Nivo Controls 127
7. Next-Gen Legacy: RP–Sanjiv Goenka Group 144
8. A Temple of Modern India: SAIL 166
9. Journey to 'World-Class': Sona Group 192
10. The Perennial Pioneer: Tata Steel 215

Notes 246

Acknowledgements 256

Index 257

FOREWORD

The world stood at a precarious juncture at the start of the decade of the 1990s. Unprecedented geopolitical developments, accompanied by a shift towards globalization and advances in technology, set the scene for huge changes in the global economic order. The Indian economy, inadequately aligned with emerging economic forces, faced major macroeconomic challenges in the years preceding 1991. It was against this backdrop that the Indian government undertook the process of reforms that has continued uninterrupted for more than twenty years.

On 24 July 1991, the Government of India presented the Statement of Industrial Policy and the Budget of 1991–92 that were to transform the economic environment of the country. Resulting in substantial economic and social change, liberalization and globalization have firmly placed the nation on a stable and sustainable path to inclusive development.

The changes that began in 1991 encompassed the entire range of industry in India. The fundamental principles were to infuse competition and efficiency in industrial activity and to align it with the global economy. The new institutional paradigm for growth encouraged industry and entrepreneurship through a facilitative business climate.

Economic liberalization shaped a new growth and development model. This is most evident in the elevation of the growth trajectory, which rose from a 5–6 per cent average annual level to an 8–9 per cent level at the peak. Poverty ratios, too, have improved substantially, recording a considerable fall in absolute numbers of people below the poverty line. Human development indicators, such as life expectancy, literacy and the infant and maternal mortality ratios improved as well.

A modern Indian economy has been crafted over the last two decades since the reforms began. Today, India is respected for its knowledge economy as reflected in its iconic information technology (IT) industry as well as in innovation, management styles and sunrise sectors. India is carving a place for itself in new talent-rich manufacturing industries such as automotives, aerospace and life sciences. The globalization of the economy and integration with global flows of goods, services, people and technology have turned India into an attractive destination for the world's corporate leaders.

Within the overall transition, the experiences of Indian business present an interesting and instructive paradigm. Instead of being overwhelmed by the onslaught of global competition, Indian industry embarked on restructuring itself. The entire model of doing business that companies were accustomed to was changed, within a very short time frame.

Several key trends are evident in Indian industry sector in the reform era. The corporate sector's contribution to growth, savings and investment as well as taxes increased. Competitiveness, efficiency and productivity of the industry greatly improved over the years. Many companies exceeded global benchmarks of quality, and indeed are setting the pace today. New industry sectors led by advances in technology, such as IT, telecommunications, automotives and pharmaceutical have decisively entered the industrial scene. Finally, globalization of the Indian economy took off, as measured by openness indicators relating to export–import ratios and foreign direct investment (FDI) inflows and outflows.

I am delighted that the Confederation of Indian Industry (CII) has taken the initiative to present the stories of change for Indian businesses in this book. I believe that this publication will be useful to readers for learning more about how this section of society has converged with the overall aspiration for inclusive growth. It would also serve as a guide and inspiration for future entrepreneurs and managers.

The task of development and reforms is by no means complete. The next few decades will remain busy for policymakers and Indian industry alike as India fulfils its promise of inclusive growth. We look forward to partnering the government in meeting national development imperatives.

July 2013

Adi Godrej,
President 2012–13,
Confederation of Indian Industry and
Chairman, Godrej Group

PREFACE

Three months before the momentous announcements of July 1991, the Confederation of Indian Industry (CII) held its annual general meeting (AGM). As in every year, we had a theme for the two-day discussions. For this AGM, it was 'Challenge of a Free Economy'—at a time when a free economy was barely a vision. At the end of the conference, we brought out the usual manifesto for economic reform, without much hope of change.

But shortly afterwards, change hit the Indian economy like a whirling tornado. The July 1991 policy shift was far more sudden and comprehensive than anyone could have anticipated. Licensing, the mainstay of the industrial policy environment for more than four decades, was cast aside, not in diffident steps or by half-measures, but completely and irrevocably. Of course, a few sectors were still covered by licensing, but only due to security and other considerations, rather than to restrict the access of the private sector. This was accompanied by drastic slashing of import duties and allowing entry to multinationals, which exposed Indian industry to foreign competition.

As Tarun Das, secretary of the Confederation of Engineering Industry (CEI), as CII was then named, often said, the walls for Indian industry were hammered down overnight, just as the Berlin Wall had been knocked down. We understood that we were balanced at the threshold of a bold new era, an era that would demand total re-engineering of the way we did business, but that would bring rich rewards for our country.

In the years since that July, much progress has been made to infuse competition, efficiency and productivity in the system. Apart from abolishing licensing, the Statement on Industrial Policy also addressed foreign investment, foreign technology agreements, the public sector and the Monopolies and Trade Practices Act. Foreign direct investment (FDI) was allowed up to 51 per cent in certain sectors and this was progressively increased until almost all sectors were open to 100 per cent foreign investment, a situation that continues today. The role of the public sector was redefined and over time, sectors reserved exclusively for it were reduced to enable the private sector to enter practically every field of industry.

To say that the industry was taken aback by the speed of the reforms is to put it mildly. But its 'animal spirits' rebounded quickly. While in the early months, the industry raised concerns about policy decisions coming too fast—leaving it little time for adjustment—in later years, roles were reversed and policymakers felt that the industry was pushing for too much.

The story of how Indian companies adapted to the changed circumstances is replete with passion, courage, innovation and high aspirations. Undaunted by competition from overseas, they shifted track midway to undertake a range of strong initiatives to build quality and competitiveness. Simultaneously, they entered new fields and stepped out onto the world economic stage.

Small shifts had taken place in the policy environment in the late 1980s, encouraging Indian industry to plan for the future. AIEI, an association of Indian engineering companies, was at the time a relatively small and unknown organization. (We mark our history from 1895, when five of the then largest engineering companies had formed a lobby to petition the colonial government for local manufacturing orders.)

In 1974, some of the leading industrialists of the day came together in an unprecedented manner and merged two major industry engineering associations—one with its roots overseas and the other that of Indian manufacturers. Thus, AIEI came into being, an umbrella organization representing all manner of engineering firms, small and large, domestic and foreign, public and private.

The new association moved its central office from Kolkata to the national capital, and took up the task of supporting the Indian engineering sector through policy recommendations and advisory services. In 1986, AIEI became a national-level body termed the Confederation of Engineering Industry (CEI), representing the engineering industry as a whole.

During the 1980s, CEI was aware that a fresh economic breeze was in the air for Indian industry. Leaders like Rahul Bajaj, K.N. Shenoy, Dr J.J. Irani, Dhruv Sawhney and many others supported CEI in taking initiatives for quality circles, environmental awareness, technology upgradation and other competitiveness solutions. We had already started taking steps in many directions, including overseas networking, when the 1991 reforms were announced.

In the ensuing years, the industry association, which became CII in 1992, worked hard to devise a smoother transition for Indian industry during challenging times. Opening up to the world was not easy. Indian manufacturers had been accustomed to operating in an economy of shortages, where production decisions were based on what quantities we had got licensing capacity for, and what raw materials we had access to, rather than what consumers wanted. The quality of goods produced was far from international standards, but this is what we were used to in those days. Compare that with the relentless design of products by global companies, their unremitting marketing efforts, their massive resources, their sheer volume and scale across the world. Indian companies were puny in contrast, expected to compete with imports and with multinationals in an environment that, despite liberalization, was still complex and subject to high costs.

CII basically took up the challenge on four fronts. The first was the very important one of making recommendations to the government for new policies. This was absolutely necessary as Indian industry felt it needed time to align with global enterprises. We knew that the opening of the economy should be done in a calibrated manner so that our firms could adjust. So, for example, CII made recommendations on tax reforms, financial sector reforms, FDI and so on, the idea being to evolve the best set of policies that would give domestic firms a level playing field. To be sure, CII's suggestions to the government were often more liberal than what the industry captains wanted, leading some to complain that CII was going too far and too fast!

The second set of initiatives was to build a consensus for reforms within the industry, still shellshocked by the developments. Discussions, conferences, meetings and sustained interaction with members took place all across the country. It was often a task to convince industry members that opening up and lifting protectionism was good for the country, good for the economy and, above all, good for business.

The third set of initiatives was to build closer connectivities with the outside world. This we did through conferences and exhibitions with foreign participants as well as through dedicated business missions overseas. I must say that while in the beginning, governments and top global companies were lukewarm about meeting a delegation from India, this changed quickly and we were welcomed wherever we went.

But it was on the fourth front that CII truly became a pioneer. This was in assisting a beleaguered Indian industry to scale up the competitiveness ladder so that it could be on par with global companies. At a time when these terms were not in the lexicon of Indian industry, Total Quality Management (TQM), Total Productive Maintenance (TPM), cost management, energy efficiency, technology adaptation, and many other areas that would make a manufacturer do more with less became CII's expertise.

Some of these competitiveness solutions were introduced by us, such as the quality movement which CII initiated through its TQM division. Cajoling twenty-three reluctant industry heads into joining the committee on quality in 1986, CII built this up into a national endeavour. This was a time when the benchmarks of the International Organization for Standardization (ISO) were hardly familiar in the country, and we worked on getting the first ISO 9000 certification for a member company. The movement involved much persuasion, working with industry and the government alike, partnering with Japanese institutions and setting up new systems and processes, including the CII Institute of Quality. But these initiatives were rewarded in 1998 when an Indian company—for the first time ever—won the Deming Prize for Quality, the international gold medal for quality attainments. The honour went to Sundaram-Clayton Ltd of TVS Group.

Today, CII's centres of excellence offer a full spectrum of services for competitiveness, from agriculture and sustainable development to water and green buildings. Supported by top Indian companies, these centres are hubs for research, consultancy, innovation and training. They reflect the wish of Indian industry to align itself to global benchmarks of performance.

The task of economic liberalization still stretches before us. Many sectors of the economy would benefit from greater participation of the private sector. For example, the Twelfth Plan has projected an expenditure of $1 trillion in infrastructure alone, aiming to build roads and highways, ports, railways, power plants and so on. It expects half of this investment to come from private companies—up from a third in the earlier Plan—and has mobilized the model of public–private partnership for encouraging private spending. To actualize this investment, tax reforms, land acquisition, resource allocation and a facilitative business environment would have to be tackled effectively. As we saw in the high-growth period of 2003–08, private sector investments, encouraged by low inflation and contained government spending, can be the key engine of growth.

Indian industry has truly come a long distance from the days when its products were seen as substandard and of poor quality. These days, it is not unusual for Indian companies to be studied at top global management schools for their unique ways of doing business. Words like 'frugal engineering', 'jugaad', 'doing more with less' and 'diversity management' have come to be associated with our distinctive style of operating.

Most important, Indian industry has transformed lifestyles for people in all walks of life, and is driving change in an India of multiple transitions, across social, economic and cultural spheres. It has demonstrated how a robust and dynamic segment of society can propel growth for all, given the right conditions. As India continues to progress rapidly on its way to inclusive development, industry will be in the driving seat.

The Big Leap: How Indian Companies Leveraged Reforms for Success presents the fascinating stories of some of these companies, all from diverse fields such as traditional sectors, family business, public sector enterprises, and small and medium enterprises. I take this opportunity to thank the participating companies for sharing their experiences for this book. We hope that the book will shed some light on the remarkable turnarounds effected by Indian companies after liberalization, and will inspire fresh thinking on their role in the evolution of a new and inclusive India.

July 2013

Chandrajit Banerjee,
Director-General,
Confederation of Indian Industry

INTRODUCTION
'WINNERS AND CHAMPIONS'

When I type in 'India companies' in the Amazon book search website, the first few results bring up the East India Company. Change the terms to 'Indian companies' or 'India business' and the titles that come onscreen are either about native Americans or tell me how to do business in India. Then there are the management and case studies' books on other websites. But a recent historical reference on how individual Indian companies shifted gears after liberalization of the Indian economy is missing.

I started working with CII in 2004, and its then director-general, N. Srinivasan, asked me to write the industry association's history. 'It should be within the context of India's economic growth,' added Tarun Das, the charismatic director-general who had just stepped down after thirty-six years in the position. The research for the book, *Building India with Partnership: The Story of CII 1895–2005*, was fascinating. Following the Indian economic story during one of the most transformational periods in the nation's history, with a ring-side view within India's major industry association, I marvelled at the profound changes that Indian companies had experienced and dealt with in these two decades.

How did they cope with the sudden influx of competition? Why did they not just wither away to cede space to multinational conglomerates and how did they actually end up so successful? What strategies did their leaders think of to tackle the changed conditions? Twenty years after economic reforms became part of the landscape appeared to be a good time to answer these questions. As Chandrajit Banerjee, director-general of CII since 2008, pointed out, CII was in the best position to take up this task since it had worked so closely with both the government and the industry during this period. And so, we embarked on this project. We were fortunate to have the guidance of the then CII President, B. Muthuraman of Tata Steel, and the whole-hearted participation of a diverse group of companies.

This book focuses on the massive efforts that Indian companies undertook, first, to become competitive, and then to race up the global business ladder in an entirely new economic environment. Industry was a major beneficiary of the reforms process, but the readjustment process was not easy; in fact, it was painful and protracted. Accustomed to lack of competition, Indian companies had become inefficient and suffered from a lack of productivity. As the walls of protection around Indian industry crumbled, companies had to restructure completely to keep pace.

Be it industrial delicensing, reduction in import duties, opening of financial markets, or liberalization of foreign investment and technology agreements, Indian companies had to internalize the changes and adapt continuously. CII worked with the government to create the most conducive atmosphere for companies to do this. Led by some of the most progressive industrialists of the day, the industry association had over the years carved a name for itself in representing the views of Indian industry. CII now took on the mantle of acting as an interlocutor between the government and industry. Its members knew that liberalization was imperative for economic growth; however, policies needed to balance the playing field, so that, in the words of Jamshyd Godrej, chairman of the board of Godrej & Boyce

Manufacturing Company Ltd, Indian companies had the chance to emerge as 'winners and champions'.[1]

While, on one hand, it worked with the government, on the other hand, again due to the initiatives of its far-sighted members, CII created capacities in areas that would help companies restructure themselves. Competitiveness was the defining mantra for progressive industry in the years following economic liberalization. Says Chandrajit Banerjee, 'The competitiveness journey never ends—there is always another barrier to cross and another milestone to achieve.'

The ten companies covered in this book are diverse, representing different sectors such as the traditional steel industry and the modern banking sector. And they represent different organisational structures, including a public sector company, a company that migrated from the public sector to a multinational status, and companies that started out in the SME (small and medium enterprises) category.

These companies set new benchmarks for success, not just in India, but globally. Some of them completely transformed industries, while others created new sectors practically from scratch. The broad span helps us get an idea of the variety of challenges that Indian industry as a whole faced, as well as of the strategies that companies prioritized in their journey to success. Each of these companies has been closely associated with CII, driving the landmark initiatives of the industry association as its leaders at a time of change.

The Indian Growth Model

The story of the evolution of the Indian economy is well documented. After half a century of stagnation under colonial rule, the country achieved a jump to a 3.6 per cent annual rate of growth of gross domestic product (GDP) in the first thirty years of Independence.[2] Industrial growth averaged about 5.3 per cent each year in this period. And so, India painstakingly built the foundation for manufacturing from a virtually non-existent base, creating a diversified and thriving industry sector that could produce anything from steel to machinery and equipment to consumer goods.

Post-Independence, the Indian private sector industry was in no position to pitch in the required resources for building this base. The famous Bombay Plan, brought out in 1944 by leading industrialists of the day, stressed the dirigiste role of the government and the need to lay a strong foundation of core and basic industries. We may argue about the control regime, the statist model, the insulation from the global economy and other economic policies; but we must recognize that circumstances as well as the popular mood of the day governed the choices made in the early years after Independence.

The Indian model of mixed socialism created space for both the government and private industries to function, with the Planning Commission working out the modalities. The idea was to be self-reliant, which is why high duties and import controls were imposed on foreign goods. Everything the country required could well be produced at home, reasoned policymakers. But at the same time, there were just not enough funds, and it was more important to spend the available resources on steel and machinery and equipment than, say, on cars and refrigerators, which few could afford.

Basically, the public sector took command of sectors that entailed huge funds, while the private sector was allowed to flourish in designated areas. To begin with, seventeen sectors were reserved entirely for production by the government, such as heavy machinery and machine tools, iron and steel, and coal. In twelve other sectors, the government planned to set up new units, but the private sector was not debarred completely. In all other sectors, both the government and private companies could operate. Business was regulated across all operations, including the supply of raw material, use of foreign exchange and technology.

Above all, a firm had to acquire a licence before it could enter the sectors where private industry was permitted. According to the Industries (Development and Regulation) Act, 1951, all enterprises using power and employing fifty workers, or not using power and employing 100 workers, had to apply for a licence, which specified how much a firm could produce and where it could operate. Technology and inputs, such as steel and cement, depended on annual applications. The product could not be changed without applying for a fresh licence and getting new permissions. Over the years, the licensing system further evolved to reserve certain sectors for small-scale enterprises, prevent monopolies and take into account a balanced regional development.

A Licensing Committee, made up of officials from the Ministry of Industry, the Planning Commission and various concerned departments, examined each application for a licence. The committee recommended the size of the project, along with inputs and imports that would be needed, then sent on the applications to the Directorate-General of Technical Development (DGTD) for allotment of raw material. In case imports of raw materials or machines were felt necessary, permission would again have to be sought.

In later years, certain industry segments were demarcated for production only by small enterprises, defined by the amount of investment in the plant and machinery, to encourage entrepreneurship. Over 800 items were reserved for production exclusively by these enterprises at the peak of this policy, creating further restrictions. The Foreign Exchange Regulation Act (FERA) and the Monopolies and Restrictive Trade Practices Act (MRTP) also came into being, narrowing the space for larger enterprises.

The system thus served to curtail competition. Further, if firms obtained licences for producing certain quantities of an item, they were deemed to be meeting the demand as calculated so new licences for the same product were not issued. In this way, the existing firms enjoyed protection in their markets. But the system also led to shortages of various products, given that matching of demand and supply was not always accurate and the availability of inputs and imports were limited. For consumers, this meant much planning ahead and long waits to acquire items such as two-wheelers, telephone connections, refrigerators and gas cylinders, while there was little or no choice in the market due to the limited number of brands available at the time.

What was the impact of this situation on firms? Getting ahead in the business meant obtaining licences, rather than becoming more competitive, innovative, or efficient. It meant traversing the corridors of various ministries and departments to get clearances and permits, rather than spending time on the shopfloor. In fact, the shopfloors of most factories in those days were untidy, messy places, laid out haphazardly with little regard to efficiency. Firms with licences were generally content to maintain the status quo, sheltered from competition both from imports and local entrepreneurs, and as a consequence, substandard products were churned out, depending on the quality of inputs rather than the needs of consumers.

As Nadir Godrej, managing director of Godrej Industries, and chairman, Godrej Agrovet, wrote in one of his delightful poems:

'A licence then was a sinecure
A perfect method to ensure
A steady stream of easy dough
And this went on and on, you know.
The dinosaurs that roamed the land
I'm sure that you will understand
Had no need to innovate
For after all they were doing great.
But in '91 the meteor hit.
And stirred things up quite a bit.'[3]

By the 1980s, enterprises were aware that such a lackadaisical approach could not be sustained for long and the government, too, came to this realization. The lack of progress in alleviating poverty and examples of other emerging economies led to rethinking on the industrial licensing policies.[4] Some policy adjustments and fine-tuning of procedures led to a sudden jump in the industrial and GDP growth rates during the decade of the 1980s. Economists who like to compare pre-liberalization and post-liberalization growth experiences have ascribed this jump—in the absence of notable economic reforms—to various factors, such as a rise in productivity,[5] untapped demand, or, as Dani Rodrik and Arvind Subramanian put it, the 'pro-business attitude' of the government.[6]

The Revolution

Despite this spurt in growth, as the 1990s approached, the Indian economy reached a crisis point, with government finances in the danger zone and foreign exchange reservoirs close to depletion. Further, Indian industry was still hobbled by severe regulations and was pretty much closed to outside influences.

And then dawned 24 July 1991.

'Pandit Jawaharlal Nehru laid the foundations of modern India,' began the innocuously termed Statement on Industrial Policy issued that morning. Reiterating the government's commitment to welfare, the statement stressed 'continuity with change'. And then it went on to completely redefine the parameters for doing business in India.

'The winds of change have been with us for some time,' the document went on, '...In the above context, industrial licensing will henceforth be abolished for all industries, except those specified, irrespective of levels of investment.' With that, the forty-year-old way of doing business was relegated to the sidelines of history, and Indian industry awoke to a new era.

The statement went on to re-frame the structure for business in the country. It is useful to spell out some of its salient points, as it reveals much about prevailing sentiments that still continue to baffle policymakers. 'The Indian entrepreneur has now come of age so that he no longer needs such bureaucratic clearances of his commercial technology relationships with foreign technology suppliers,' it said, opening the way for automatic approval of foreign technology agreements.

The policy for the government's involvement in industry was revamped, recognizing that sick private companies taken over by the public sector accounted for a third of the losses of central public enterprises, and that the sector had strayed somewhat from the original intention of 'commanding heights' by entering consumer goods and services industries. Henceforth, sectors would no longer be reserved for the government, barring a few, and existing public enterprises would have more administrative powers.

The draconian MRTP Act was laid to rest by absolving MRTP companies from pre-entry scrutiny of investment decisions. Mergers, amalgamations and takeovers were also liberalized, and companies no longer had to look at the Act for acquisition and transfer of shares. Foreign investments of up to 51 per cent were invited for 'high priority industries', which included a 'long' list of thirty-four sectors.

But this was only the beginning. Later in the day, Dr Manmohan Singh, the then finance minister, rose to present the budget for 1991–92. 'In sum,' he pointed out in the speech, after mentioning a long list of troubles, 'the crisis in the economy is both acute and deep. We have not experienced anything similar in the history of Independent India.' Recognizing that it was imperative to increase competition among firms domestically to raise productivity, the finance minister added, 'The time has come to expose Indian industry to competition from abroad in a phased manner.'

In the next few months, this task was carried out with a fair amount of determination, despite a chorus of protests from the industry. A new policy for integrating the Indian economy with the global economy was progressively instituted, including partly freeing the rupee from strict foreign exchange controls, rapid reduction in customs duties and complete disbanding of import and export licences. With each passing year over the next two decades, a slew of steps was taken to open up the Indian economy, invite private sector participation and raise foreign investments.

The range of measures covered taxation, the financial sector, initiatives for individual sectors, disinvestment of public sector enterprises, competition, foreign exchange deregulation and other areas of the economy. Interest rates were liberalized, allowing markets to set them rather than administering them through policies. Share bazaars were opened up so that companies had new avenues for obtaining funds, both from domestic sources and from overseas.

All in all, the implications for companies in India were enormous. Simply put, this was akin to putting a trundling Ambassador car on the race track and expecting it to compete with racing Ferraris.

After the initial shock had worn off, industry captains responded with enthusiasm to the sea change in the environment. The risks were high in an uncertain environment, but in the next twenty years, Indian entrepreneurs proved they could take on the Ferraris of global business.

Progress after Reforms

India's business journey after 1991 is broken up into distinct segments.

In the first phase, which lasted from 1992–93 to 1996–97, the stress was on capacity enhancement and putting funds and inputs into new ventures. So, for example, Tata Steel went in for modernization, while the Godrej Group entered into agreements with multinationals. The R.P. Sanjiv Goenka Group's flagship

CESC doubled its power generating capacity and the Bhartia brothers went into newly-opened industry sectors. Companies also dealt with internal management conflicts, as did ITC, or went into new sectors altogether, like ICICI Bank. In the overall context, GDP growth was rapid, deriving from strong expansion in all three sectors of agriculture, industry and services. More important during this period, however, was the shift in the mindset of the industry, which led to greater investments.

The boom in industry in these first few years came as companies expanded and also from the setting up of new companies. Profits went up and so did the productivity of workers, as their wages increased. Freed from licensing for the first time, firms happily spent a lot of money to cater to what was thought to be a hidden iceberg of unmet demand. The idea was just to do more.

But in 1997–98, the tide changed suddenly. The Asian financial crisis swept the fast-rising Asian 'tiger' economies into a deep slowdown, threatening to engulf the global economy. This was compounded later by the dotcom bubble burst and the 9/11 attacks that, taken together, contributed to the slide in global growth at the turn of the millennium. In India, the government's excessive expenditure led to a rising fiscal deficit, while the nuclear test in 1998 led to sharp reactions from many nations which cut off aid and imposed other economic restrictions. Failure of the monsoons further added to India's woes.

The second phase was characterized by low growth that lasted for as many as five years. GDP pace faltered from 6.7 per cent annually to 5.5 per cent, and industrial growth came down from a rapid clip of 7.6 per cent in the period from 1992–93 to 1996–97 to just 4.4 per cent per year in the period from 1997–98 to 2001–02.[7] Fixed investments as a proportion of GDP remained at more or less the same level for several years, as resources were limited. Moreover, there were three general elections in a span of just over three years. Although the reform process continued with landmark policy changes in succession, the economic slowdown hit firms in the country.

Consumer demand just did not match up to business expectations and firms found that their investment spree had led to surplus capacities. This was a period of intense introspection by India Inc. Acknowledging that the situation called for a new response, companies now examined their internal processes, going all out to target productivity and innovation. They concentrated on consolidation and carefully planned out new strategies, putting in greater time and effort into the exercise. 'It was only as growth fell and profit margins were squeezed that firms started to seriously restructure,' pointed out Naushad Forbes, consulting professor at Stanford University and director, Forbes Marshall.[8]

So when the global economy started on the path to recovery from 2002 onwards, Indian companies, now leaner and fitter, were set to aggressively expand. The archaic vehicle of Indian industry was still small, but its engine was now toned and tuned.

And expand they did—not just in India but all over the world. The third phase in the liberalization journey is visible in the five years from 2002–03 to 2007–08. Income growth was never as rapid in India as it was in those halcyon years, as the average annual pace raced to a peak of 8.7 per cent. For three years, in fact, the GDP rate was well over 9 per cent, an achievement which enhanced the confidence and transformed the mindset of Indian industry—and placed the Indian economy decisively on the global map.

Several new factors coalesced to make this truly a phase of remarkable ascendancy for the Indian economy. The steady growth process of the last decade had gained momentum and a new class of consumers was now in the market, both in urban and rural areas. Interest rates had come down, while the banking sector had spread, making more goods affordable to more people. Growing incomes, changing lifestyles and preferences for branded products characterized the market. A younger population, rapid urbanization and an increased allocation for rural development schemes like the Mahatma Gandhi National Rural Employment Guarantee Act (MNREGA) and Bharat Nirman also added to the momentum. Further, technology and communications added to this potent mix. Cell phone connections soared at the rate of some 20 million a month, and software services became India's forte.

At the other end of the market, manufacturing and services, too, had transformed and Indian firms had realized the value of innovation. They also had accumulated resources internally, which they used again to build new capacities. This time around, they looked at opportunities and devised plans to take advantage of them. The positive growth drivers for Indian industry were focused initiatives and strategies of companies, such as mergers and acquisitions, overseas expansion, new product and marketing innovations and aggressive rural market penetration.

Although the share of manufacturing in India's GDP remained the same post-reforms, important changes took place in what was produced. For example, traditional industries using lower technology have given way to modern industries with more technology input. Similarly, more than two-thirds of manufacturing is now carried out by the organized or registered companies, and the share of public companies has dipped. Goods such as textiles, food products and paper products have declined in importance, and sectors using more funds and technology, like petroleum products and cars, have gone up. Significantly, technology use has changed after liberalization, with more capital-intensive goods coming out of India's factories.

Also in this period, more liberal policies allowed Indian companies to operate overseas and to access increasingly greater funds from foreign sources. This was the time when globalization became part of the lexicon of every large company—and many small ones as well—which thirsted to make it big. The big-ticket overseas acquisitions that took the world by storm came in this period: Tata Steel's acquisition of Corus, Hindalco's acquisition of Novartis and many other smaller takeovers that emphatically brought Indian companies to the attention of global investors. Looking for new horizons, India started punching above its weight when it came to overseas investments.

But it was not just investments that companies undertook overseas. Confident about their capacity to address new markets, specially markets of relatively poorer consumers, they went all out to sell their products in the international arena. India's exports zoomed from just $64 billion in 2002–03 to $305 billion in 2011–12. Exports to Asia, Africa and Latin America rose even faster.

The global economic crisis in 2008 halted India Inc.'s rapid expansion plans in its tracks, bringing the fourth post-liberalization growth phase. Funds simply dried up, booming overseas markets shrivelled up and trade contracted. The storm that hit the financial sector savaged the global economy. India recovered quickly, but just as soon lost steam once again. The GDP rate came in at an average of 7.5 per cent in the four years from 2008–09 to 2011–12, but dropped to a decadal low of 5 per cent in 2012–13. Even after liberalization, a high growth trajectory will require consistent efforts from policymakers and industry alike.

Going forward, there is little dispute that India is set to become one of the top three economies within the next couple of decades. And Indian industry will play a big role in this journey.

The Consumer is King

The biggest gainer from the reform process has been the consumer, across all income bands, from the poorest of the poor to the growing numbers of the middle class. The infusion of competition in the markets meant that companies had to actually look at what consumers wanted, rather than at what could be produced under the licensing regime.

In entire sectors, the choices offered to consumers shot up. As the number of players, both domestic and overseas, went up, prices dropped drastically, and the variety of models available in the markets rocketed. Refrigerators, air-conditioners, motorcycles, cars... the markets for these simply exploded. Innovation offered better and better products. For example, cars that earlier came only in three models now straddle each and every segment, from entry-level hatchbacks to SUVs. Food products, soaps and shampoos, and other fast-moving consumer goods (FMCG) seem to address every personal need, from branded snacks to suit every taste to shampoos for all manner of hair types.

In other sectors, consumers gained by targeted marketing efforts from companies, particularly in villages. The shampoo sachets that took rural India by storm are one example of goods made affordable to a larger section of consumers through innovation. Small packaging is now a staple of accessing markets in the hinterland, from phone subscriptions to fairness creams to spices. Similarly, innovation in products brings out interesting new items, such as the phone with a torch, widely used in villages. Easy funding options also brought more consumers into the market. The term EMI or 'equated monthly instalment' entered the household and quickly took over its spending decisions.

Rural markets have completely transformed under the impact of new goods and new models of delivery as companies reach out to tap changing lifestyles. For example, instant noodle sales are growing nearly twice as fast in rural India compared to urban areas in both penetration and frequency. Seemingly 'urban' brands in categories like deodorants and fabric softeners are growing much faster in rural India than in towns.

And then there were the sectors that metamorphosed

under the impact of new technologies, aided by the advent of liberalization—software, banking, telecommunications, pharmaceuticals, media, civil aviation, and many more. Who would have thought that India would become one of the world's biggest producers of medicines, manufacturing one of every five tablets, capsules or injectable doses of generic drugs? Or that it would offer the cheapest cell phone rates anywhere in the world? Or that its small cars would astound global markets?

How They did It

As the structure of the Indian economy and its manufacturing and services sectors shifted, the turnarounds engineered by the Indian companies covered in this book are inspirational. Indian companies have attained scale and quality benchmarks today that could not have been imagined before liberalization. Their engagements in the Indian market as well as overseas compare well with companies of other emerging markets. In fact, in certain respects, such as management of diversity, innovation and sheer hard work, Indian companies fare better. The term 'jugaad' (innovative idea) is being studied in management schools all over the world and terms like the 'Indian model of management' or 'the India way' are cropping up.

It must be kept in mind that the business climate in India remains quite challenging, despite the many steps to unshackle constraints over the last twenty years. Infrastructure continues to be a major deficiency, compelling companies to think of ways to ensure a regular power supply, move goods across the vast country and create supply chains practically out of thin air. While reforms opened up many opportunities, other sectors like education and skill development remain under-served, which means that a trained workforce is scarce. Administrative systems are not the smoothest in the world, and a project can require managers to make the rounds of hundreds of officials for certifications and clearances. The taxation architecture is complex and requires much navigation, while the financial sector is still not deep enough to facilitate financial engineering. In fact, in its Doing Business report, 2013, the World Bank has ranked India at 132 of 185 economies. But Indian enterprises hardly allow such challenges to deflect them from their aspirational path to growth.

So what are the takeaways from the experiences of the unique companies we learn about in this book?

To begin with, leaders made it all happen. Whether it was Ratan Tata or Dr J.J. Irani, K.V. Kamath or Y.C. Deveshwar, Adi Godrej or Sanjiv Goenka, each of them simply said, 'This can be done.' Then they went all out to get it done. The targets they set were never easy, but they came out with strategies to meet them. With the fervour of the obsessed, they drove, inspired, encouraged and supported their teams through their varied leadership styles towards a single objective—to be the best in the field.

Second, the leaders knew early on that they needed the complete commitment of each and every employee at each and every level, whether it was the management or workers. So, for example, Tata Steel managers talked to staff members to explain the new direction the company was headed towards and the role they were expected to play, driving a 'mindset change', as Dr Irani put it. Godrej Industries placed their employees' needs above all else, while Sona Koyo in its quality circles encouraged all its workers to contribute new ideas for improving processes. The Steel Authority of India Ltd (SAIL) instituted a set of incentives to fit tasks to the specific abilities of people and get them to put in their best effort. The one lesson from looking at the experiences of these ten companies is that every single employee of an organization is made to feel that he/she is part of its vision and that his/her contributions can make a difference. The human factor is the key to all achievements. 'If you want to be a good leader, it is not enough to just deliver growth and profits. You must also grow your people,' Adi Godrej tells his top managers.

Third, quality was a common underlying factor for all the companies. It is perhaps little realized that firm-level competitiveness played a huge role in the industrial progress of the country after liberalization. The one major transformation arising from reforms was to thrust international competition into the market landscape. This was not accompanied by a similar transformation of the Indian business environment in terms of better infrastructure, lower regulations, labour reforms or other 'ease of doing business' parameters. In this scenario, the only way for companies to improve their productivity and counter global competitors was to relentlessly upgrade efficiency and lower costs.

Fortunately, there was plenty of space to do so.

Some of them went so far as to make TQM the defining mantra for their firms, relentlessly striving for perfection in all processes. But all of them developed a strong quality culture as part of the DNA of their total functioning. So, for example, while Maruti started off with the Japanese commitment to quality, it worked later on with its suppliers to inculcate the same practices so that its entire supply chain became faster, smoother and leaner, with minimal disruptions.

With the concept of quality comes efficiency and productivity, reduction in costs, least wastage of time and energy as well as process stability. It has to be accompanied by minimizing the use of energy, water and other inputs that contribute to the sustainability of an enterprise. 'Continuous improvement' is the credo of quality. The story of Sona Koyo, which internalized quality and sought nothing less than the ultimate Quality Award, the Deming Prize, highlights the unyielding determination that goes into making an enterprise a winner and champion. India, at one time, had the most number of Deming awardees outside of Japan, and this was no flash in the pan.

Fourth, innovation is imperative for success. The companies covered here all drove innovation through various means, either in the way they did business, like, for example, ITC, or in what they produced—as for Maruti—or the customers they addressed, like ICICI Bank. Research and development (R&D) is an essential aspect for the Jubilant Bhartia Group, whose business in pharmaceuticals is propelled by research, and for companies like Tata Steel and SAIL, which are always looking for more efficient and cleaner ways of producing steel. R.P. Sanjiv Goenka Group digitised a massive music library. For Nivo Controls, a company in the Small and Medium Enterprises (SME) segment, innovation was key to tapping domestic and overseas markets. New frontiers, as these companies have shown, can only be tackled through innovation, and a business culture that fosters and nurtures creativity proves to be agile, flexible and ahead of comparable entities.

Fifth, all these companies engaged deeply with society as a matter of strategy. Traditionally, Corporate Social Responsibility (CSR), derived from ancient social practices of charity, is entrenched in Indian business enterprises. In modern times, TQM incorporates CSR into the overall operations of an enterprise, so that a company that strives for quality awards is invariably judged on how it reaches out to society as well. And then there are the companies that redefined CSR to make it the heart of their business. ITC's social forestry and e-choupal initiatives impact 5 million people, and its sustainability and climate change efforts are part of its Triple Bottom Line approach. The Godrej Group has made environment a central passion, initiating an entire movement for green buildings in the country. Similarly, ICICI Bank's business extends to financial inclusion and microcredit in remote villages, which are as much a part of its general operations as its huge corporate credit facilities.

All these and more are defining features of the Indian

way of doing business, a way that considers business to be an integral part of society and operates in conjunction with the requirements of the nation in the larger context. The companies we learn about in the following pages are exemplars and award-winners. They have excelled in the new open, liberal economic environment. But they are by no means alone in their success. The Indian industry scene is replete with such outstanding and inspirational enterprises. They can now truly be counted amongst the 'winners and champions' of the business racecourse.

In their book, *The India Way: How India's Top Business Leaders Are Revolutionizing Management*, four Wharton School professors delineated the Indian management ethos as a 'holistic engagement with employees', 'improvisation and adaptability', 'creative value propositions', and 'broad mission and purpose'. 'India has a way of doing business that brings together business leadership with national leadership and societal leadership,' they write in an article, '...Indian leaders care as much about national purpose as about financial results.'[9] The narratives in this book fully illustrate this premise through the experiences of individual companies that have come a long way to define themselves in a brave new India.

This publication is part of CII's efforts to take the story of Indian enterprise to a wider audience. I am grateful to all the participating companies for their support and, of course, patience, in answering my many queries. A second volume is planned that will focus on the globalization experiences of Indian companies. As such, companies with a strong outward orientation, such as those in the software and automotive sectors, will be covered in the next publication.

The task of nation-building is incomplete and it cannot be achieved without the participation of industry. As India strives to evolve into a modern developed nation where each citizen is able to meet her potential, the fullest involvement of all enterprises, from the individual entrepreneur to the massive conglomerate, will be a central factor. The economic environment must be geared towards sparking and nourishing entrepreneurship—the small ideas that germinate in the minds of enthusiastic individuals and grow into sturdy businesses, creating livelihoods and changing lives.

1 BORDER-DWELLERS

GODREJ GROUP

Step into the Godrej corporate headquarters at Vikhroli in Mumbai and you enter a soothing room of green, nestled in a self-contained cocoon. You encounter a white and glass 'Space' office. Walk in, and you see swing chairs and multicoloured bean bags. Look around, and your eyes fall on a central mural in the shape of a heart. Look closely, and you notice it is made of miniature replicas of Godrej products and little snippets of its long history. You find books on design scattered here and there. While this new-age building may be more like something you would expect of an Apple or Google office, this is, in fact, the prototype for the Group's new global headquarters.

Is this the Godrej company of yore? For someone who has grown up in India, the Godrej corporate giant conjures up an almost symbiotic association with trust, as it immediately evokes the images of almirahs, those sturdy steel cupboards synonymous with bridal gifts at Indian weddings.

This is an exciting time of transformation for Godrej. The company's 115-year 'young' legacy is meeting up with India's promising future; it is innovating, building on its key imperatives and charting the course ahead.

In fact, the associations in the public mind are so strong that few know that the fledgling start to this Group, established way back in 1897, lies not in its signature locks, but in surgical instruments. From then to now, the company has branched out into everything from consumer durables and aerospace to processed chicken and real estate. Today, it is giving an unprecedented spin to this enviable heritage.

Like numerous other Indian enterprises, the Godrej Group, too, had its antecedents in the indomitable will of self-driven nationalists of the colonial era, who wished to prove the point that India was very much capable of developing its own industry.

Ardeshir Godrej, son of a businessman, trained as a lawyer in Bombay. Strongly believing that freedom from colonial rule depended a great deal on economic independence, he took a loan to make surgical instruments. Why surgical instruments, a difficult sector to undertake? The answer was simple—no one else in India was making these at the time. Ardeshir then embarked on lock-making. Instead of the traditional hand-tooled locks, he went in for mechanized manufacturing, setting up the Godrej & Boyce Manufacturing Company Ltd for the purpose.

The overriding characteristic of the locks was an extremely high level of security, thus ensuring complete peace of mind for the consumer. They should be 'absolutely unpickable,' Ardeshir believed. And so, right from its inception, the name Godrej went on to symbolize safety and quality. The solid Godrej steel safes, almost universally used by banks and companies, came to represent the ultimate in secure storage, so much so that 'Godrej' became the generic term for a steel cupboard.

From the beginning, diversification was the Group's mantra. Steel furniture, hospital equipment, toffees, detergents, refrigerators, office automation equipment, chemicals, real estate, aerospace... the list of products is long. Today, the Godrej Group, in its various avatars, can justly claim to touch the lives of 500 million consumers daily. At the heart of all products, binding the various companies together, is the Group's legacy of ethics and customer service.

'Antevasin'

Not so long ago, in 2008, Godrej undertook a rebranding exercise with the global brand consultant, Interbrand. The reason for this, quite simply, was the fact that while the Group was getting older, its consumers were getting younger. The iconic Godrej logo was recast in a new tri-colour and the Group adopted 'Brighter Living' as its mantra, showing a resolve to appeal to customers with original products and outstanding service.

'Brighter Living' was developed through intense dialogue and debate with scores of people across the Group companies and has now become the cornerstone for all people and process innovations. Tanya Dubash, executive director and chief brand officer, who led this rebranding exercise, says that by placing progressive consumers at the centre of their product and brand development, Godrej has created a contemporary and aspirational lifestyle brand, one that has appeal in both domestic and international markets.

At Godrej, the leaders refer to the Group's position today as 'antevasin' or 'border-dwellers', walking the line of trust, integrity and humility on which they have built their credibility. At the same time, they are learning to be young again as the Group rejuvenates itself to connect with younger consumers.[1] Nisaba Godrej, president, human capital and innovation, sums it up best when she says, 'Being authentic to who we are is very important, even as we progress and change. So, while trust, integrity... are important, we are also trying to be more edgy, quirky and more creative...'[2]

Walk the Talk

Adi Godrej is a man who wears many hats, each with equal aplomb, mainly because he functions in such a structured way. Discipline for him is not a creativity-stifling, mechanical routine, but the way to generate a structure and form patterns.

A popular part of Godrej lore is how early his days start. He is at his office by 8 a.m., a habit he began years ago when his children were little and had to leave early for school. He used to make it a point to always have breakfast with them before they left. After breakfast, he, too, would pack up and leave for work. Another practice that he follows is making detailed daily checklists for himself and sticking to them meticulously, so that he stays up-to-date on important matters. This is something that he has been doing for a long while now and it's a habit quite intrinsic to his personality and success.

A self-confessed fitness freak, Adi exercises for at least ten hours a week. He has always been very fond of sports and spends most of his time on water sports, the weekly Sunday water-skiing date with his grandchildren being a priority on his calendar. His other passion is travel. He enjoys exploring different parts of the world and happily juggles business and personal schedules to make the most of his time.

Being authentic goes much further than mere lip service in a company where Adi, as chairman, strives for reliability and genuineness. Looking back to when he first went to study in America, he talks of how he had to push himself really hard to make ends meet, something that he never had to do back in India. At that time, according to the rules, only a fixed sum of money per month from India was allowed to a person living abroad. He had no choice but to do several part-time jobs—and this had a great impact on him. First, he worked as a research assistant for Franco Modigliani, who was to later win the Nobel Prize for Economics in 1985, an exposure that was tremendously valuable to him. Then he worked as a bellboy at a resort hotel, which awoke him to the importance of providing services and the dignity of labour.

It may come as no surprise then that the Godrej Group was probably the first to introduce the 360-degree feedback as a process in India, at a time when it wasn't a fad. The 360-degree feedback comprises an evaluation of work performance where a manager receives inputs from not only his seniors, but also from his juniors in the company.

Talking about that defining period, Adi recalls how this bold new process thrust a feedback at managers and pushed them into learning how to accept it. Even he, as the leader, was not exempt from the process. During his own feedback, he was told rather bluntly that he was a poor listener, did not encourage inputs and reactions from others, was arrogant about his ideas and interrupted people too much when they were speaking. This made him sit up and start thinking long and hard about the kind of leader and colleague that he was projecting himself to be, because as he saw it, the worst thing that a leader can do is to not listen. The 360-degree appraisal is still one of the foremost people-oriented processes that Godrej runs today, encouraging a culture of feedback across different levels, and championed strongly by Adi himself.

Since discipline has always formed such a vital part of Adi's approach to work, he naturally tried to extend it to the functioning of the Group and how it approached its systems at Godrej. In his opinion, one of the most effective ways in which the Group has hardwired discipline is in the financial prudence it follows. The concept of 'Economic Value Added', or the measure of profits after deducting the cost of capital from operating profits, is used to measure the financial performance of the Group's businesses. This metric has enabled it to be much more disciplined about how it approaches capital employed in the businesses and remain focused on returns to the shareholders than it would have been otherwise. As he often says, 'For us, sales is vanity, profit is sanity and cash is reality.'

Vision 2020

Godrej evolved considerably in the second decade of the reforms process, enabling it to set ambitious targets as part of 'Vision

2020', the umbrella goal. Vision 2020 has four parts to it: (1) Grow ten times in the next ten years (2) Be the most trusted and innovative Indian brand (3) Foster an inspiring place to work in and (4) Create shared value through 'Godrej Good and Green'.

The whopping 10 x 10 proposition, to grow ten times to clock the magic figure of $33 billion by 2021, is an example of the aggressive dreams the Group is chasing. This translates into a compound annual growth rate (CAGR) of 26 per cent year-on-year and will be contributed to by both organic and inorganic growth by the two arms of the Group—Godrej Industries Ltd and Associate Companies, GILAC (which comprises the FMCG, real estate, agriculture and chemicals businesses) and the Godrej & Boyce companies (with fourteen divisions, including appliances, locks, precision engineering and process equipment).

Just having a vision, however, is never enough. If people are confused about what it encompasses and what exactly they are supposed to do with it, it fails to hold water. So Godrej has tried to make sure that its vision is translated into specific performance goals and that each team member is aligned with them.

Design-driven Innovation

Pick up any of the Godrej Aer air fresheners, which announce themselves as being 'here to change the air—the way it smells and the way it spells', and you will be struck not just by the sleek look and feel of the product, but also the funny, quirky slogan that introduces it. The bigger surprise is that this is not the handiwork of an external agency, but a 'Godrej baby' in every sense of the term, crafted and pieced together by an internal team of designers and production experts. This then is the hallmark of the 'new' Godrej and one of the biggest changes that the Group is making, as it embraces design-driven innovation.

Determined to leverage innovation as a key differentiator and have a strong innovation pipeline in place to create exciting new products, Godrej is pushing boundaries. For example, its Hit

Magic Paper launched in Indonesia is a paper-based mosquito-repellent, which burns only for a couple of minutes, but is as effective as a mosquito-repellent coil.

'We are constantly re-engineering our offerings on the innovation plank with the objective of serving the evolving needs of our consumers,' explains Vivek Gambhir, chief strategy officer, on the company's heritage brand, Cinthol soap. This enduring brand of personal care has been recently refreshed with a new personality and proposition, 'Alive is Awesome', to connect with a modern and vibrant young India.

Godrej refrigerators have always been a trusted buy. In a recent twist, the team created a variant, which plays music through a radio and an MP3 player. Offering a traditional white-goods product that doubles as an entertainment hub is a first. Innovation, however, is not new to Godrej and every contribution to this field comes with its own story. This is the Group which scored for the swadeshi movement by creating the first soap in the world to be made from vegetable oil, a reaction to the tallow-based soaps of yesteryear, which went against Indian sentiments. They also created the ballot boxes for Independent India's first elections.

Godrej is very proud of its Indian roots. Much of the inspiration for the company's first set of products came from Ardeshir's commitment to the freedom movement. A note from Mahatma Gandhi to a competitor finds a place of pride in the Group. Translated, it reads: 'I hold my brother Godrej in such high regard, that if your enterprise is likely to harm him in anyway, I regret very much that I cannot give you my blessings.'

The Group has always promised value-for-money, quality products. Today, this takes the form of the interesting Godrej Expert Rich Crème hair colour, crème offered in the sachet format for the first time in India, at a surprisingly affordable price point.

Godrej & Boyce has set up a 25,000-square-foot incubation

zone, the idea of Navroze Godrej, son of Jamshyd Godrej, chairman and managing director, Godrej & Boyce, who is currently a director at the company. This space is meant to encourage people and get them inspired by what consumers want. One of its big achievements is the oft-quoted example of 'ChotuKool', the unconventional cooling solution of portable, low-cost refrigerators, targeted at the bottom of the pyramid segment in India, which has become a *Harvard Business Review* case study.

So, whether it is the stylish-cum-friendly Godrej Interio furniture, the imaginative spaces being built by Godrej Properties, the world of gourmet food retailing at Godrej Nature's Basket or even ergonomically designed bars of bathing soap, Godrej is actively reimagining and remaking itself.

Simple, Authentic, Edgy

With so much change, it comes as no surprise then that the biggest focus in the Group is people. Godrej has always been known for its old-school charm and stability, but these qualities, like the rest of the company, are evolving into something much greater. The ambitious vision and thirst for being bigger and better has meant that the culture at Godrej needs to be more oriented towards innovation and customer-centricity.

In line with the 'Brighter Living' philosophy, Godrej has also recalibrated its values and what it will stand for. These are now articulated as Progression ('from small steps to giant leaps, we believe in constantly moving forward'), Expression ('thoughts and feelings; hopes and dreams; the things that make you who you are; they should always be expressed'), Empathy ('a deep understanding of people, their life and their situation is the foundation of any good relationship') and Experience ('everything we do creates an experience for someone, let's make them good ones'). Tying this all together is Trust ('Godrej is not what we say it is, it is what our customers believe it is').

'Trust is the first word that you associate with Godrej. For us, this is a huge source of advantage in attracting not only customers and partners, but also the right kind of people who want to work with you,'[3] says Pirojsha Godrej, managing director and CEO of Godrej Properties. The Group's new Human Resources philosophy, 'Tough Love', is designed to speak to these right kinds of people. It encapsulates a basic principle—the onus of growth will now lie with both Godrej and the employee. While Godrej commits to providing whatever resources it can to aid opportunities and development, the employee will be held equally accountable for coming forward and making the most of what is on offer.[4]

What is it that the team hopes to achieve by this? In a nutshell, outstanding people-performance by being simple, authentic and edgy. For them, 'simple' translates into elegant and aligned processes, strongly backed by technology. In 2011, the Group introduced the Godrej Capability Factors, a set of key capabilities to help build a brighter and future-ready Godrej, in line with Vision 2020. The three pillars that define leadership capabilities at Godrej are, 'Leading Self': being self-aware and self driven, 'Leading Others': collaborating with and developing people, and 'Leading Business': acting strategically to deliver results. These form the basis of all people processes and are used to hire and identify talent, review performance, provide feedback and structure development efforts for growth.

'Authentic' means that the Group will stick by its 'Tough Love' philosophy, continuously raise the bar and differentiate on the basis of meritocracy and potential. At the same time, it will make it a point to hold its values sacrosanct, inspire its people and make real commitments, not just lip service. The understanding is that talent management at Godrej will be as rigorous as tax management.

Though a family-owned business, and one which generation after generation of Godrej family members have opted to work for, leadership is not a rite of passage but a position that is earned. All family members who work at the Group are qualified individuals in their own right, have trained in the businesses and worked their way up the ladder. Adi majored in management from the Sloan School of Management, Massachusetts Institute of Technology. His daughters, Nisaba and Tanya, graduated from Harvard Business School and son Pirojsha from Columbia University. Their cousin Navroze has studied design at the Illinois Institute of Technology.

The youngsters who have grown up with the companies in their background are passionate about the Godrej brand values, and fully cognizant of the ethics and philosophy that stand behind the brand. Business was often discussed at the dinner table and the children, who now have senior positions in the companies, visited the Vikhroli premises regularly with their parents. Their deep and strong identification with the family business was the major reason why each of them chose to join the Group rather than take up other occupations. They felt it their responsibility to contribute to a family business that had the heritage of a century behind it.

Combined with their energy and enthusiasm plus a desire to innovate, the fourth generation has infused a new dynamism into the Group. The older generation has allowed them to devise their own paths and follow their interests within the overall structure of the organization. Interestingly, while the older generation was more attuned to manufacturing, technology and finance, the focus of the younger generation has been on brands, marketing and people, shifting the organization's DNA towards innovation and a consumer-centric approach. New ideas are discussed and elaborated, and the family selects those they agree are workable.

Nevertheless, the family part of the business has been institutionalized through dedicated interactions. 'It's likely they will be more jet-lagged and stressed than in the past, but with luck there won't be any food fights for a while,' commented *The Economist* in an article on Godrej's overseas acquisitions.[5]

Interesting new initiatives have been taken by the younger generation. While the brand makeover was led by Tanya, new packaging and premium new products were also launched. For example, hair colour powder, available as sachets for Re 1, was relaunched as Godrej Expert Hair Dye with a conditioner and a new fragrance at a higher price of Rs 9. The global acquisitions coordinated by Nisaba helped bring in younger brands, which in turn invigorated products such as Renew hair colour. Pirojsha is leading Godrej Properties' new growth model, tapping the need for housing among the middle class. Navroze's emphasis on new products that meet the needs of consumers in the Indian context has led to the establishment of the new-age incubation centre for innovation.

'They've grown up whilst India has been very successful... So they are very ambitious about what the company can do. I feel all my three children have the best of both, old-world values and new-world approaches,' said Adi in an interview.[6] And quite possibly, that is the best way for a family business to emerge strongly into a new era.

One of the much talked about stories at Godrej is the number of young thirty-something leaders who have climbed the ranks in recent years. Whether it is the head of Mergers and Acquisitions, the head of Godrej Consumer Products' largest international business, Godrej Indonesia, or the head of Corporate Human Resources, the company is living out its commitment of valuing potential over tenure.

The 'edgy' Godrej is being crafted at many levels. As part of a conscious drive to encourage diversity and build 'whole-brained', complementary teams, Godrej is actively hiring people from different backgrounds like the arts, design, or anthropology, to mix with a steady stream of engineering and management graduates. In a break from the traditional recruitment drill at business schools, the Group pleasantly surprised many when it launched ‘Godrej LOUD’ (Live Out Ur Dream), a project which sought to fund unfulfilled personal dreams. Winners were awarded with not just funds for their dreams, which ranged from a painting holiday in Spain to solving the water problem in a remote village, but also got offers to spend a summer working with one of the Group companies. The idea behind this programme is to find passionate young people, encourage their ideas and then invite them to bring that drive to the workplace.

Bringing people together from varied walks of life and encouraging sharing of ideas and healthy debates is ensuring that the Group’s culture becomes more creative, experimental and change-oriented. You have to work hard to create the right conditions for teamwork—it does not happen by itself. The Group focuses on ensuring that their senior management lead by example and act as guides, a philosophy which ties in with their company-wide policy of ‘Bedhadak Bolo’, which encourages uninhibited speaking out.

The ‘Design and Innovation Cell’, which has led the recent product innovations at Godrej Consumer Products, is a good example of how this encouragement of collaboration is impacting business. The Group also set up the ‘Godrej Culture Lab’ a couple of years ago. A think-tank of sorts, this lab is exactly what its name suggests—an experimental space that aims to interrogate the textured nature of Indian modernity by cross-pollinating the best minds working on India from across the academic, creative and corporate worlds. One of the much looked forward to series of events that the Lab hosts are ‘Friday Fundas’, Friday evening sessions with people from the performing arts, sports, technology, literature and science.

Learning at Godrej is taken very seriously. High-potential talent is now being trained by world-class professors, Bharat Anand of Harvard Business School and Hitendra Wadhwa of Columbia Business School, at exclusively tailored workshops on a range of topics, from personal growth to business strategy. Aspiring young leaders from across the Group also have the opportunity to apply for the coveted 'Godrej Fellows Programme'. The one-of-its-kind year-long programme offers promising youngsters a chance to work on high-impact projects, while being closely mentored by senior leaders. Apart from the tremendous exposure and learning, this programme is about thinking big, and encourages a meaningful questioning of the status quo.

Footprints on Distant Shores

For a company so rooted in the Indian business scene, it is easy to overlook the fact that about a quarter of the turnover comes from exports and overseas markets. From 2005, Godrej Consumer Products Ltd (GCPL) started acquiring enterprises in different markets that they thought would deliver. The acquisition strategy, called 3x3, focuses on three key developing markets of Asia, Africa and South America in three core areas of hair colour, household insecticides and personal care.

Keyline, the toiletries and personal care company that owns the Cuticura brand, among others, was taken over in 2005. Kinky and Rapidol, hair products, gave GCPL a foothold in South Africa, while the Group continued its outward expansion after buying out the Argencos and Issue Group in Argentina, Tura in Nigeria and Megasiri in Indonesia, all household product manufacturers. The company is placed at the top or at number two for various product lines in five countries.

Despite these overseas acquisitions, the company is focusing on domestic growth, especially in the exploding middle and bottom-of-the-pyramid markets. The international business is expected to contribute not more than 30–40 per cent of GCPL's revenues and profits.

Adi explains that GCPL's technology, products and business processes have translated very well into the international businesses. For example, per capita sales in Indonesia are higher than in India as Megasiri is a company of significant size and scale. In the hair colour segment, GCPL brands are leaders in twenty-one countries.

No Easy Journey

The Godrej family was one of the most vocal and ardent supporters of the 1991 economic liberalization. Jamshyd Godrej was vice-president of CII in 1992–93 and president the following year, at the cutting edge of the industry's response to the fusillade of policy actions. He recalls that most CII members were used to operating in a shortage economy without much competition. But CII under his stewardship, and that of other progressive office-bearers, emerged as a major proponent of economic reforms and went on to become a widely respected voice of Indian industry. The stance of the industry body was that liberalization was critical to economic growth; however, reform measures needed to be carefully calibrated so that Indian companies had an adjustment cycle.

Unfortunately, the government contended that given the economic emergency, there was no time to judiciously sequence policy actions. Indian industry, therefore, barely had advance notice to put its house in order before it was forced to compete against multinational conglomerates.

As president of CII twenty years later in 2012–13, Adi Godrej was part of a new era in the industrial experience of the nation. Reforms and governance were part of his agenda for the Indian economy, supported by the continuing drive for global competitiveness, inclusivity and sustainability as well as engagement with society.[7]

As a largely family-owned conglomerate, the Godrej Group faced several challenges after the 1991 industrial reforms. For a Group that enjoyed high brand value and well-diversified portfolios, the opening of the economy came with many new opportunities, yet it was not always easy to leverage these.

BUILDING A NEW FOUNDATION

At the time of liberalization, the Godrej Group was still privately held, managing the businesses with one supporting the other. 'We survived by having one company use its cash flow to buy the family's shares in another company,' said Adi Godrej. 'That way we kept control, and the family got the cash to pay taxes.'[8]

Openness inevitably meant competition. While Indian companies were small, sluggish and inefficient, protected by high tariffs and entry barriers, they faced immediate competition from huge multinational conglomerates used to managing in a cut-throat global environment and having the experience and resources to manage global complexities. The scale of the Indian companies was just a tiny fraction of these large transnational companies. The cry of protest that went up from Indian industry when tariffs were slashed was by no means unjustified—there was a real possibility that Indian companies would just shrivel up and disappear as global giants with their massive strength and funds took over the Indian manufacturing space.

But it was not so easy to crush Indian industry. In an unfamiliar environment and a new market, multinationals were looking for partnerships, and Indian companies, apprehensive about being swamped, deemed it better to team up with them.

The Godrej Group went in for a double-pronged strategy under the new regime to begin with. On one hand, it decided to strengthen its internal organization, processes and systems; greatly boost efficiency and quality; and add to its management capabilities. On the other hand, it went in for several joint ventures with large multinationals. While the strategy of strengthening systems proved to be highly successful, some of the joint ventures did not fulfil expectations.

Adi looks at the positives of joint ventures between Indian and multinational companies and believes that the many partnerships that the Godrej Group undertook in the first few years of economic reforms served it well, financially as well as in terms of bringing in new strategies. These partnerships were necessary for Indian companies which, for the first time, were exposed to overseas entities.

First Steps: 1991–97

Even before the reforms were announced, Godrej & Boyce had felt the need to deal with what was considered as a deficient functional approach that was bureaucratic and non-responsive. The company was streamlined into product divisions, with key persons allocated the tasks of product groups, a process termed as 'divisionalization'. A further development was a strategic partnership with the US consumer appliance major, GE, for the durables segment.

The Godrej refrigerator story is an example of the changes undertaken by the company. The Godrej fridge was a preferred household appliance for new entrants to the middle class, and the innovative use of polyurethane foam (PUF) insulation—Godrej was the first in India to use PUF and that, too, at a low cost—helped it become a market leader in the late 1980s. When the economy was liberalized, Godrej brought out new refrigerator models in a regular stream to meet the requirements of different classes of customers, from the 390-litre double-door for hotels and large families, to the 100-litre model as an entry-level fridge. In 1994 and 1995, the company introduced four new models each year, which was a remarkable achievement. Later on, it was also the first company to introduce refrigerators completely free of greenhouse gases: chlorofluorocarbon (CFC), hydrochlorofluorocarbon (HCFC) and hydrofluorocarbon (HFC).

Godrej Soaps, second among the three FMCG majors in India, was already used to stiff competition from its peers. Adi, who joined the company in 1963–64 and was responsible for launching a large number of brands since then, recognized that a different way of doing things was needed. Moving from operational affairs, Adi shifted into a more strategic role, working with a team rather than in a 'boss–subordinate' relationship.

A major decision was taken by Godrej Soaps in 1994 to go in for public listing. Debt was the main instrument for raising finances, but the cost of interest was high. It was the first time that family equity was diluted, but it is a credit to the company that the public offering was fully subscribed at an uncertain period. Listing the company unlocked some of the brand value and infused funds for undertaking new initiatives. Part of the restructuring exercise was to shift decisively to professional management. Family members chair strategic business units, but decision-making is based on consultation and defined criteria.

Diversification was the strategy that Godrej Soaps espoused for dealing with liberalization. Building on the brand and the Group's reputation for quality products, the edible oils used in soaps led to food products, while oil cakes, a residue from edible oils, led to animal feed. Godrej Agrovet, a fully owned subsidiary of Godrej Soaps, was already a market leader in animal feed, plant growth promoters and urea coating agents, cementing a strong relationship with farmers.

Real estate also went up in importance as the company owned a large plot of land in Vikhroli. The chemicals business, too, was diversified. Throughout the decade of the 1990s, Godrej Soaps continued to spin off new companies. The list was long: Godrej Capital for investments and finance, Godrej Agrovet for animal feed and agriproducts, Godrej Plant Biotech for tissue culture, Godrej International for trading overseas, Godrej Properties and Investments for construction and housing, Sahyadri Aerosols and Godrej HI-Care for household insecticides, Tahir Properties for construction, Puran Plastics and Chemicals for investments, Godrej Oil Palm Konkan for plantations and Ensemble Holdings and Finance for investments. Through amalgamations and acquisitions, Godrej Soaps demarcated the various businesses clearly.

Partnerships

A key decision was to partner with Proctor & Gamble, the new entrant in the FMCG market. The arrival of the global multinational meant that Godrej could lose its market position and cede share. Rather than go under, Godrej decided on an alliance with P&G, a venture that would bring in additional funds, knowledge and expertise as well as R&D. 'P&G was a great MNC and we learnt a lot in terms of business processes and marketing research,' said Adi about the Group's first joint venture.[9]

However, the Godrej Group's experience of joint ventures with global multinationals was mixed. The end of the partnership saw P&G retaining the sales force and distribution network built by Godrej Soaps Ltd over decades, which gave it a huge advantage. But for GSL, distribution pipelines for other products helped it to maintain its marketing chains. Adi regrets that too much was expected from the distribution network, which was geared towards a much smaller turnover, and the distribution quality suffered until it was painstakingly rebuilt.

G&B's 1994 alliance with GE fell through after six years as it did not meet its performance expectations, and G&B bought out GE's stake. Some of this may have had to do with the recessionary conditions in the Indian economy that set in after political developments in the second half of the 1990s.

However, other partnerships such as with US companies—Sara Lee, Tyson's and Pillsbury's—worked out well. Nevertheless, in 2010, Adi Godrej observed that few joint ventures are long-term 'marriages' and that globally, most do not last as long as a decade.

A New Strategy: 1997–2012

GSL began the second round of restructuring in the late 1990s. The focus this time was on the consolidation of core businesses, concentrating on a deeper engagement with customers and innovation. At the time of strategizing for a new leap ahead, consumer products comprised 47 per cent of Godrej Soaps' total turnover of Rs 695 crore.

Several measures taken at the time helped the company turn around its operations towards better growth and profitability. To begin with, the company zeroed in on four specific areas, namely, consumer products, chemicals, agro-based goods and properties. These were viewed as sectors where high growth could be expected, where Godrej had proven strengths and natural advantages to build upon and where the Group could emerge as market leader.

In December 2000, the board of directors approved a plan to demerge the consumer products business and form a new company. This initiative was meant to create a focused FMCG entity, concentrating primarily on a single business demarcated from the business in chemicals and other Group companies, such as properties. As a result of the demerger, GSL became two new companies—Godrej Consumer Products for FMCG products and Godrej Industries for the others. As part of the restructuring exercise, some key brands such as Cinthol, Godrej Fairglow and Godrej No. 1 were transferred to the consumer products company.

Simultaneously, the idea was to divest part of the GSL stakes in Godrej Sara Lee, which by then was the leading household insecticide enterprise in the country. Turning Godrej Sara Lee into a listed company would bring in more resources to reduce GSL's debt and improve its debt-equity ratio. It would also lower its interest burden. In a later move, Godrej Sara Lee became a hundred per cent subsidiary of GCPL as Godrej Household Products.

Several reasons were behind these two decisions. For one, the company had been prone to high debts, which was not considered efficient in terms of interest costs and financial ratios. Second, as a separate company, Godrej Consumer Products, which had been dragged down by less profitable businesses, would be able to achieve better sales. Third, the brands were not able to realize their full value in terms of capitalization. The various brands had a makeover, with Cinthol, for example, extended from soap, deodorant and talcs to handwash, shower gel and other cleaners. Also, Godrej Sara Lee repositioned its repertoire of mats, coils and refills under the Goodknight and Jet brands.

The Group has articulated its approach to business in the acronym 'CREATE', where the first four letters refer to its four core businesses of Consumer and Chemicals, Real Estate and Agribusiness. The T stands for Transformation to strive for the realization of the full potential of the companies, and the E represents Emergent or focused incubation of new businesses.

After 114 years of uninterrupted operations through various difficult business climates, the Group enjoyed a turnover of $3.3 billion in 2011 and employed over 25,000 people. It is India's leading supplier of a range of items such as household insecticides, hair colour, animal feed and processed chicken, ranking second in soaps and third in sugar confectionery. Its product lines reach final consumers through a vast supply chain that embraces some three and a half million retailers and its footprints are etched in sixteen countries through marketing and production lines, with brands that are as popular there as the Indian ones are in India.

Good and Green

As a Group, Godrej has always actively championed social responsibility. Over the years, it has focused on education in a big way, through its Udayanchal schools, the Dr B.P. Godrej Research Centre and contributions to Teach For India programmes and the Indian School of Business, Hyderabad.

Being environmentally conscious is another strong theme in the Godrej set-up, including close associations with India's largest conservation NGO, the World Wide Fund for Nature, and the construction of the CII–Sohrabji Godrej Green Business Centre, led by Jamshyd. It was the first building in the world to receive the Platinum Leadership in Energy and Environmental Design (LEED) award for being so environmentally advanced. Godrej also owns, conserves and protects the largest privately managed belt of mangroves in Mumbai, supported by the Soonabai Pirojsha Godrej Foundation.

Godrej has worked closely with the World Health Organization to eradicate malaria, an initiative that ties in closely with its household insecticide business, and has also built the Godrej Memorial Hospital in their township at Vikhroli in Mumbai. The 'Heroes Project', which convinces societal leaders to work as champions for a cause, is another unique project that the Group backs. It has also instituted the Indian chapter of the 'Table For Two' initiative, aimed at addressing the problems of hunger and malnutrition in the developing world.

In conjunction with the vision for Brighter Living for all stakeholders and Vision 2020, the team leaders at Godrej spent a whole year exploring what they could do to strengthen their commitment through shared value initiatives to create both social and business benefits. In line with this aim, the Group is now focused on playing its part in creating a more inclusive and greener India and have named this effort 'Godrej Good and Green'.

Godrej Good and Green is founded on 'shared value' initiatives. Here, the concept of shared value is defined as policies and operating practices that enhance the competitiveness of a company, while simultaneously advancing the economic and social conditions in the communities it is associated with. As part of Godrej Good and Green, the Group aspires—by 2020—to create a more employable Indian workforce by teaching various skills to 1 million rural and urban youth, to reach global best standards in environmental sustainability.

On the employability front, Godrej Consumer Products

has initiated pilot programmes to train under-privileged rural youth in sales. Participants certified by Godrej through this programme will be given the opportunity to get jobs with Godrej distributors or sub-stockists in these areas. The beauty, hair care and mehendi programme, 'Godrej Salon-i', has been launched in partnership with NGOs and equips women to operate as self-employed beauticians and hairdressers and also aids with training in entrepreneurship.

All the Group's companies are committed to Greener India goals and are striving towards reducing specific energy consumption, utilizing a higher proportion of renewable energy sources, becoming carbon-neutral and water-positive and eliminating solid waste dumped in landfills. Godrej Properties' projects are all LEED-certified and, in fact, its Ahmedabad township, 'Godrej Garden City', was selected as one of sixteen projects from around the world to partner the Clinton Climate Initiative with the goal of creating a Climate Positive development.

An example of how two goals have been achieved in a product—one that is not just environmentally friendly but also made affordable to under-privileged groups—is ChotuKool, a battery-operated container that cools food without compressors. To further help under-privileged groups, Godrej & Boyce is also making benches that can be used in low-income schools. It will be interesting to watch how the Group works with all its products to bring them to different levels of compliance with these good and green ambitions.

The Next Chapter

The story of Godrej goes hand in hand with the resurgence of India, now prominently marking its place on the global map. The Group's leaders believe that the tremendous potential of today and the unparalleled opportunities promised for tomorrow means that they have an increasing responsibility regarding how the future will shape up.

Take a look around at how societal issues are clearly gaining attention: citizens across emerging countries are boldly taking stances, acting as moral police and voicing their discontent. Whether it is an oppressive dictatorial regime, growing environmental backlashes or closer home, the uproar against corruption, the writing on the wall is clear. Success isn't determined by mere economic growth or profit figures; companies will need to build more sustainable models, complete with irrefutable corporate governance, and then live up to them.

Godrej looks all set to do just this. Armed with its big dreams, the Group will need to ensure that it continues to turbo-charge talent development, improve R&D effectiveness, keep up innovation and preserve agility and sharpen its focus even more, as it prepares to deliver the promise of 2020 as the year in which it will fulfil all its potential.

What better way to conclude this story than an excerpt from a poem on the Group's vision, penned by the lively Nadir Godrej, managing director, Godrej Industries and chairman, Godrej Agrovet:

Last year turned out to be quite good.
And yet it should be understood
The future too will be bright
If we always keep in sight
Our vision for 2020.
India will be a land of plenty.
...
And this we call **10 x 10.**
Our claim then will be very bold
In ten years' time we'll grow tenfold!
Now this can easily be stated.
But how is it to be created?

...

And yet the message should be sent
That values will be paramount.
When in doubt nothing else should count.
Newer values we should gain
But older values must sustain.
And let us live with ***Progression***
Empathy, Experience *and* ***Expression****.*

...

We should remember as we grow
That big is strong but could be slow.
We must acquire the ability
To react with great agility.
If we do all that is expected,
If our brand is loved and respected,
If all stakeholders benefit,
Our strategy will be a hit!

2 REINVENTING BANKING

ICICI BANK

Not many companies blaze a trail that redefines an entire industry. Certainly not a company with antecedents in India's state-led system of enterprises in the early years after Independence. And particularly, not in a traditional and conservative sector such as banking. Yet that is what ICICI Bank managed to do within a very short time as India's economic liberalization got under way.

In 1993, when an account-holder wanted to withdraw cash or save money in fixed deposits, she would have to physically walk into the bank. Generally, there was a long queue until the account-holder reached a (usually surly) staff member at the counter, who condescended to take the cheque. Another long wait followed as cash withdrawals typically took at least half an hour, while applicants for demand drafts to transfer money or for fixed deposits were asked to come in the next day. In rural branches, prospects for banking services were even dimmer.

A visit to a bank, therefore, required much planning and could take up an entire day or two, relegating other important matters to the back-burner. Any company that had to deal frequently with a bank had to keep at least one employee free for the job of running between the bank and its own offices.

It is astonishing how a single person's charisma and ideas can shape new paradigms in different fields. Narayanan Vaghul was one such person—he continually distinguished himself in his professional career through his innovative thinking, changing precepts and processes, and initiating ventures that would have a lasting impact. After an outstanding performance in various positions in different banks, including being the youngest ever chairman of a public sector bank, N. Vaghul came to ICICI Ltd in 1985 as its chairman and managing director.

The Industrial Credit and Investment Corporation of India Ltd (ICICI) was one of the financial institutions initiated by the government to make funds available for the private sector industry. Post-Independence, the country needed huge amounts of resources to finance its development but banks, then mostly in the private sector, did not have the necessary funds.

The government thus created an entire infrastructure of term-lending institutions such as the Industrial Development Bank of India (IDBI), the Industrial Finance Corporation of India (IFCI), state industrial financing corporations, and later on, insurance and unit trust companies. The history of the Reserve Bank of India gives an interesting account of the deliberations that went into creating some of these formidable institutions—a committee set up under A.D. Shroff of Tata Sons to examine the issue of financing private industry concluded that the then general opinion in the country 'discouraged and discredited' private enterprise. But the RBI was not convinced that banks should be allowed to offer long-term loans to companies.[1]

Nevertheless, ICICI Ltd was set up in 1955 to help the development of private industry in India and, just as important, to encourage overseas institutions to invest in Indian companies. However, unlike IDBI and IFCI, which were set up through Acts of Parliament, ICICI was a private sector development finance institution under the Companies Act. Private parties from the US and UK as well as the World Bank, the Government of India and Indian shareholders contributed to its resources. A British general manager was in charge of operations and the board of directors included overseas representatives. Right from the beginning then, ICICI was known as an innovative and dynamic private-sector-led finance institution.

Over the years, ICICI diversified its financing activities from providing equity and foreign currency loans to leasing, deferred credit and asset credit. Its repertoire of services included project counselling, capital issue management and syndication of loans, among others.[2] It also helped set up other institutions that served private industry in India such as the Credit Rating Information Services of India Ltd (CRISIL) and the Over the Counter Exchange of India (OTCEI).

With this background, ICICI in 1994 spun off its own bank, ICICI Bank. Within a few years, the new bank soared to become the market leader in technology-led growth and the second largest bank in a country where the banking sector was dominated by public sector banks.

The Banking Sector after 1991

I remember working in a public sector bank in the late 1980s. At the branch level, the atmosphere was quite lethargic, and we staff members treated customers as minor irritants in the important task of reporting figures to the regional office. We did everything by hand, from entering transactions, totalling long columns of figures and calculating interest that was due, to balancing the ledgers. Our bank branches then did not even have automatic calculators, let alone computers. The staff left soon after lunchtime, leaving us apathetic officers to put red tick-marks against the calculations. By the late-1990s, however, computerization of accounts in cities was complete, although transactions were still manually entered.

Private banks and foreign banks were present in the Indian financial sector from the 1860s onwards. After Independence, RBI became the regulatory authority for banks and the State

Bank of India (SBI) took over eight banks of princely states. The banking sector underwent a major upheaval in 1969 with the nationalization of all banks with deposits of more than Rs 50 crore. The rationale was to spread banking facilities to small towns and villages and to make it easier for small enterprises to get finance. Rapid expansion followed as the number of branches and amount of deposits grew phenomenally. This was followed by a second round of bank nationalization in 1980, which brought about 90 per cent of assets, deposits and credit under the control of the government.

The government then set the interest rates for deposits and different types of loans. Banks had to keep a certain proportion of funds in government bonds and other mandated instruments. They had to allocate another percentage—going up to as much as 40 per cent over the years—of their loan portfolio to defined priority sectors such as agriculture and small enterprises at low interest rates.

The entry of new banks was practically impossible and branch licensing policies were highly restrictive, leading to low competition. All these strict controls naturally resulted in inefficient and unprofitable banks, poor risk management and high rates of faulty loans.

In 1992–93, the twenty-seven public sector banks which dominated the banking sector faced bad loans, or non-performing assets (NPAs), of almost a quarter of all loans, with half of the banks falling into negative net worth. As with most other sectors of the economy then, there was little incentive to improve and drive competitiveness.[3]

Interest rate deregulation started tentatively after 1985. But the reforms process that commenced in 1991 was a game-changer for the industry. The 1991 reforms marked a complete shift in the mindset of policymakers, bringing not just incremental changes in policy, but setting off in an entirely different direction. Market forces were now to be progressively incorporated in the banking sector, and competition and international best practices were to be the objective.

Chanda Kochhar, MD and CEO of ICICI Bank, recalls those early days, 'It was clear to us in ICICI that the 1991 announcements marked a major shift in the Indian economy and the trajectory of the economy was going to be very different in the years ahead from what it had been in the past.'

The Narasimham Committee was set up to examine financial sector reforms and in 1991, it came out with path-breaking recommendations for a systemic change in the banking sector. In 1998, a second committee established under the chairmanship of M. Narasimham brought in the second generation of reforms.

For K.V. Kamath, non-executive chairman of ICICI Bank, the scenario in ICICI was different, 'At the time of the economic reforms of 1991–92, I was working with the Asian Development Bank and was not involved with ICICI. However, even from a distance it was clear that there would be a paradigm shift in the way ICICI and its clients would need to operate going forward, in terms of meeting the challenges that came with globalization and, at the same time, in being a first mover in capitalizing on the benefits of the liberalization of the economy.'

Among the plethora of banking reforms, the entry of the Indian private sector, foreign banks and FDI led to a new banking era. The idea was that these new banks would bring in the latest technology, offer better customer service and be more competitive and efficient. Most importantly, public sector banks, too, were allowed more freedom as government ownership came down and shares were sold in the markets. So public sector banks significantly improved their financial health, and the entry of private sector banks led to greater efficiency and productivity.

In 1993, RBI started accepting applications for a preliminary approval of new banks. These were mainly promoted by leading government-led financial institutions—ICICI Bank by ICICI

Ltd, Axis Bank by the Unit Trust of India (UTI) and insurance companies, HDFC Bank by the Housing Development and Finance Corporation, among others. The share of private sector banks steadily went up under the new environment.[4]

ICICI Bank

The winds of change were already whispering through the Indian economy at the time Narayanan Vaghul took over as chairman of ICICI. He sensed the direction of change and moved to set up many new institutions that would place ICICI in a leading position. The Shipping Credit and Investment Company of India was set up in 1986; CRISIL, India's first credit rating agency, was incorporated in 1987 with the partnership of UTI; the Technology Development and Information Company of India Ltd (TDICI), India's first venture capital company, was set up in 1993; and ICICI Securities and Finance Co. Ltd in 1994 with JP Morgan.

Even before joining ICICI, Vaghul came across a young manager, K.V. Kamath. Here is Kamath's account of that meeting: 'I was responsible for ICICI's leasing business, and Mr Vaghul called to ask me whether we were looking at a large aircraft leasing transaction that was being talked about. I gave him several reasons why we could not do the deal—it was too large; we had a limit of Rs 1 crore per deal; we did not finance public sector enterprises, and so on. He heard me out patiently and simply said, "If that is the policy, perhaps it is time to revisit it." We ultimately did not do the deal, because it was indeed too large for us then, but we learnt a lot from just studying it. This was the beginning of ICICI's culture of challenging the status quo.'[5]

Kamath, who joined ICICI Ltd as a new graduate of the Indian Institute of Management (IIM) Ahmedabad in 1971, went on to transform banking in India. In his first stint in the corporation, which lasted till 1988, he helped set up its new ventures for leasing, venture capital and credit rating. He was also instrumental in leading the computerization programme.

In 1988, he shifted to Manila to work in the Asian Development Bank, an entirely new experience that gave him international exposure and a vision of the global scale of banking. Indeed, Vaghul was largely instrumental in getting him back to ICICI. He gave the young manager a ringside view on key elements of the functioning of ICICI Ltd and its subsidiaries.

For Kochhar, liberalization was a particularly exciting time. Speaking animatedly on the immediate aftermath, she notes, 'There were three major changes that we had to deal with. First, the change in the policy environment meant that we would have to look at new project financing proposals differently. It meant that we had to now assess their global competitiveness, and not just their ability to compete with other domestic players.

'Secondly, many of our existing clients were impacted by the changes in the economic environment from a protected to an open economy and we had to decide how to deal with them. We could either treat them as unviable and write off the debt, or we could handhold them through this transition phase and help them emerge stronger. In many cases, we took the second path, and that indeed proved to be the right one as many companies which were stressed at that time went on to do well later.

'Thirdly, and this was perhaps the most exciting part, was that along with the reforms came the opening up of the financial sector. I was personally involved in this because when the new bank licences were announced in 1994, I was given the task of setting up ICICI Bank as a subsidiary of ICICI, and creating a new commercial bank from scratch. This was a tremendously exciting learning experience for me.'

ICICI Bank was envisioned by ICICI Ltd as a commercial bank and was incorporated in January 1994 after obtaining the preliminary approval from the RBI. It applied for a banking licence and received it in May 1994. In June that year, with a carefully selected staff strength of less than 200 people from diverse financial institutions, it commenced operations with its first branch in Chennai. In five years, it had sixty-four branches across the country.

THE CHALLENGES

It could not have been easy to enter what was essentially an entirely new business for ICICI. The bank would have direct dealings with depositors and borrowers on a much lower scale than it was accustomed to with its premier corporate clients. This required a totally different set of strategies. As Kamath stresses, 'We had no competency in banking because we were a term lender, not a retail player. Nor did we have any products, or distribution, or processes, or people. In fact, we had nothing except confidence in our ability to use technology and leaders who we thought could drive the business.'[6]

But in the very first year of inception, the bank displayed its intrinsic avant-garde way of doing things.

According to the first annual report, 'The Bank has been alert to the emerging market trends. When interest rates on deposits were deregulated by the RBI in November 1994 with a cap on the maximum rate of interest payable, the Bank was the first to offer the highest rate, setting thereby a trend in favour of the depositors.'

It also developed a reputation as an active participant in the domestic money market, calibrating its funds deployment carefully to maintain safety as well as to ensure quick funds when required at short notice for credit. International treasury operations, too, commenced in the first year with the operationalization of its dealing room and again, it was the first bank in India to be accorded the status of 'designated' bank to handle accounts of foreign institutional investors.

Elaborating on the key challenges faced by the new bank, Kamath says, 'When I came back to India and to ICICI as its CEO in 1996, there were clearly three things I saw as priorities. The first was diversification. This itself had two legs: one was diversification of our bread-and-butter corporate business from pure project finance to the full range of corporate finance and banking, and expanding our client base to include companies we would not have had significant dealings with earlier since they did not require project loans. This was driven by the fact that our project finance clients were going through a lot of pain as global competition came in and the country became more exposed to global risks like the Asian crisis.

'The next leg of diversification was our entry into retail, which was a completely new and untested area—but our entry was driven by the diversification imperative as well as my firm belief, based on what I had seen in other Asian countries, that retail banking booms as a country crosses a certain level of per capita income. The second priority was to get in the right quantum of capital to strengthen the balance sheet and support growth diversification, which we did proactively very soon after I came back with our GDR (Global Depository Receipt) issue.

'The third was to have the right organization structure, right people and right HR processes to be able to build these new businesses and compete and grow in this new environment.'

Kochhar adds, 'I think the key challenge was that we had to transition from being a company that only gave loans for manufacturing sector projects to diversifying into many new areas in the financial sector. This was important not only from the perspective of sustaining growth, but also to maintain a healthy risk and financial profile.

'The good thing was that there were so many opportunities to expand—be it in asset management or commercial banking or infrastructure financing or retail. But we had to build the capabilities required for each of these areas. In those years, the organization adopted a strategy of entering each and every area of financial services and backing these ventures with people and capabilities.

'Even though I was a relatively young business head at that

time, the organization gave me full empowerment to build new businesses. I was given the responsibility of expanding our existing corporate project finance business to a comprehensive corporate banking business, covering all products and services and building new relationships with companies that were not our clients in the past because they were not taking project loans. This ability and willingness to empower young leaders to build businesses in new areas was our major distinguishing factor.'

Setting Forth

By the time the bank completed its first five years of operations, it had achieved great success and was ready to take business to a new platform. The second half of the 1990s was not a good period for the Indian economy, which was witnessing a comprehensive slowdown.

However, Kamath and his team were not going to let a minor hiccup like widespread GDP deceleration detract from their plans. A new aggression and drive marked its growth during 1998–99, described as a watershed year. McKinsey and Co. was hired to advise on Group restructuring, and new synergies were harnessed through a new logo. Several new initiatives came about in the next five years, placing the bank at the top position among private banks.

To begin with, the parent company, ICICI Ltd, became the first Indian company to seek and obtain a listing on the prestigious New York Stock Exchange. This was not an easy process, requiring compliance with the US accounting principles audit, but with determination, the financial institution achieved it in only four months. On 22 September 1999, Kamath started the company's first trading session in New York, when it became only the second Asian bank to be listed. Within six months, ICICI Bank too followed suit, raising $175 million through the American Depository Receipts (ADR).

Indeed, ICICI Bank first went in for a $125 million fund-raising approval, which was later increased to $175 million. This meant that all approvals that were in place had to be obtained all over again for the increased amount. Officials at the RBI, the Securities and Exchange Board of India, the Department of Company Affairs, the Foreign Investment Promotion Board, etc. had to be again taken through the entire paper work. The whole exercise, from taking the decision to tap international markets to the day on which the bank received its funds, took a record short period of just sixty-nine days. After the ADR issue, the increase in its net worth propelled the bank into the top ten ranks of banks in India in terms of net worth.

Another innovative development in its progress was the structuring of its operations into three units to meet specific requirements: corporate banking, retail banking and the treasury. Leveraging the parent company's various divisions such as the Major Clients Group, the Growth Clients Group and the Personal Financial Services Group, ICICI and ICICI Bank together were able to take advantage of a combined corporate client base to market their diverse products and offerings.

Among the new initiatives that the bank took was acquisitions of existing companies. It bought out the Shipping Credit and Investment Corporation of India (SCICI), ITC Classic Finance, and finally, the Bank of Madura in 2001. The Bank of Madura was fifty-seven years old and had a wide reach, especially with small businesses. With this move, ICICI Bank emerged as the largest private sector bank in the country with 355 outlets. From just over six lakh customer accounts, the number of accounts went up to 32 lakh. Retail deposits, aggregating thousands of savings and current bank accounts, now soared to Rs 16.4 crore, moving from 31 per cent of total deposits to over 60 per cent, and affirming the bank's customer-orientation.

Here is what the reputed international magazine *The Economist* had to say about this development: 'India's banking industry is a land of state-owned zombies, shared by a handful of little private banks that attempt to dodge their footfalls. There was a brief stir in this land last month, when one of India's most go-ahead private banks announced that it would swap shares with one of the country's oldest. ICICI Bank and Bank of Madura plan to create India's largest private bank, with hopes of taking on the zombies.'[7]

A key advantage of the acquisition was the erstwhile Bank of Madura's strengths in micro-credit, a new form of customer finance targeted at the poorest of account-holders and a concept that was just beginning to take shape in India. This would provide the launching pad for ICICI Bank's entire rural credit drive that was to come in later years.

Finally, the natural conclusion of its phenomenal expansion was at hand. In 2002, ICICI Bank conducted a reverse merger—it subsumed its parent company ICICI Ltd into itself. It also merged two of the parent company's subsidiaries, forming one new entity, which Chairman Vaghul referred to as a 'virtual universal bank'.

This could happen after the central bank permitted financial institutions to convert themselves into banks. Taking full advantage of this, the ICICI Group moved quickly to create a new financial institution that would provide multiple formats of service delivery, from retail customers to large corporate clients. Within six months, it had completed all the requirements of raising the required finance, meeting regulatory criteria, getting approvals and managing staff. As Kamath said, 'We adopted the Silicon Valley's ninety-day rule in banking services. This was the first time that a business was placing speed—speed to market, speed to execute—as an important component of business success.'

Where did all these ideas come from? Kochhar explains, 'One of our core philosophies has been an openness to learning from anywhere (including from organizations outside the financial sector), and creating an environment within the organization that encourages innovation and a free flow of ideas.

'For example, when I was the head of the retail business, I learnt about service from the airline and hospitality sectors, and process efficiency from the automobiles sector. In some areas—like the use of technology in retail banking—we took our own calls. At a time when there were only 100 ATMs in the country, we said we will set up 1000 ATMs and we believed that the customers would use them. And our call proved right when customers embraced the convenience of technology and we saw a dramatic shift in transactions from branches to alternate channels. This actually triggered a transformation in the banking industry in India.'

The early successes evoked larger aspirations. By this time, the continuing reform process had opened more avenues for entrepreneurs and in the banking sector. Restrictions on foreign exchange transactions were falling, and Indian companies were being permitted to make overseas investments and tap overseas sources of funds. This brought an entirely new category of customers to Indian banks. Thus, the bank formulated a three-pronged strategy for growth—retail banking, international banking and cross-selling. All this was to be achieved with technology as the bedrock.

In 2000, ICICI Bank obtained an in-principle approval for setting up a representative office in New York. The idea was two-fold: the first, to tap the growing and increasingly wealthy community of overseas Indians who were now looking to the new resurgent India for opportunities, and the second, to enable Indian companies to expand on the global stage. The New York office came up in 2002, and a representative office was set up in London as well the same year. The overseas expansion continued the next year with a subsidiary in Canada, offshore banking in Singapore and representative offices in Dubai and Shanghai. As of 2012, ICICI Bank had operations in nineteen countries.

As Kamath puts it, 'The ideas came from my experience of what had happened in other countries, and what we saw happening around us and how things were changing as we went along. For example, the entry into retail was based on the experience of how the retail banking opportunity had opened up in other countries as they crossed a certain level of per capita income. The retail delivery model—combining technology and feet-on-street—in a way was something that foreign banks operating in India were already trying to do; we took that model and scaled it up in a much more cost-efficient way.

'The ninety-day rule came from a session with Silicon Valley entrepreneurs, and I at once asked my team, which was then working on an e-trading platform, to deliver it in ninety days! They didn't meet the ninety-day deadline, but they did deliver it in a much shorter time than was originally planned.

'In some areas, we had nothing to go by and took our own calls—for example, our belief that a distributed technology architecture was the way to go and not mainframes, was untested and based on our understanding of how technology was moving. I think these approaches led to some major success: we transformed the way retail banking was done in India, created a technology architecture that matched the capabilities of global banks at a much lower cost, and achieved our organizational goals of diversification and becoming a universal financial services provider.'

Building Customer Recall

It was in the area of conventional banking, in the form of mass deposits and lending, that the bank redefined the industry's business model. The bank moved quickly to identify gaps in customer service and initiated its mission for providing a new customer focus to banking and bringing efficiency and responsiveness into interactions with clients. For ordinary account-holders, long used to being supplicants rather than customers, this new banking experience was a fresh breeze.

Speed, innovation, technology, range of products and high quality of service—all of these were novel to bank customers.

It was important to attract as many depositors as possible in order to build the base for profitable operations. Three years after it commenced, the bank had almost 50,000 accounts. It went all out to add customers and mobilize deposits.

With the slogan of 'We make banking a pleasure', the bank systematically wooed depositors with advertisements and new products. The different types of deposits were given classy and attractive names, 'Money Plus' for current accounts, 'Treasure Chest' for locker facilities and so on. Within six years, before the merger with the Bank of Madura, the number of retail customers had soared to 6,37,000 and deposits were close to Rs 10,000 crore.

With intense campaigning, ICICI Bank literally 'blanketed' the market. Direct mail, telemarketing, TV, hoardings, newspapers... the company pulled out all stops, notching up among the highest expenditures on ads by private banks. It was well on the way to becoming an iconic brand and a household name.

'We used a technology-intensive model to develop delivery channels like ATMs and the Internet. The effect on the customer was significant. For the first time, the Indian customer was able to carry out his/her transactions without even visiting a branch. We rolled out similar propositions for our large, medium and small corporate customers. Convenience became a key element of our customer proposition,' says Kamath.

Year after year, in the initial period of operations, the bank added new feathers to its cap. Accessibility and convenience were its driving concerns, creating an enhanced customer interface by being present 'everywhere'. It designed products specifically targeted at niche customer groups, such as NRI services for overseas Indians, Kid-e-bank to teach children banking and Bank@campus for college students. And it delivered these services through different platforms that were just beginning to emerge—actual branches, ATMs, call centres, the Internet and mobile phones.

ATMs were a special attraction. Starting in the first year with five ATM machines, ICICI provided customers—who were used to 11 a.m. to 2 p.m. bank operation hours till then—a 24-hour facility for cash withdrawal. This was unheard of and generated much interest, especially among younger account-holders for whom the flexibility of the service was a lifestyle feature. By the turn of the millennium, the bank had set up 175 ATMs, and as of 2012, it had over 9,000 of them across the country, from petrol pumps to malls, from colleges to hospitals, making life much simpler for the general customer.

'We believed that the Indian customer was prepared to look at technology,' writes Kamath, 'So we said, let's put in the ATMs, Internet banking and a call centre... I think we have the ability to read what will happen a little faster than the competition...'[8]

The bank also came up with innovative ideas to increase the reliance of the customer on their products. They encouraged a business–customer relationship, with vendors as well as their clients holding accounts. This enabled seamless and problem-free payments from large companies to their suppliers. Working with electricity and other utility companies, the bank also facilitated online bill payments for households and small businesses. Pre-paid mobile recharges online attracted more depositors and a state-of-the-art call centre, the largest in the country, handled 2.5 million calls every month, providing services in 355 cities.

Says Kamath, 'In a nutshell, one has to read the market early, read all the available proxies and take a decision, often with limited information.'[9]

Leveraging Technology

Information technology was what distinguished ICICI Bank from its peers and it relentlessly pursued best practices—and indeed, invented practices—to forge its distinct identity. 'The technology choices made by the bank leverage the advantage of not having the baggage of the past "legacy" systems,' noted the first annual report. The latest software and systems were brought in, even as rapid technology advances included the risk of obsolescence.

From the beginning, technology was the bank's USP, and the first branch was fully computerized with state-of-the-art systems. Networking under the Very Small Aperture Terminals (VSAT), facilities were set up through a satellite link for data transmission. It provided a highly reliable and flexible platform for the bank's new value-added services such as funds transfer, 'Anywhere Banking' and ATMs. The bank also enabled connectivity with the international Society for Worldwide Interbank Financial Telecommunication (SWIFT) system. Thus, it was able to offer seamless domestic and international banking services in addition to conventional personal and corporate services.

The adoption of IT in banks in the first years of liberalization was not an easy task. To begin with, bank unions had fiercely resisted any kind of automation, fearing job losses. On the other hand, RBI insisted that technology be the centerpiece of the proposed new private banks. Additionally, there was no software that banks could buy off the shelf that was suited to Indian conditions and ways of doing business. In fact, the entire communications network infrastructure was still in its infancy. How then was a bank, entering the business for the first time with grand visions of being the best, to set up a whole network that would meet its needs?

Kamath's earlier work in the digitization of ICICI Ltd's leasing department was a useful experience. He recalled, 'That was way back in 1981 when all we had was an eight-bit machine with 20 MB of storage running on a 8086 processor.'[10] Before leaving for Manila, he had organized the establishment of Oracle in the bank, but when he returned in 1996, he noted that nobody was using it.[11] He observed that incomplete communication and inappropriate ownership were the biggest problems and realized that user groups should own and implement their own IT to avoid failure and reduce time and expenses. The decision was taken that instead of relying on software companies, the bank should have its own in-house software development—which is when ICICI Infotech was tasked to implement solutions.

To begin with, although ICICI Bank had the latest technology and professionals who were conversant with IT, the problem was that each branch was operating on its own. ATMs, too, were linked with individual branches. Networking was limited to email, but branches were able to transfer funds with the help of the VSAT-based wide area network.

The bank adopted a 'click and brick' strategy of organic growth. On one hand, revenue would be generated using Internet facilities; on the other, technology would be deployed to relentlessly bring down costs. Thus, both branch expansion and the roll-out of technology were the instruments used to expand the bank's market presence.

'Anywhere Banking' was the target and to achieve it, core banking solutions needed to be worked out. Infotech designed a network with a hub-and-spoke architecture to centralize procedures and, more importantly, to centralize data. A number of designs were developed, using the different modes of technology available. The final design included VSATs, radio-links, Integrated Services Digital Network (ISDN) and leased lines to match the regional disparities in technology.

'All our technology implementation took place after the mainframe era, and we could take advantage of the huge breakthroughs in computing power at the time when our customer base was exploding from 10,000 customers to 600,000 to 2.5 million to 5 million to 10 million today,' explained Kamath.[12]

In 1997–98, ICICI Bank launched Infinity, its Internet banking service. It was the first bank to use this kind of service in India, and one of the few in the world to offer this facility at the time. This was to drastically change the model for the bank–customer interface and go on to become one of the most widely used and advanced technology options for banking.

ICICI Bank's website had already taken a lead in keeping non-resident Indians in touch with their facilities, and NRIs flocked to open accounts. Infinity allowed customers to access information about their account balance and transactions and garnered more than 1000 registrations in the first few months. The next year, customers could actually transfer funds between their different accounts in different locations. 'Anywhere Banking' had arrived in the country.

The launch of Infinity was a landmark in the annals of India's banking history, opening for the first time a portal into the potential of technology and banking convergence. Within three years, the Internet customer base shot up to 5.5 lakh. It once again illustrated ICICI Bank's innovative capacities. Today, for urban customers and overseas Indians, Internet banking and its even newer off-shoot, mobile banking, are the accepted mode for transactions.

Sitting in Colombo, Sri Lanka, I often used to get desperate calls from my college-going son based in New Delhi, 'Mom, I'm on my way to the mall and have no money in my ATM. Just send me some cash!' and I could immediately use my ICICI account to transfer money to his ICICI account. By the time he reached the mall, the funds were available for him to draw. Such convenience was just not available earlier.

The following year, however, Y2K fears gripped the banking industry across the world. Most banks had commenced work to tackle the upcoming crisis much in advance, and ICICI Bank was no exception. By March 1999, it estimated that it was Y2K-compliant in most segments by taking stock of the status, and testing software and hardware. Nevertheless, afraid that any glitch anywhere could lead to a complete breakdown of the system, it instituted a back-up plan that included manual banking. Fortunately, the transition to the new millennium was smooth, and the staff did not have to resort to entering transactions by hand.

Creating an Entirely New Market

No bank can operate profitably without a healthy portfolio of loans and advances. In the early period of the reform process, it was not easy for entrepreneurs to get loans. It was not enough to merely have an excellent business proposition; banks then required monetary guarantees and guarantors of proven worth, collateral security to back up loans, an array of financial and supportive documents, and much begging and pleading with the loan officer before the application was considered. The application would then go up and down the chain, depending on the amount requested, but more often than not, after the customer had gone from pillar to post with his documents, it would be rejected.

In current times, the situation has completely reversed. Now loan officers call prospective clients on their mobile phones and try to sell them the latest credit product, be it a credit card, a car loan, or even housing loans. Loans are available for trips abroad, purchase of consumer durables, or just because some extra cash would be handy.

For ICICI Bank, innovation in credit was another defining characteristic. One of the primary obstacles to easy loans in the 1990s was the high interest rate. While companies were forced to take loans at the elevated rates, ordinary consumers faced no such restrictions, and could avoid taking loans altogether. Moreover, the economy of shortages had inculcated a deep philosophy of 'save first, then spend' so that entire generations of consumers built up savings before purchasing a refrigerator or two-wheeler.

But a major transformation was under way. Industrial delicensing had created large capacities across sectors such as automobiles and consumer durables, but demand was still flagging. In the mid-1990s, surplus capacity led to an investment slowdown, bringing down the high pace of income growth that the first round of economic liberalization had generated.

A new way had to be found to revive demand and investment. RBI thus started progressively lowering the prohibitively high interest rates in an effort to make demand and investment the drivers of growth. By early 2000, the interest rates were deregulated and reserve requirements were substantially eased, providing new opportunities for the banking sector.

Kamath anticipated this cut in interest rates, and believed that a new consumer mindset could be shaped. Thus, the era of consumer finance emerged.

As Kochhar puts it, 'When we rolled out the retail strategy in a big way... the entire consumer finance business was very nascent for the country as a whole. So, we really had to create a vision of what this business was going to be like... One was really moving in uncharted territories and taking decisions... learning alongside.'[13]

When interest rates were actually gradually brought down, ICICI Bank was well positioned to take advantage of the boom in consumer credit that took place in India for the first time. Systematically, melding technology with new products tailored to suit the requirements of the ordinary person, the bank diversified from its traditional loan avenues to target retail customers. Home loans, automobile loans, commercial business loans, personal finance and credit cards—the proportion of retail credit to total loans spiked phenomenally as the bank tapped this new segment with innovative new products.

Kochhar, who joined the bank in 1984 as a management trainee, was given the responsibility to lead its retail banking revolution. Within a single year, in 2002–03, retail credit zoomed up from 6 per cent of the total to 18 per cent and it kept skyrocketing to more than three-fifths of aggregate advances by March 2006.

From the beginning, ICICI Bank was the acknowledged market leader in the segment, but more importantly, it created a market for the first time. Says Kochhar, 'The challenge was to think beyond the boundaries of our business, recognize the under-penetration of retail lending and importance of the segment and identify the key growth opportunity for the future, ahead of competition. In fact, the challenge was not only to create a new market but also achieve scale.'

The growth was driven by a strategy including: 1) focus on customer needs, 2) creating innovative product designs, 3) competitive pricing, 4) convenient delivery and 5) strong systems for delivery and back-up. The advantage of being an integrated financial services provider, which derived from its backward merger with ICICI Ltd and other Group entities, was that it could cross-sell its diverse range of credit services.

For example, a company would have a suite of credit facilities with ICICI Bank for its various finance needs, while it would also encourage staff to open accounts with the bank under the Power Pay account. Thus, the bank could address this Group for credit requirements as well, benefiting in terms of credit information of staff members.

The concept of monthly instalments completely changed the way consumers saved and spent. Not only did these instalments transform lifestyles, particularly in urban areas, but it also led to a huge new demand for consumer durables and revived Indian industry at the time of the global 2000–01 slowdown. Even young householders could envisage equipping themselves with refrigerators, washing machines, microwave ovens and, most important of all, cars. It can be said that ICICI Bank was a pioneer in this class of retail lending, enabling millions of people to meet their dreams of an upwardly mobile lifestyle on affordable terms.

In 2003–06, retail loans grew at a rate of about 30 per cent annually, but from 2006 onwards, persistence of inflationary pressures in the economy led to a slow but inexorable rise in interest rates by the RBI. The proportion of retail loans in ICICI Bank's overall advances portfolio, therefore, started going down, reaching 40 per cent in March 2012 from a peak of 65 per cent in March 2007.

Corporate Affairs

The bread-and-butter of banks lies with corporate clients, and this segment was not neglected in the drive to garner small borrowers. In fact, ICICI Bank's inherent strength derived from its long association with corporate customers from its project financing days. But the changes in policy and its own blue-ocean way of thinking led to restructuring of its credit offerings for large clients.

Again, technology was the main instrument for delivery of improved services. The bank set up centralized processing facilities for back office operations that helped it reap benefits from large transaction volumes. ICICIebusiness.com was a single-point portal for all corporate products. No longer did companies have to designate a person to carry cheques and letters to a bank branch—they could rely on the Internet, which provided secure services.

Companies now received tailored solutions to their financing challenges. Structured transactions and channel financing options were available through the bank's Structured Finance, Credit and Markets Group, which not only offered expert services for financial structuring and related legal, accounting and tax issues, but also worked with clients to devise financial products.

For small businesses, too, ICICI Bank pioneered a new customer interface. As early as 1999, it offered free cash remittance, free delivery and pick up of cash and documents, and automatic transfer of idle deposits between current accounts and time deposits. In 2006, it helped set up the 'Emerging India' awards for recognizing achievements of small businesses, and also partnered in launching a rating agency specifically for SMEs.

It was no wonder that during a single year, 2002–03, barely eight years after commencing operations, ICICI Bank was showered with accolades from global and domestic institutions. It was ranked Bank of the Year 2002 in India and Bank of the Year from the Emerging Markets by *The Banker* magazine in the UK, Best Consumer Internet Bank in India and Best Foreign Exchange Bank in India by *Global Finance*, and was rated as India's Top 5 Most Respected Companies by *Businessworld* magazine.

Looking far ahead of the curve, the bank saw opportunities arising in a new India. While its retail lending transformed households, it avidly viewed the potential in sectors such as telecommunications, power, roads and highways, iron and steel, and manufacturing. Although the share of advances in these sectors declined concomitantly with a rise in the share of retail lending, its assistance grew in proportion with India's progress. Between 2002–03 and 2011–12, its loan portfolio went up fourfold from Rs 84,000 crore to Rs 262,000 crore.

No White Spaces: Rural Agenda

One of the main reasons why the Indian government resorted to bank nationalization in 1969 was the fact that existing banks of the time had not reached out to villages and small towns in which the majority of the population resided. Who could have believed at the time that a private bank would make the rural market its groundswell of operations just three decades later!

By the time the Indian economy recovered from a series of global slowdowns and droughts, the new phase of banking pioneered by ICICI Bank had taken hold. The bank now was looking for new opportunities, and it hit upon the increasingly vibrant rural markets.

After more than a decade of reforms, a higher growth rate had raised per capita incomes across the country but the rate of financial inclusion, or the number of people who had bank accounts, was still dismally low. In addition, the government, to deal with the slowdowns, had initiated a number of new reforms across sectors such as infrastructure, industry and, particularly, banking, which allowed companies to tap new markets.

In his characteristic style, Kamath thought of rural India as the next big opportunity of growth for the bank at a time when hardly any company was seriously addressing it.

Apart from its sheer geographical spread and huge population, the Indian rural segment throws up a variety of challenges in financial inclusion. Ordinarily, village denizens are subject to fluctuating incomes, raising risks for banks. They have a wide range of financial needs, from savings and crop credit to insurance, health and personal expenses. Further, little information is available about the credit histories of individuals.

ICICI Bank went in for an inclusive rural banking strategy for supplying financial services to farmers, traders and small businesses. Again, technology solutions, instead of setting up bank branches, were its modus operandi. Multiple products catering to all savings, credit, insurance and investment needs were devised, to be delivered through web and mobile platforms. Business facilitators and business correspondents, or 'vikas sahyogis', were appointed as intermediaries. Local institutional facilities, such as cooperative banks, NGOs, or non-banking financial companies, were also harnessed. The term used for its strategy was 'no white spaces', implying a comprehensive coverage with the partnership of all players.

To de-risk its rural portfolio, ICICI Bank decided to shift risk from the credit-worthiness of the farmer to collateral security. In this case, collateral security was the crop. A complex formula was devised, taking into account the price of the crop, the warehouse where it was stored, future price possibilities, the borrower's track record, and so on. The e-Commodity-based financing model that was developed tracked all these parameters to determine how much finance could be accorded to a particular farmer, trader or agri-company against the collateral of an agricultural commodity. Warehouse management agents would interact with farmers, supported by a web-based system that would look at all accredited warehouses.

For creating a data bank of customers' credit information, the bank helped develop the Financial Information Network and Operations Ltd (FINO), a technology platform that would collect data on savings, credit and investment habits of individuals. Smart cards with biometric capabilities and handheld devices were devised and could be used for many different products and applications. A robust back-end technology infrastructure would capture transactions for monitoring and performance management.

The financial products offered included index-based rainfall insurance, health insurance for accidents, working capital finance for traders and artisans, credit and savings for low-income families. The bank also set up rural Internet kiosks and low-cost ATMs for maximum access. The idea was to have an ICICI Bank 'touch point' within 10 kilometres from any customer. Constant innovation remained the defining characteristic of the bank's rural interface, with new products such as rural housing finance and rural educational institution loans being added.

Microfinance was another route in the growing industry for maximizing financial inclusion. Starting in 2003, ICICI Bank developed several models to work with local non-government organizations and microfinance institutions in setting up self-help groups and bank linkages. Self-help groups are groups of ten or more persons, usually women, who jointly guarantee repayment of a loan taken by any one of them, a model that has proved to be very effective in giving the poorest of the poor access to loans.

In three years, the bank achieved exponential growth. It increased lending from $1.2 million and 20,000 clients to over half a billion dollars and some 3 million people.

In 2007, the bank had to re-examine its rural operations and undertook a comprehensive change in line with its experiences. A robust risk management structure was put in place to manage credit, operational and fraud risk. RBI was stressing financial inclusion through the Business Correspondents model, leveraging new technologies. It also suggested opening 'no-frills' accounts for under-privileged persons, with zero-balance or low balance and limited transaction facilities.

By 2012, ICICI Bank had opened some 9.8 million accounts for financial inclusion. New products continued to be placed in the market to meet the needs of rural and agri-businesses. Says Kochhar, 'Our vision encompasses not only participating in all aspects of the Indian economy and its international linkages, but also catalysing India's growth. We are executing a focused financial inclusion plan leveraging information and communications technology and enabling a regulatory framework to provide basic banking services to the unbanked.'

Dealing with the Crisis

The day was 16 September 2008, a date most bankers will have imprinted on their memories. That was the day that the legendary investment bank Lehman Brothers collapsed practically overnight, the culmination of a slow process of unravelling credit markets in advanced economies that had already resulted in several massive financial institutions going under. But this was only the beginning of a huge wave of bankruptcies and closures that engulfed the entire global financial system, manufacturing industries and workers over the next few years. Entire economies found themselves at the edge of a precipice with their very survival at stake.

Concerted global action to flood the markets with liquidity and undertake monumental bailouts helped avoid the impending disintegration. By all accounts, the financial sector was in the throes of a complete reorientation of its operations, with governments taking on a larger role as owners, monitors and regulators. By March 2013, major advanced economies were recovering from a second phase of recession, the euro was pulled back from the brink of collapse, several large economies were in a state of near-default and emerging economies were slowing down.

The era of effulgence was over.

In 2008, ICICI Bank had announced its own transition. After twenty-four years, it was decided that Chairman Vaghul would step down and Kamath would move from the posts of MD and CEO to non-executive chairman. Chanda Kochhar, joint MD and CFO, would then take over as the new MD and CEO. The changes took place in April 2009.

But before that, the ongoing financial crisis had to be tackled. Once again, the bank proved itself to be ahead of the curve.

As early as February that year, Kochhar had shifted the bank's high-growth strategy into a consolidation phase that would impart stability. Realizing that retail loans, which were the bank's forte, could prove to be risky owing to rising defaults, she added a note of caution to the unbridled expansion.

As large corporates faced a liquidity freeze, they turned to their fixed deposits, withdrawing money to meet regular operational needs. The bank also held $80 million of bonds in Lehman Brothers—and this was enough to spark all kinds of stories. A rumour floated that the bank was facing a run on deposits, and thousands of customers queued up at branches and ATMs to withdraw their money. The situation amounted to a crisis and the bank had to move quickly to quash this baseless news.

According to a *Fortune* article, ICICI Bank rented 'virtually all' the armoured trucks in the country to supply cash to troubled branches. There was no question of refusing depositors. Each customer who wished to withdraw cash was permitted to do so, even if it involved ferrying people to other branches where cash was available. The RBI stepped in to assure depositors that ICICI Bank was safe and had enough liquidity to meet their needs.

In the event, the second largest bank in the country also suffered the largest losses arising from the global financial crisis. It reported the steepest fall in quarterly profits in six years as it scaled down loans and overseas operations to avoid exposure to bad assets. But it was still among the banks with the highest capital adequacy ratios and its strong risk management systems helped to minimize the impact of the crisis.

Says Kochhar, 'The events of 2009 showed business was becoming increasingly complex, and business leaders needed to be constantly aware of the speed of change and be agile and quick to react to different situations while planning their strategies. It also highlighted the need to constantly re-assess market environment and plan for long-term growth even if it resulted in a period of adjustment over the short term. ICICI Bank had enjoyed a period of unprecedented high growth for several years and the challenge was to realign the organization's strategy to the new environment and shift gear from growth to consolidation.'

Since then, the bank adopted a more cautious strategy of reducing its retail loans and increasing its current and savings deposits to reduce costs. 'The five-year strategy started with a significant shift of gear from growth to consolidation in the initial phase. Even though this strategy resulted in moderation in business volumes in the initial period, it placed us in a better position to participate in the renewed growth cycle,' says Kochhar.

The Four-Cs strategy was formulated: growth in Current and

Savings Accounts (CASA), driving down costs, improving the quality of credit, and capital conservation. Within a year, the CASA ratio went up by thirteen percentage points. Operating costs were pared to a quarter of the level it had reached two years earlier.

Khayaal Aapka

The last two decades have seen a transformation of a fundamental aspect of the Indian economy—its banking system. Nowhere is the mindset overturn as evident as it is in this sector, both from banks as well as customers. The government and the central bank together rolled out a model of prudent and calibrated reform, a process that, though seen by many as too slow, helped protect the banking sector from the worst financial crisis the world had faced in eighty years. The progressive dismantling of government control and administered mechanisms while regulating capital adequacy and, at the same time, ensuring the right conditions for growth and financial inclusion, is viewed as one of the best models in the world.

Kamath's leadership style certainly helped in ICICI Bank's success. In his words, 'I would say that one lesson is definitely that you should not get boxed in by challenges but should rather look for opportunities. In our own case, we could have allowed ourselves to get bogged down by the challenges in the project finance portfolio, with our clients feeling significant pain in the 1990s; but we instead chose to focus on new areas of growth and opportunity, and transformed ourselves from a project finance company into a universal bank.

'Another lesson would be that you should have the courage to dream and imagine the future. Very few people in the late 1990s could have envisioned what India and Indian banking would be ten years later, but those who did were able to capture the opportunity.'

As new markets opened up in the emerging India, it needed

a dynamic and innovative bank to recognize and leverage new opportunities. ICICI Bank met this need completely, forging ahead at a tumultuous pace. Innovation was its primary preoccupation. As Kamath puts it, 'Every day at 8.30 a.m., a new idea would come up.'[14]

The factors contributing to the bank's success can be summed up as follows:

Identifying new markets: As the growing Indian economy brought more households into the consuming classes, ICICI Bank was ready to offer them the financial products that they needed. Globalization made overseas markets accessible, and NRIs became a new market. The growth of Indian companies offered a natural growth avenue which the bank was quick to capitalize on.

Innovating on products: A wide range of products was developed to address the whole life cycle of customers, from children's needs, to students, workers and employees to retired people. Similarly, the integration of corporate clients up and down the supply chain, and a cross-selling model helped add to financial product offerings. 'You need to take that innovative spirit and push it to a level where change, learning and knowledge sharing become a regular part of your company's structure,' emphasizes Kamath.[15]

Leveraging technology: From the beginning, technology was the key determinant to the bank's success. It deployed new technology models as they came out, and helped create new products that would meet its requirements. ATMs, mobile phones, call centres, the Internet, and a constant flow of tailored software were all major areas of growth. A secure banking platform was instituted that provided comfort to customers.

Building the brand relentlessly: Dissemination of information and 'in your face' advertising supplemented by telemarketing helped make customers aware of the products on offer. The bank was always willing to go the extra mile to reach the customer. Its 'everywhere' strategy meant that it was always easily accessible and its vibrant red and orange logo enjoyed the confidence of customers.

Human resources: Finally, the bank tapped the best people in the business for its growth. Its leaders over the years are virtually household names who sized up opportunities and operationalized ideas with exemplary drive and vigour.

'The most important thing for an entrepreneur, based on my experience of building businesses over the last two decades, is to combine vision and execution,' sums up Kochhar. 'What happens with most business leaders is that they go to one extreme—they are either so visionary that those ideas sometimes don't transform into reality—or they get so involved in day-to-day matters that they don't allow their team to breathe, or they themselves do not have the time to think of the next big step.'

She adds, 'It is important for a leader to always dream big and create a vision for the organization, and at the same time keep checking with reality to ensure that the vision is getting translated into action. The other learning is that the quality of management and leadership is critical for the success of a company. I always say that a bad project can survive with good management, but a good project can fail with bad management. So the quality of the entrepreneur makes a big difference to the performance of a business.'

As ICICI Bank takes on the next growth trajectory, it will continue to do whatever it takes to meet its promise of 'Khayaal Aapka' for each one of its 25 million—and growing in numbers—customers.

3 TRIPLE BOTTOM LINE FOR THE NATION

ITC LIMITED

The story of ITC Ltd in the post-liberalization era symbolizes how a company can overcome adversity and completely reorient itself to achieve success. It is also a journey of transformation to create an exemplary 'Indian enterprise' aligned to the national goals of inclusive growth; a diversification story that blends internal capabilities with the opportunities thrown up by the economic progress of an emerging economy.

Most of all, it is a story of how ITC pioneered a new model that radically changed the way businesses contribute to creating value for societies, a model that covered the entire gamut of social development from rural empowerment to growing natural resources. ITC's Triple Bottom Line approach converges the three imperatives of people, profits and the planet—a philosophy that the company's chairman, Yogesh Chander Deveshwar ('Yogi' to all), passionately espouses and calls 'a commitment beyond the market'.

ITC's journey has been one of challenge and change. The day after Deveshwar took over as chairman of ITC in 1996, a tax tribunal slapped a charge of Rs 803 crore on the company for excise dues pertaining to the 1980s. It was 2 January 1996, and the amount was over three times the company's profits for the fiscal year ending March 1995.[1]

This was just one of the many trials and tribulations that ITC was confronted with in the immediate aftermath of liberalization in 1991. To begin with, a series of very public disagreements unfolded between ITC and its foreign shareholder. Under the new liberal FDI entry norms, the British tobacco giant, British American Tobacco (BAT) Industries, tried to regain control of the company by raising its shareholding to 51 per cent. However, ITC's shareholders, led primarily by public sector financial institutions, rallied to ensure that ITC retained its identity as an Indian corporation committed to serving national priorities. The takeover attempt was, therefore, unfruitful. Investigations by the Enforcement Directorate further compounded ITC's woes in November 1996, when two former chairmen were remanded in custody under the Foreign Exchange Regulation Act.

So, in 1996, five years after liberalization, ITC Ltd was facing a severe crisis with smear campaigns damaging its reputation together with challenges emerging from the competitive landscape as a result of economic liberalization.

Cut to 2012.

ITC was recently conferred the World Business and Development Award 2012 at Rio+20 United Nations Summit on Sustainable Development. The list of recognitions from global and domestic institutions stretches long on its website, ranging from the Development Gateway Award to the inaugural World Business Award for companies creating sustainable livelihood opportunities in developing countries. These awards are a fitting tribute to ITC's leadership in corporate governance, business and innovation, and sustainable development.

In 2011, Deveshwar was honoured with the Padma Bhushan, one of the highest civilian awards given by the Government of India for distinguished national service. As chairman of ITC from 1996, he has led the visionary transformation of the company as an Indian enterprise, a company which strategically aligns itself with India's economic growth.

ITC has evolved, embraced and aggressively championed a

new way of doing business—the concept of the Triple Bottom Line. This business strategy goes beyond financial achievements to also encompass social and environmental issues. ITC believes that by making societal value creation the core of its business strategy, it is able to contribute much more meaningfully to the nation, its people and the world around it. This strategy also makes excellent business sense and reaps richer rewards than a narrow focus on profits.

According to the company's worldview, working sustainability and inclusive growth into business strategy adds to corporate profits. By empowering the lives of people at the bottom of the income pyramid, joining hands with rural communities and building competitiveness, a company also ensures better rewards for its shareholders. Over the years, Deveshwar, the longest serving chairman of ITC, has unequivocally demonstrated the efficacy of such a strategy.

'...our strong belief in creating an organization to serve national priorities led us to reaffirm our strategy in creating multiple drivers of growth that could leverage the opportunities of an emerging economy by matching it with the strengths and core capabilities of the organization,' wrote Deveshwar about the ITC route to growth.[2]

Early Years

ITC's history is deeply intertwined with India's overall economy and industry. In 1905, BAT established the Peninsular Tobacco Company to enter the cigarette industry in India and in 1910, it set up the Imperial Tobacco Company of India Ltd for sales, and the Indian Leaf Tobacco Company (ILTC) in 1912 to ensure raw material supplies. Peninsular and ILTC were integrated into Imperial Tobacco in 1919, and the latter became BAT's main subsidiary in India. The white colonial headquarters of ITC—the elegant Virginia House at 37, Chowringhee, one of Kolkata's heritage buildings—came up in 1928.

Like all other foreign-led companies, Imperial Tobacco, too, underwent a change after the institution of Monopolies and Restrictive Trade Practices Act, 1969, and the Foreign Exchange Regulation Act, 1973. BAT had to reduce its stake to below 40 per cent and for the first time an Indian chairman, A.N. Haksar, assumed charge.

His vision was to build an Indian enterprise that would derive its inspiration from the needs of Indian society. This led to ITC's initial diversification into the hotel business in 1975, followed by its entry into the paperboard business in 1977. These were nation-building interventions, with hotels serving to earn critical foreign exchange, and paperboard enabling ITC's expansion into the plantation sector with opportunities to create livelihoods in a backward area. Reflecting these aims, the company's name went through several changes, from Imperial Tobacco Company to Indian Tobacco Company in 1970 to I.T.C. Ltd in 1974 and finally to ITC Ltd, without the full stops, in 2001.

In the decade and a half following the initial forays into hotels and paperboard, the company ran into severe problems because these were highly capital-intensive businesses, which placed huge demands on the company's resources. Since these businesses were structured as separate companies during this period—also at the bidding of the overseas shareholder—their ability to raise capital and achieve a meaningful scale was limited. Consequently, they remained on a slow growth path.

Cigarettes, however, continued to be the company's primary business segment in those years, contributing 80–85 per cent of its gross turnover at the time of liberalization. Its prestigious brands, from India Kings to Gold Flake and Classic, were market leaders. Its factories at Munger, Saharanpur and other places deployed sophisticated technologies and research to meet customer aspirations.

The decade from the mid-1980s to the mid-1990s witnessed

feverish strategic activities under the chairmanship of J.N. Sapru and K.L. Chugh. The company entered the financial services business and set up ITC Classic Finance Ltd. Almost simultaneously, it went into the edible oils business and set up ITC Agro Tech Ltd, which was to later launch the popular brand, 'Sundrop' oil.

During this period, the hotel business took its iconic restaurant 'Bukhara' beyond the shores of India into New York and Chicago, while ITC acquired the specialty paper company Tribeni Tissues Ltd. Aspiring to become an international trading house like the Japanese 'sogo shosha', ITC Global Holdings Pte Ltd was set up in Singapore. Additional capital was raised through an issue of Global Depository Receipts to finance the company's expanding profile.

When he assumed office as chairman in 1996, he inherited a 'crown of thorns'.[3] '...I was confronted with a mix of challenges,' remembered Deveshwar. 'The company's earlier diversification into hotels and paper was faltering. Before that could be put on a firm footing, a slew of new businesses were launched in edible oils, financial services and international trading, which turned out to be disasters.'[4]

Therefore, ITC was under severe pressure in the initial years of the economic reforms introduced in 1991.

'When I took over as chairman of ITC, two of our businesses were facing tremendous competitive pressures, perhaps even the threat of closure,' said Deveshwar.[5] The agri-business, based on an export-oriented model of selling tobacco overseas, was threatened by large international companies that had better access to risk arbitrage. Similarly, ITC Bhadrachalam Paperboards faced competition as customs duties came down and overseas players accessed the Indian market. The overwhelming view of analysts was to shut down these two businesses.

'We disagreed,' he recalled. 'Today, with many years of perseverance and conviction, we are proud that we could prove the cynics wrong. Behind these two amazing turnaround stories lies a great transformational idea: of becoming internationally competitive by empowering [the] entire value chain.'[6]

Indeed, the challenges for ITC in 1996 were immensely daunting. Responding to this mix of old burdens and fresh opportunities, the newly constituted Board of Directors, led by Deveshwar, launched into a purposeful phase of rationalizing, restructuring and repositioning the company for international competitiveness. The new team stood steadfast in its resolve to preserve ITC's Indian identity and its strategy of 'creating multiple drivers of growth'. A new structure of corporate governance, based on the principles of trusteeship, transparency and distributed leadership, was put in place.

Recognizing that ITC was not well positioned to create long-term value in businesses such as edible oils and financial services, a responsible exit from these businesses was executed in 1998. In what was one of the most turbulent periods in the company's history, huge financial outlays were incurred to wind up Classic Finance and make a pre-deposit in the excise duty case for the period of 1983–87. Subsequently, with the winning of several legal cases, ITC's stand was vindicated, marking a very important step in the rebuilding of its reputation.

A Story of Transformation

It has been a journey of sheer persistence and innovation since then. By the time ITC celebrated the century of its incorporation in 2010, its transformation was indeed very apparent. By 2013, its gross income had surpassed Rs 43,000 crore, a near eight-fold increase from 1996. Post-tax profits also grew almost twenty-eight times to over Rs 7,400 crore. Market capitalization multiplied over forty-five times to cross Rs 260,000 crore.

Going beyond cigarettes, it has become the largest player in the paperboard and packaging industry, the second largest in the hotel space and a market leader in FMCG (fast moving consumer goods). ITC has also been a pioneer in rural transformation through its e-choupal initiative, a path-breaking rural empowerment and agri-business strategy, bringing big gains to millions of farmers and hailed by top management gurus like C.K. Prahalad as an innovative way of integrating marginalized groups of society into larger markets.

But most importantly, ITC has become the acknowledged leader in sustainable business practices, the only company in the world to be carbon-positive, water-positive and solid waste recycling-positive. Its ITC Grand Chola Chennai is the world's largest LEED (Leadership in Energy and Environmental Design) Platinum-certified green hotel. It published a sustainability report in 2004, one of the earliest to do so.

'The contribution of companies needs to be more comprehensively measured along three dimensions, commonly referred to as the "Triple Bottom Line",' wrote Deveshwar in the introduction of the report. 'These dimensions are: economic, ecological and social.'

Supporting over 5 million livelihoods, empowering nearly 40,000 rural women, greening more than 1.4 lakh hectares and irrigating nearly 116,000 hectares, ITC has truly become a national asset.

Shifting the Strategy

Deveshwar joined ITC in 1968, after graduating from IIT Delhi. After getting his start with A.N. Haksar, the first Indian chairman of the company, and running three ITC divisions, he was nominated to the board as director of the company at the young age of thirty-seven. In 1996, he became the chief executive and chairman of the board amid a highly public battle with the parent company, BAT, for control of the board.

In his first address to shareholders at the company's annual general meeting in August that year, Deveshwar spoke on the issues confronting the cigarette industry, which was the primary business of ITC at that point of time. India was the third largest tobacco producer in the world, but had failed to capitalize adequately on this sector. The share of cigarettes in India's tobacco consumption was just about 20 per cent—far from the 85–90 per cent share in mature markets. Although 200 million people in India used tobacco products, only 12 per cent smoked cigarettes, the rest preferring cheaper products like bidis, chewing tobacco and gutka. Moreover, the cigarette industry had been hit by high taxation and had barely recovered to go back to the levels of production prevailing in the mid-1980s.

It was in his next speech the following year that Deveshwar talked about 'complete re-evaluation', 'reshaping' of businesses and a new strategy that would match the 'strengths of ITC with the growth opportunities in the marketplace'.

During the year, the ITC board worked hard to identify the new trends in the Indian business scene. It mainly looked at how the entry of large, fund-rich international companies would impact Indian business houses. The conclusion was that Indian companies would need to use their understanding of local markets and differentiate their brands from international brands. Equally, they would have to build their international competitiveness through innovation.

So the board delineated four core businesses—tobacco, travel and tourism, packaging, and paper. The strategies it identified were the following: to work with overseas companies for technology, know-how and best practices; address global markets; and leverage its prestigious brands for new lines of business. International competitiveness was always top of the agenda for the Group.

With its strategy of strengthening its growth drivers, the company restructured its portfolio of businesses, based on matching market opportunities with its best performing segments. The paperboard business was merged with ITC, infusing it with new life. The business, instead of being shut down as analysts propounded, was expanded, with modernization of the paper mill at a cost of Rs 675 crore. For packaging, the target was no less than a leadership position in the Asia–Pacific region.

A deep commitment to the creation of growing and sustainable value in the country inspired ITC to swim against the tide and fashion a comprehensive turnaround strategy, drawing upon the diverse skills within the ITC Group. For example, the paperboard segment was significantly stepped up to embrace more small farmers and poor tribals.

It was in travel and tourism, at the time the largest industry in the world, that Deveshwar announced an expansion programme to offer a more complete and attractive hotel chain to upmarket international and domestic travellers. He said at the 1999 AGM that these investments were being viewed as 'a significant contribution to the development of infrastructure for trade and commerce in the country'. In addition, the proposed investments would 'stimulate large direct and indirect employment besides supporting substantial foreign exchange earnings'. It was estimated that the company's investment programme would generate about 20,000 additional direct and indirect jobs.

Subsequently, the hotel business was folded back into ITC in 2004. Renewed efforts to create one of India's finest hospitality chains have today resulted in an internationally acknowledged business with best-in-class operating margins, with discerning guests that include heads of state as well as global corporate leaders.

Quality and productivity in the tobacco business were targeted through increased investments in leaf-processing plants and storage. A new state-of-the-art cigarette plant was planned at Bangalore involving a fund outlay of Rs 900 crore over five years. Despite the global glut in the tobacco market, ITC worked with farmers to enhance the competitiveness of green leaf tobacco and upgrade its services to them.

However, given the social challenges in the tobacco sector, it was obvious that the progressive leadership of ITC would look beyond cigarettes and embark on a very arduous journey to create new drivers of growth. As it is, the excise component of cigarettes kept going up exponentially, placing it out of reach of most tobacco consumers. The share of cigarettes in tobacco consumption was below 16 per cent in 2001, as taxes amounted to over 80 per cent of the value added. Three-quarters of the excise revenues from tobacco emanated from the cigarette segment. In addition, as was often pointed out by the company, the high tax rates encouraged cigarette smuggling—across the world, one-third of the total cigarette trade was estimated to be contraband.[7] The Indian government passed new cigarette laws in 2003, banning smoking in public places, and further restraining advertising and promotion of cigarettes. State governments, too, imposed additional duties.

According to ITC, tax differentials between cigarettes and other tobacco products shifted consumption to bidis, chewing tobacco and gutka, which were produced mostly in the unorganized sector and were not subject to content and packaging regulations. The company continued to present its case for more rational and non-discriminatory tax structures in the interests of government finances, farmers and the industry, but while retaining its thrust on tobacco and the cigarette industry, ITC accorded high importance to its other three core businesses as well.

A New Path

'If I were to set out a single key priority for Indian companies, it would be: to rapidly reposition the companies for extreme competitive preparedness and support their successful transition from an era of regulation and protection, to the fully globalized market of the twenty-first century,' stressed Deveshwar in his AGM speech in 1998.

The second phase of the Indian economic experience had commenced, and it was not a happy one, coinciding as it did with the Asian financial crisis. Although ITC had performed well in the past two years, Indian industry was in the throes of anaemic growth and despondent investor spirits.

Deveshwar, always a clear and concise orator who meticulously weighed each word of his speeches, zeroed in on essentials of the strategy for ITC. Aiming towards the original idea of concentrating on its four core areas, ITC exited from the financial services and edible oils segments, which had been rashly set up in the first exuberance of reforms.

This was not an easy decision, since closing Classic Finance required a cash outlay of Rs 800 crore at a time when the company had to also deposit Rs 350 crore with the government under the ongoing excise case. But both the segments were haemorrhaging cash and the alternative would have been worse for the company. ITC used the internal resources that came from added operating cash flows from the previous two years as well as borrowings. ICICI Bank bought over ITC Classic Finance, as we noted in the previous chapter, and the international agri-business major ConAgra took over edible oils.

As globalization unfolded with the economic reforms of the 1990s, ITC saw this turning point in the country's economic history as an opportunity to invest in the businesses for tomorrow. A strategic choice was made to enter new businesses by leveraging internal competencies that best matched emerging market opportunities.

Driven by the aspiration to become the country's leading FMCG company, ITC created a bouquet of businesses which spawned several brands that are popular household names today. The expansion strategy in FMCG saw ITC making an entry into lifestyle apparel, branded packaged foods, educational and stationery products, safety matches and incense sticks and, more recently, personal care products.

The carefully thought-through diversification strategy was designed to create unique sources of competitive advantage by deriving synergies from its different businesses. For example, Deveshwar pointed out that empowering farmers could not be successful until there was a good market for their produce. From this understanding was born the idea of enlarging the food processing business, such as the Aashirvaad atta, which buys wheat directly at the farm-gate, or the Kitchens of India ready-to-eat products. And, in turn, this derived from ITC's hotel chefs whose expertise could be used to concoct flavourful dishes such as Dal Bukhara. Says the chairman, '...our packaging business is part of the supply chain for our FMCG business. Our agri-business is the supply chain for the foods business.'[8]

With this clear enunciation of its intentions, the ITC Group set forth on the overriding priority of competitiveness. ITC steadfastly maintained its character as an 'Indian enterprise' as Deveshwar referred to it, as distinct from a company operating in India. 'The difference,' he pointed out in a speech, 'lies in the depth of commitment to the Indian economy'.[9] Such an enterprise would partner with other sectors of the economy for maximum value to Indian society, regardless of the source of its funds.

It was on the strength of this vision, and the overarching commitment to subserving national priorities, that ITC came up with its pathbreaking rural transformation flagship innovation, the ITC e-Choupal.

Electronic Meeting Place

Time was when the word 'choupal' evoked images of languid farmers relaxing under shady trees after a hard day's work and exchanging village gossip. No longer. Today, the concept is of e-choupals, or the Internet-enabled meeting places created by ITC to transform the way a farmer interacts with the market.

An Indian farmer spends an entire year preparing his land,

planting seeds and nurturing crops. At the end of this long, hard labour, he is forced sell his full crop to the nearest mandi, or government-regulated wholesale agricultural market, through an agent. The agent advises him about the price, which is usually non-negotiable and is only a fraction of what the produce costs the final consumer. The farmer doesn't know any better and is unable to get the right price. In the absence of an efficient market and institutional framework, farmers are at the mercy of intermediaries and extremely vulnerable to exploitation.

But in 40,000 villages across the country, a new story of farmer empowerment was emerging with the launch of the ITC e-Choupal initiative. This unique programme brought together information technology and customized extension services to enhance agri-productivity and quality. It also linked farmers to markets and global supply chains for their soya, wheat and other crops. At the touch of a button, they could access the latest prices in markets around their villages, understand weather conditions, and even the prices prevailing at the Chicago Board of Trade. Armed with these valuable inputs, they could now make an informed decision on whether to sell their crop or wait for better prices.

S. Sivakumar, the chief executive of ITC's erstwhile International Business Division, which was later restructured as the Agri-Business Division, was tasked by Deveshwar in the late 1990s to rejuvenate the agri-business. After careful analysis, his team identified multiple hurdles for farmers in terms of costs, middlemen, infrastructure availability and so on.

He noted that farmers had to cart their produce to the mandi for price discovery and sales, but then go to the moneylender for crop finance and to the extension centre for inputs and know-how. Without access to real-time information, the farmer had little bargaining power and was dependent on agents. And so, after a brainstorming session, an entirely new model for buying and selling crops was devised.

After studying various options, Sivakumar's team decided to deploy the Internet to take information to the farmer. But how could this be done, given that not all villages had electricity access to begin with, let alone Internet connectivity? So satellite-connected dishes and solar panels had to be brought into the model. This was how the ITC e-Choupal came into being.

ITC e-Choupal was a natural outcome of the company's involvement in agri-business coupled with the emerging importance of the information and communications technology business. The company was quick to realize that rural India would be the fulcrum of growth, both driving growth through its resurgence as well as benefiting from higher incomes.

Leveraging its experience in farming and deep understanding of rural India, ITC had also been working with other crops—soya, rice, coffee, etc.—and entering international markets with agri-exports. The Agri-Business Division and the IT business came together to create the unique 'click and mortar' model of e-Choupal, which converges traditional 'mortar' shops with new-age IT or 'click' transaction formats.

To begin with, the two divisions created a 'soya choupal' in Madhya Pradesh, a virtual soya market. Through electronic connectivity, farmers could get a range of critical information regarding weather, prices and farm practices. They could also purchase inputs and sell their produce at optimum prices at their doorstep. Soya farmers found this to be an eye-opener for producing and marketing their crop, and encouraged by the response, ITC scaled up the model to six pilot projects in June 2000, covering other crops as well.

Within a year, the project had surged to encompass 120,000 farmers in more than 1,000 villages through 235 e-hubs. 'This communication miracle—the empowerment of India's agricultural poor—began simply enough as a company's effort to re-engineer the process of more efficiently and fairly getting the farmers' soya crop to market,' observed the late Professor C.K.

Prahalad in his path-breaking management book, *The Fortune at the Bottom of the Pyramid: Eradicating Poverty Through Profits*.[10] This book revolutionized the way companies all over the world viewed markets, for the first time seeing low-income consumers as a business opportunity rather than as a difficult market to be avoided. ITC's e-Choupals were a major reference point in Professor Prahalad's book.

'ITC devised a strategy to systematically deploy information technology to change the game,' commented Professor Prahalad. A critical differentiator of ITC e-Choupal, which till date has ensured the empowerment of farmers, is its focus on first strengthening the farmer—enlarging the wallet, rather than fighting for a larger share of a small wallet—and freeing them from a formal contract, thus giving them the option to sell to whoever they think fit. In this manner, farmers could derive full gains from the e-Choupal network but were not tied to it through contract, providing them the much-needed empowerment and market linkages.

In the e-Choupal model, a sanchalak is identified from the local farmer community and trained in computer operations and business skills. He enjoys the trust of the community and can thus effectively interface with farmers on the one hand and ITC on the other. The sanchalak provides relevant information to farmers, such as the price of the crop at the mandi, and arranges purchases and sales after making quality checks on produce brought to him. The farmer then transports the produce to the nearest ITC procurement centre.

The venture quickly became the largest Internet-based initiative in rural India. In 2013, 6500 e-kiosks were present in ten states of India. They acted as hubs for 40,000 villages and catered to some 4 million farmers, mostly set up at walking distance from target villages. That's an outreach of 20 million family members.

At the other end of the e-Choupal model is the Choupal

Saagar, ITC's innovative one-stop integrated rural services' hub for farmers. Twenty-four of these large warehouses-cum-outlets deliver a range of tailored services to farmers, from training and testing to provision of inputs such as seeds and fertilizers. They are also an organized retail format, selling every item that a farmer's household might need, including clothes and shoes, soaps and shampoos, refrigerators and mixies, and even tractors. Fuel stations, food outlets and medical services, too, are part of the offerings, making the Choupal Saagar a veritable hypermarket for rural areas.

The network further includes outsourced warehousing hubs, or choupal pradarshan khets, which bring the latest technologies to farmers through demonstration farms, and choupal haats, which are rural platforms for consumer engagement.

For ITC, the benefits have been immense. Its supply chain has been streamlined with respect to costs, quality and traceability of goods sourced. It has been able to gain access to under-served rural markets, and has built up trust and loyalty with farmers. It has also been able to synergize e-Choupal with its other businesses, offering its own FMCG products on the platform as well as tying up with other companies for a wider range of goods for farmers. For example, delivery of agri-inputs, consumer goods, insurance, healthcare and education has been possible through the Internet-enabled platform. ITC is one of India's largest exporters of agricultural products, including marine products, processed fruits and coffee and spices, selling frozen and pulp fruits to markets in the US, Europe, Japan and West Asia.

The e-Choupal model has received wide international acclaim, being recognized through awards and citations such as the Stockholm Challenge, the UNIDO Award, and many others.

Multiple Drivers of Growth

A driving force behind ITC's strategy of transformation was its vision to revitalize the company into a vibrant engine of sustainable growth with a substantial and growing contribution to the Indian economy.

It was for this reason that a portfolio of businesses was carefully chosen. The corporate strategy of creating multiple drivers of growth was put in place with ITC entering new FMCG businesses as well as IT in addition to revitalizing and growing its existing businesses of cigarettes, paperboard and packaging, hotels and agri-commodities.

In the FMCG space, the company looked to expanding its presence in sectors other than cigarettes. As mentioned earlier, the items ranged from branded packaged foods, personal care products, lifestyle apparel, educational and stationery products to safety matches and incense sticks.

By 2002–03, revenues from this segment had crossed Rs 100 crore. In 2012–13, sales had gone up to Rs 7000 crore, bringing down the share of cigarettes in the overall product mix—and the aggressive branding and promotion strategies of the company raised quite a few eyebrows.

A key strategy for FMCG was to build Indian brands so that India could gain intellectual property and a brand premium. The idea is to grow by a multiple of three within five years.

'Distributed leadership' was the solution that Deveshwar found to manage the different operations of ITC. Fortunately, ITC had always been a preferred option in the private sector for management graduates and it had loads of talent.

Deveshwar established a three-tier structure for management. The chairman and board of directors were responsible for 'strategic supervision'. The next tier was the Corporate Management Committee (CMC) responsible for 'strategic management', and then the executive management team for each strategic business unit, headed by a CEO who reported back to the CMC.

This strategy of organization allowed ITC to diversify and focus simultaneously by ensuring that each division was run like a separate company but at the same time derive benefits from the institutional and enterprise strengths of the parent company. The CMC was like a venture capitalist, investing in a business but giving each chief executive enough room for his own management style. 'For example, the CEO of the paperboard division has just one concern—to produce world-class paperboard,' according to Deveshwar.[11] 'Our whole concept is of distributed leadership. My role is like a wholetime non-executive chairman of all the businesses.'[12]

Today, ITC is one of India's largest professionally managed companies, neither a government enterprise nor a family business. As a professionally managed company, ITC is led by its board. Since there is no single dominant shareholder, the ownership is differentiated from the management. Everyone works as part of a team driven by shared goals and objectives and a superordinate vision. Of the three executive directors, Nakul Anand joined the company in 1979, P.V. Dhobale in 1977 and Kurush N. Grant in 1980.

In the branded packaged food business, ITC foresaw a shift in market preferences at a time when little processing was carried out and Indian brands in the segment were limited. The company already had an excellent supply chain for agri-produce and a strong distribution base as well as the culinary expertise in its hotels business. Putting these advantages together, it, as mentioned earlier, ventured into branded foods with readymade packaged food called 'Kitchens of India'.

It then expanded the portfolio to create winning brands such as 'Aashirvaad' in atta and salt, 'Sunfeast' in biscuits, premium cookies and pasta, 'Candyman' and 'Mint-o' in confectionery, 'Yippee!' in instant noodles and the range of 'Bingo!' snack foods—all an outcome of the constant focus on consumer aspirations and research in food products.

Beginning in 2001, the brands quickly sped up the sales graph. Within a short time, ITC's foods business enjoyed the market leadership in staples and confectionery, came in second in instant noodles and third in biscuits. Its advantage? End-to-end supply chain capabilities, including sourcing the best wheat for its atta, to world-class manufacturing facilities driven by an obsession with quality, and thousands of outlets serviced by its extensive trade marketing and distribution infrastructure for its FMCG products. And the talents of some of the best chefs in the business.

Similarly, soaps, shampoos and other personal care products entered the company's repertoire in 2005. Essenza di Wills, Fiama di Wills, Vivel and Superia stepped into the highly competitive industry armed with years of research and a deep understanding of consumer preferences. The idea was to identify various groups of consumers, the upper end of the mid-segment, the young and the aspirational, and devise tailored marketing strategies for each group.

For example, the Vivel soap has been developed with a range of variants, Satin Soft, Young Glow, Silk Spring and so on. Deodorants, fairness creams, fragrances are part of the portfolio, and celebrities are brought on board to build awareness of the products. Within a short time, these brands have developed a high recall value, growing their share of a rapidly expanding market.

Wills Lifestyle, ITC's fashion arm, which sells apparel and premium personal care products, is taking on global brands such as Mango and Tommy Hilfiger. The apparel collection, meticulously crafted with the help of top designers, targets the entire cycle of an adult's day, including clothes for office, relaxed times and evening engagements. Innovative garments, such as shirts with a UV coating and temperature control, and new designs are constantly being introduced in the flagship eighty-six stores across forty cities. Designed for the new upwardly mobile generation of high-income earners, the apparel segment is already a significant contributor to ITC's market presence.

The Spring–Summer 2013 collection of top fashionista, Ritu Kumar, was welcomed with oohs and aahs, as glamorous models walked the ramp in colourful and innovative ensembles that highlighted Art Deco motifs in modern styles. It was the Grand Finale of the Wills Lifestyle India Fashion Week, and Ritu Kumar's show was created as part of her collaboration with Wills Lifestyle.

In the hotel sector, ITC's strategy was to step strongly into the big gap in India's tourism industry. Hotel rooms were severely deficient in the country, but corporates strong enough to invest in the long-gestation projects were limited in number. With an initial investment of Rs 1,500 crore, ITC set about expanding its room capacities. Maurya Sheraton in Delhi added 100 more rooms in its super deluxe extension 'ITC One'. ITC Grand Maratha Sheraton was launched in 2001, and ITC Grand Central came up a few years later in Mumbai. ITC Hotel Sonar Bangla Sheraton and Towers commenced in 2002 and soon became one of the finest business hotels in Kolkata. Properties in Bangalore, Hyderabad and Agra were renovated.

In 2012, it initiated a step overseas to take up a greenfield project in Sri Lanka, inaugurated the world's largest LEED Platinum-rated green hotel, the ITC Grand Chola, and outlined plans for another 5,000 rooms with an investment of Rs 9,000 crore over the next five to seven years. To meet the needs of different consumer segments, the company offers different kinds of hotels, including luxury, five-star and mid-market sectors. Altogether, it operates ninety properties with 8,000 rooms in small cities and heritage destinations as well as in the metros.

And, of course, any high-end visitor to India cannot leave without sampling the delights of its globally famous branded cuisine restaurants, Bukhara and Dum Pukht. 'Since that first meal, in 2000, so many customers have uttered some variation of "Give us what the president had," that the restaurant has started serving a mixed-meat sampler—a one-off prepared for Mr Clinton and his guests—as a nightly special,' wrote the *New York Times*, referring to President Bill Clinton's visit to Bukhara during his trip to India. 'The Bill Clinton platter ...is an aromatic spread of mixed meats, lentils and oven-baked bread.'[13] Hillary Clinton, too, got a platter named after her in 2009, prompting President Obama to also clamour for an 'Obama Platter' during his visit to the restaurant.[14]

A recent venture of the company has been its foray into IT through ITC Infotech India Ltd and its subsidiaries in the UK and US. Within a short period, it has emerged as one of the fast-growing mid-tier IT companies in India.

Interestingly, since the ITC repertoire of products also includes safety matches and agarbattis, the natural question is why these items are produced by a company that looks at luxury hotels and high-range FMCGs as its breadwinners. Again, this derives from ITC's engagement with society, in this case, cottage enterprises that are mainly staffed by women. The manufacture of agarbattis is outsourced to households and micro-enterprises where women are trained and supported. Women in rural hinterlands of states across the country are finding it a way to earn incomes at their own convenience—and this is just another way of empowerment for ITC....

For the Planet

Sustainability is a passion for Deveshwar. 'It is my deep conviction that both the competitiveness and profitability of firms in the future will increasingly depend on their relative ability to adopt such sustainable business practices,'[15] he believes. According to him, companies need to embed sustainability as a value proposition into their operations. 'That will go a long way in creating a sustainable economy for future generations and a secure planet that will continue to nurture and nourish the billions of its inhabitants.'[16]

Early on, ITC made a commitment to sustainability, even though it could have potentially been a drag on its revenues, recognizing that it would build competitiveness in the long run. This focus on the planet and people happened in an environment when other companies were only stressing on profits. Innovation was the instrument that ITC leveraged to create new business models across its entire value chain.

Agriculture was at the heart of most of ITC's activities, and it had—over decades—built a strong relationship with and an understanding of farmers. Deveshwar knew that this was a solid foundation and wanted to build on it for a win-win scenario. The paperboard and packaging business, in particular, could be turned into a business model that would best exemplify working with society and the environment.

At the time of liberalization, the paperboard industry was faced with huge energy costs and a big shortage of wood-based raw material. Pulp imports were the only solution. At the same time, domestic mills employed low technology and used recycled fibre. ITC faced tremendous challenges due to inadequate availability of virgin fibre and, therefore, could not scale up its business and modernize operations.

The choice was to exit from the business altogether and import the end-product, paperboard, or import pulp and process it at its mills. But ITC chose the most challenging option—going to the last mile of the value chain, which were the forests. And this meant research in clonal propagation to create hardy saplings for tree cultivation, working with local populations of tribal people, managing soil and water and bringing in new technologies.

The first task was to generate the pulp. Biotechnology research was used to develop clonal saplings that could grow on degraded private wastelands owned by tribals around the mill. A social and farm forestry programme was initiated and essentially, this meant capacity-building of tribals and marginal farmers, helping them with technology and inputs and buying their produce. This involved complete dedication and courage from staff members working in remote areas, with little returns for years.

But within a few years, the paperboard division of the company was the leader of the Indian market, and had even marked out an export footprint in other countries. Not only did it meet requirements for industrial timber, it also provided livelihoods to hundreds of thousands of people in villages apart from creating a large green cover. In addition, the business' energy management solutions earned it high kudos and awards from the government and CII.

Over 1.4 lakh hectares have now been greened under the social and farm forestry programme. The social forestry programme alone, which is a small part of the entire initiative, benefits almost 30,000 people in 1,300 villages. The entire programme has enabled the creation of more than 62 million person days of employment. Vast tracts of dry, infertile land owned by poor labourers were converted into pulpwood plantations.

ITC staff help landowners to form forest-user groups, offer them loan facilities, and train them in planting and looking after saplings. These saplings are developed through research to be high-yielding and resistant to disease. Each year, tens of millions of saplings are sold and distributed to farmers.

At the other end of the value chain, this engagement in forests supports a growing paper, packaging and printing business. It supplies boxes to Nokia, copier paper to the Tatas and stationery to school students—and it is the 'greenest' paper in India.

A corollary to planting wasteland is the proper use of water. Conversion of the wood fibre into paperboard uses up a whole lot of energy and water and ITC's watershed development programme covers nearly 116,000 hectares. Working with 950 water-user groups, the company has set up thousands of structures for water-harvesting, which have helped irrigate fields, conserve soil and impart security to farmers' livelihoods.

The model was to provide three-quarters of the construction costs of bunds, trenches, check dams, tanks and other water-harvesting structures. The water-users would then contribute the remaining quarter of funds, land and labour. Close to 3.52 million man-days of employment have been created while agricultural productivity has gone up.

In water management, ITC has gone the extra mile to minimize water used per unit of production and ensure that all waste water is treated and recycled instead of adding to water pollution. The rainwater-harvesting and watershed development programmes more than compensate for the water that it uses. In fact, it helps generate more than twice the water consumed by the company's operations.

Apart from this, ITC is the only company in the world to sequester more carbon than it emits, generate more water than it uses and recycle more solid waste than it produces. The ITC afforestation programmes have added enough trees to reduce the company's carbon footprint and offset emissions from energy use. Its carbon sequestration is twice as much as its consumption.

Energy efficiency is also a major concern in the company, with continuous audits being carried out so that usage can be lowered. ITC has invested significantly in renewable energy, including wind energy. Today, over 40 per cent of its energy comes from renewable sources. Five hotels, several factories and the Infotech Park run 100 per cent on wind energy. It has been carbon-positive for seven years. Most of its facilities—factories, hotels, etc.—do not throw garbage out of the window, but have invested in systems that can recycle or reuse waste.

It is thus fully understandable that ITC continues to gather up myriad awards for sustainability, awards that are conferred after rigorous scrutiny and assessments. The feather in its cap came with the World Business and Development Award at the Rio+20 United Nations Conference on Sustainable Development for its 'transformational initiatives in social and farm forestry programmes'.

It was the only Indian company to receive this prestigious recognition among a total of five large global companies who were honoured with the award. The award was instituted by the United Nations Development Programme (UNDP), the International Chamber of Commerce and the International Business Leaders Forum (IBLF) in partnership with the Netherlands ministry for foreign affairs, the Swedish International Development Cooperation Agency and the UN Global Compact.

The Next Frontier

The relentless diversification pursued by ITC has resulted in a massive growth of fourteen times in net revenues other than cigarettes between 1996 and 2013. At the end of the fiscal year 2013, ITC's net segment revenue from non-cigarette businesses stood at 58 per cent of its net revenue of Rs 33,000 crore.

Of far greater satisfaction to the board was the fact that the company helped to generate incomes for as many as 5 million people, which in terms of households is some 25 million persons, most of them from the weakest sections of society—tribals, farmers and women. At the same time, several factories as well as its premium luxury hotels were rated for the highest Platinum LEED certification for Green Buildings.

And with this tremendous achievement comes the shareholder value creation—a market capitalization that went up forty-five times from Rs 5,570 crore in 1996 to cross Rs 2.6 lakh crore in 2013, with total shareholder returns growing at a compound annual rate of 26 per cent. This then is the Triple Bottom Line at its best.

To be future-ready, ITC envisages an investment of Rs 25,000 crore in the coming five to seven years, and has engaged intensely in R&D with a state-of-the-art life sciences research centre in Benguluru.

The chief takeaway from ITC's journey after liberalization then is that it is eminently possible to blend the larger interests of society and sustainability with creating wealth for shareholders. The Triple Bottom Line approach that has been relentlessly championed by the company is no chimera—it is an achievable aspiration, and one that each and every company must espouse if it wants to step into a sustainable future. ITC has shown that it is possible to dream big and create a national asset in the form of an exemplary Indian enterprise.

4 LIFE SCIENCES TO LIFESTYLES

JUBILANT BHARTIA GROUP

Two news items about the Jubilant Bhartia Group stood out in the second half of 2012. The first lauded a 92 per cent increase in profits for Jubilant Life Sciences, and casually mentioned in passing that during the second quarter of the financial year, the company had got approvals for four more Abbreviated New Drug Applications (ANDAs) from the US Food and Drugs Administration (USFDA).[1]

The ANDA refers to approval for a drug formulation that is already approved, but is now available as a generic. It is 'abbreviated' because it needs to show only bioequivalency rather than go through preclinical and human trials as in the case of new drugs. When the producer of the generic drug receives the USFDA certification, it can manufacture the medicine in bulk at much lower costs and sell to a huge market. Jubilant Life Sciences is India's top Custom Research and Manufacturing Services (CRAMS) provider, and among the world's leading five companies in integrated Drug Discovery and Development Solutions (DDDS).

According to the other news item, a pizza store opened in Rajinder Nagar, New Delhi, in August 2012. A routine event, one might have thought—except that this was the 500th Domino's Pizza outlet in India. After the ribbon was cut, a surge of delighted customers thronged the store. Commenting to the TV reporter, a young university student was thrilled, 'I love Domino's! And I especially love the pizza and garlic bread, and I am so glad I am here today!'[2]

Shyam S. Bhartia had a different take, 'We are in 110 cities and want to go to tier-two and tier-three cities, and the response is very exciting.' No wonder—for Jubilant FoodWorks has redefined 'hip and happening' for a market accustomed to traditional Indian fast food, and has literally created a taste for a popular Italian food item in India. Its Domino's Pizza chain is the largest in the country, the fourth largest in the world, and the fastest growing network of Domino's Pizza outlets globally.

The Jubilant Bhartia Group, led by brothers Shyam S. Bhartia and Hari S. Bhartia, is not just into discovering drugs and reinventing lifestyles—it also operates in the segments of oil and gas, agricultural products, performance polymers, and retail and consulting services in aerospace and oilfield services. One arm offers sales and services for Audi, the prestigious German car, while another arm is best known to carpenters and woodworkers for the Jivanjor brand of consumer adhesives and wood finishes—in the ad, furniture items glued together with Jivanjor are transported by being thrown into a raging river and emerging unscathed at the other end.

The Jubilant Bhartia Group shows what Indian companies can achieve in the area of science and technology, and how to deploy R&D for global success. This just could not have taken place in the pre-reform period.

Organic to Inorganic

Belonging to a conventional Marwari trading family based in Kolkata, the two brothers took up professional studies. Shyam trained in cost accountancy, and Hari completed chemical engineering from IIT Delhi. This was enough for them to set up Vam Organic Chemicals Ltd in 1979, a company making, as its name indicates, organic chemicals. As Shyam told *Forbes Asia*, 'Back then you spent less time building your business and more time lobbying in the corridors of Udyog Bhavan to procure licences and get capacity allocations.'[3]

Vinyl acetate monomer (VAM) was the product that the brothers zeroed in on, a basic compound that is used to make polymers, which in turn have wide industrial and consumer products' applicability, from glass to adhesives and packaging. Molasses, a byproduct of the sugar industry, was the unusual choice for feedstock as raw material, in place of the more generally accepted crude oil-based feedstock.

Throughout the 1980s, the company went in for several other collaborations to gain technology from firms in the UK, US and Italy, branching out into various other chemicals. Pyridine, an intermediate chemical that is widely used in medicines, was its main product.

As *Forbes Asia* noted, managers who work for them credit the Bhartias with complementary strengths ('commercial and technical wisdom', 'thinking type [versus] a quick mind') and the ability to disagree with one another while still advancing operations. 'If one brother is told something, one can assume that the other knows—they are very close,' says Ajay Khanna, head of the Group's strategy and public affairs.[4]

It was Hari who became active in CII events, going on to become its president at a time when Indian industry was recovering from the global economic crisis in 2010–11. Shyam's wife, Shobhana, is the doyenne of the media empire HT Media, which runs the prestigious *Hindustan Times* newspaper that her grandfather, iconic nationalist tycoon Ghanshyam Das Birla, started with encouragement from Mahatma Gandhi. Kavita Bhartia, married to Hari, is one of India's foremost designers and runs 'Ogaan', a fashion chain.

For their contribution to industry, both Shyam and Hari were recently conferred the prestigious Entrepreneurs of the

Year award by the President of India, Pranab Mukherjee, at the All India Management Association (AIMA), Managing India Awards 2013.

It was in 1989 that Vam Organics launched the wood adhesive that made it a household name. Vamicol was the brand, and it quickly gained a market share as a sturdy, low-cost glue used in making furniture. Reaching out to villages and small towns, Vamicol helped build the company's presence among users at the end of the chain.

The advent of the 1991 reforms left the two chairmen unfazed. For them, liberalization and opening up to the world just meant new opportunities and an easier regime, without licences, to expand in. To begin with, the brothers continued the capacity enhancement in chemicals. Organic chemicals remained Vam Organics' mainstay, with a wide variety of products churned out in its units—acetic anhydride and acetic acid, pyridine and picoline, liquid and dry ice, and so on. Construction chemicals and fertilizers, too, came into its ambit.

Other businesses also came up in the first spate of the liberalized industrial environment. In 1995, a busy year for Shyam and Hari, the food company, Jubilant FoodWorks, was set up and commenced operations the following year. At the time, food processing was an underdeveloped industry, and few ventured into it, given the complexities of working with farmers and creating supply chains. This company went on to become the master franchisee of Domino's Pizza in India, Bangladesh, Nepal and Sri Lanka. It also acquired a stake in Hot Breads, and later took up Dunkin' Donuts, aiming to spark an interest among the new Indian middle class for branded restaurants.

Also in 1995, the Group went into the oil and gas business, another industry that had just been opened up to the private sector and in which the operating scenario was yet to become favourable. The brothers began by acquiring a share of a field that was already producing oil in northeastern India. In later years, this wing of the Group built up a range of nine blocks in India in the proven hydrocarbon basins of Assam–Arakan, Cambay, Cauvery and Krishna–Godavari. It also picked up a block in Myanmar in 2012.

Jubilant Enpro was incorporated in 1991 to provide sales, marketing, repair and maintenance services for aviation products, power and infrastructure, and offshore support services for drilling rigs and supply vessels. These were sectors that foreign companies were just beginning to enter, and Jubilant aimed to provide them with assistance as a company with expertise on the ground. In addition, the Jubilant Bhartia Group also established a presence in auto, retail and hypermarkets.

The era of reforms was thus seized by the brothers to diversify and proliferate in areas where they saw opportunities. Typically, the industries they selected were not the easiest to work in, but the returns of taking the risks were higher. The promoters were ready to take on the many challenges that these ventures entailed, committed to being the best in their fields.

Vam Organics' plants and units expanded with added capital investments. With its numerous technology tie-ups, it had a strong outward orientation.

But the Asian financial crisis changed all that. The next few years were tough, as for most other companies in India at the time. Large capacities in the Asian 'tiger' economies meant a glut in the market and falling prices. Vam Organics undertook fresh investments for increasing its output and for adding to its repertoire of products. It brought in a new specialist adhesive and revamped its fertilizer plant.

But a new avenue of growth was needed. Given its existing skills and competencies, built up over almost two decades of painstaking sourcing of technology and overseas collaborations, what strategy would best suit it was the question that the two promoters asked themselves. Vam Organics had already emerged as India's largest manufacturer of alcohol-based organic chemicals, with the largest capacities in the country for most of its products, such as acetic acid and acetic anhydride. Where could it go from there?

A decade ago, the company stepped onto a path of transformation from a chemical company to a diversified specialty chemicals and pharmaceutical company, offering a wide range of products. Today, Jubilant Life Sciences has successfully transcended to the next phase of evolution—into an integrated pharmaceutical and life sciences company. The company has classified its businesses into two segments, namely, pharmaceuticals and life science ingredients.

JUBILANT!

The name 'Jubilant' symbolizes positivity, dynamism, triumph and joy, all of which guide and shape the company's collective experiences and efforts. 'Organosys' suggests life and nature, with 'sys' embodying 'the company's emphasis on systems, synthesis and science.' So went the company press release in January 2001, announcing Vam Organics' new name—Jubilant Organosys.

The re-branding under a new name was part of the entire restructuring exercise that Shyam and Hari Bhartia devised. The change in name was not just re-branding, it was a major shift towards a new innovation-led, science-based corporate avatar.

According to Shyam and Hari, the basic chemicals that Vam Organics was producing did not offer high returns. Besides, after being the largest in the Indian field already, their competition came from global giants. Assessing the outlook for India, a key advantage of operating in the country was identified—highly skilled scientific manpower that would be available at costs lower than almost anywhere else in the world.

'India is the only location in the world where you can hire 300 medicinal chemists whom you can train to become productive in two to three years,' explained Hari, when interviewed for the

Forbes Asia cover story on India's 100 richest people. Further, 'we realized that we should be in a sector where there are strong entry barriers...'[5]

In 2000–01, the company's sales were about Rs 847 crore, of which export sales were less than one-tenth. VAM was its biggest product. With technology as part of its DNA right from its inception, the company had already established an R&D lab, recognized by the Department of Science and Technology and staffed with highly qualified scientists and technicians. The lab worked in the development of organic intermediates, specialty chemicals and fine chemicals and even in biotechnology. It also carried out contract research on organic intermediates for pharmaceuticals and agrochemical companies.

Putting all these together, the rebranded company—Jubilant Organosys—moved up the chain, producing specialty chemicals with greater value addition. It clearly demarcated its areas of strength and the roadmap for the next phase of its growth. 'The general perception about Vam was that it was in the alcohol-based industry,' pointed out Shyam. 'Very few people knew that it was the flagship of a diversified Rs 1,200-crore Group with interests in chemicals, biotechnology, information technology, food and oil and gas.'[6]

According to its annual report for 2001–02, the strategy was to streamline operations, focus on a high–value global presence, and achieve a position of leadership and growth. To that end, the company restructured its overall operations into three Strategic Business Units (SBUs), to handle each product separately—organic intermediate goods, specialty and fine chemicals; performance chemicals; and plant health and animal nutrition. Each of the SBUs was further organized into growth units that looked after specific products, depending on the nature of the business.

The second objective was to become a global company. Although its products were already being sold in fifty countries, the idea was to ramp up exports. While being the largest domestic producer of pyridine, picoline and their derivatives, the company had also emerged as the third largest in the world for these chemicals. Its other products, too, ranked in the top ten in the international industry.

Innovation became the defining mantra of the new entity. R&D would continue to be a major driver for meeting consumer needs in industries such as pharmaceuticals and agrochemicals, construction and textiles, paper and packaging, and food and beverages.

Expanding its R&D activities meant that the new entity was able to launch a record number of new products in the very first year of the shift. The rewards were many and immediate—by developing customized molecules, the company signalled its knowledge-led capacities. It came to be globally recognized as a 'critical vendor' and could, therefore, increase its market share. It also addressed commercial applications in related areas.

Finally, Jubilant deployed information technology to streamline its services and delivery. It set up a supply chain management system, which helped it to take its servicing to a new level.

As for its widely recognized brand, Vamicol, this too was changed to become 'Jivanjor', which was now the 'umbrella' name for all its products: adhesives, wood polish and other woodworking products. By this time, Vamicol had cornered over a fifth of the wood adhesive market and was number two. 'The brand reflects our core value of bonding,' stated Shyam.[7]

The new name 'Jubilant Organosys' thus reflected the strategic future of the company, maintaining a strong focus on high-value-added chemicals in the international market. 'Our new corporate ID signifies our moving up the value chain and our continued emphasis on R&D,' explained Shyam.[8] The fact that the international market was dominated by huge multinational companies, such as BASF, with their large resources was apparently of little concern to the Jubilant Group. They were confident about being able to match MNCs through their customer understanding and tailored product development.

Stepping Out

That the R&D focus was an excellent option was evident after five years of rigorous product development. In the financial year of 2002–03, Jubilant Organosys notched up sales worth over Rs 710.5 crore, of which 28 per cent came from newly developed products in these five years.

The company shifted increasingly to its preferred segment of the specialty and pharmaceutical chemicals and developed research and manufacturing facilities that matched the best in the world. Within five years of changing its focus, Jubilant Organosys emerged as one of India's largest integrated drug discovery platforms, offering drug design, bioinformatics, medicinal chemistry and clinical services, among others.

Believing that the sector of life sciences was going to be a high-growth one in the future, Shyam and Hari looked at the opportunities from drugs coming off patents.

An active pharmaceutical ingredient (API) refers to a chemical that is the active part in a medicine. These chemicals have to be approved by national health regulators and authorities in individual countries after a rigorous process of application to meet the specified standards. Development of the API is complex, requiring years of research and testing, using highly sophisticated technology.

Apart from API, a medicine also contains inactive materials that make the drug easier to absorb. Any company venturing into commercial applications of science must have the requisite technical capabilities and comply with strict standards for Good Manufacturing Practices (GMP) as delineated by governments and also as set by customers.

So the chairmen decided to enter this market. As a first

step for inorganic growth, Jubilant acquired Max India's API operations. Max India was running an advanced manufacturing facility in Nanjangud near Mysore, which had the potential to get USFDA approval. It produced drugs for the central nervous system therapeutic segment as well as other formulations for gastrointestinal diseases, among others.

Shyam pointed out that this acquisition was a natural corollary of Jubilant's excellent position as a supplier of advanced intermediates to the international pharmaceutical players and would help the company to expand its market presence. The acquisition also accelerated Jubilant's shift into pharmaceuticals and shortened the learning curve for the promoters.

Thus, the Group set off in a different direction, moving from bulk chemicals to an integrated pharmaceutical manufacturing and research company. Investing in a new drug discovery centre in Bangalore and a phase I clinical development centre in Noida, Jubilant went in for both organic and inorganic growth models.

In the next few years, it made headlines by acquiring four overseas companies, two in Europe and two in the US. The Belgian acquisitions helped it to go into unbranded finished dosage forms for markets in Europe and gain expertise in handling the complex regulatory environment of the European Union.

In the US, it started with a small manufacturing company to produce dosage forms. A fifty-two-bed hospital and a clinical research centre helped it to carry out the requisite bioequivalence tests. Another US Contract Research Organization (CRO) company that it acquired in 2005 led its clinical trials in phase II to phase IV of the drug discovery process.

Taking over the Max India API operations, Jubilant's spending on research went up from 0.6 per cent of net sales to 1.2 per cent. In 2003, it employed as many as 150 scientists in its labs and centres. Nineteen patent applications were filed in the US and other countries. The quality and environmental systems went in for ISO standards, and received certification from the

Department of Scientific and Industrial Research (DSIR). But it continued to invest in new R&D facilities in Uttar Pradesh.

Jubilant Biosys was spun off in 2001 to provide bio-informatics research services for the entire drug discovery and development process. It developed bio- and chemo-informatic services as databases that helped speed up drug discovery for medical ills such as Alzheimer's disease, arthritis and cancer. Jubilant Clinsys was set up in 2004 to focus on entry into the clinical research industry with the US acquisition.

International business remained the focus, with exports growing rapidly due to market expansion and new product development. Jubilant had reached fifty countries, with Europe as the largest market for its products. China was also on its radar, and it set up an office to take care of its distribution there. In the early years of the new millennium, this again was a strategic decision that most Indian companies of the time had not taken cognizance of. It showed once again that innovative thinking was the first step to global status.

Another hectic year for the two chairmen was 2007, as they went in for multiple acquisitions and joint ventures. Hollister-Stier Laboratories in the US was taken over to give the company a presence in injectable contract manufacturing and allergy and immunotherapy areas. Draxis Specialty Pharmaceuticals of Canada was another contract manufacturer, engaged in radiopharmaceuticals. While announcing the completion of this acquisition, Jubilant stressed that it was a niche, high-entry-barrier business. But the prospects were considered to be excellent for the sector.

The cost of these two acquisitions ran into several hundred millions of dollars, with Draxis itself at over a quarter billion dollars. Later, the two acquisitions were brought together to consolidate Jubilant's contract manufacturing operations in North America.

Today, Jubilant Life Sciences Ltd is one of the largest

investors in North America with an investment of about $600 million, including over $300 million in the US. It is one of the largest employers amongst Indian pharmaceutical companies in the US with around 1,000 employees, of whom 99 per cent are US citizens. The company has more than half its assets based in North America, spread across the US from Spokane in Washington to Salisbury in Maryland to Bedminster in New Jersey and Raleigh in North Carolina.

The partnership with Eli Lilly, a fifty-fifty R&D initiative in 2008, was the first time that a global drug discovery company had come together with an Indian firm in a joint venture. The two companies already had a pact for sharing any discovery since 2005, but in the new joint venture, both would contribute molecules to go through the pre-clinical and phase II stages of the development of new drugs.[9]

Dating back to 1876, Eli Lilly is based in Indianapolis, and one of the first in the world to start pharma research. A top ten global company, it enjoys excellent credibility for its medicines. This joint venture leveraged Jubilant's research capabilities in its Biosys arm, and offered Eli Lilly the chance to take its early-stage compounds to the next phase. The two companies decided to work on medicines for cancer, diabetes and cardiovascular conditions.

That the partnership worked well and brought gains to both sides was evident when two years later, it was extended for five more years and expanded. Many discovery milestones and pre-clinical possibilities had been arrived at during the four-year partnership.

The year 2007 saw another landmark venture, committed to create an affordable, world-class healthcare delivery system for the middle- and lower-income-group people in West Bengal, including those living in districts and villages. Jubilant First Trust Healthcare Ltd was set up at Kolkata. West Bengal became the new frontier of operation for the company and the Jubilant Kalpataru Hospital came up in Barasat, Kolkata, in 2009.

The 120-bed superspeciality hospital was inaugurated by Pranab Mukherjee, then finance minister. The idea was to create an infrastructure of 1,000 beds in seven hospitals across the state that would cater to low-income populations in a hub-and-spoke model of healthcare. A fifty-bed medical centre is also being managed at the same time (Rabindranath Thakur Diagnostic and Medical Care Centre).

And finally, as part of all this diversification and restructuring, Jubilant Organosys further changed its name to Jubilant Life Sciences Ltd in 2010, consolidating its focus exclusively on pharma and life sciences.

'Almost a decade ago, we had stepped onto this path of transformation,' said Shyam, 'and today we have successfully positioned ourselves as a life sciences company with a presence across the value chain,'[10] which in the case of the Group ranged from the beginning of creating molecules right up to the delivery of healthcare.

It enjoys strategic positioning in the pharma and life sciences industry, across products and services in many countries, with continuous investments in different areas and total commitment to innovation. The company has ten world-class manufacturing facilities, seven in India and three in North America, with around 6,400 staff members belonging to diverse nationalities, and serves customers in as many as ninety countries.

In November 2010, the agri and polymers part of the company was split off into Jubilant Industries Ltd. The new company would handle all products related to crop nutrition, as well as adhesives and wood-finishes, and the application polymers of emulsions, food polymers and latex for the automotive industry in its five factories scattered across the country. Jivanjor continued to be the second largest brand in consumer adhesives, but Jubilant was also a top-three player in single superphosphate fertilizers, and ranked second in the world for producing chewing gum base and latex for automobile tyres.

With all of these initiatives, continuously adapting business models to enter into new 'high-barrier' fields, the life sciences and chemicals companies of the Jubilant Bhartia Group are all set to compete globally.

In its latest initiative, the life sciences' arm set up a special economic zone (SEZ) over 300 acres in Bharuch, Gujarat. While inaugurating the SEZ in April 2012, chief minister Narendra Modi lauded the Group for its strong emphasis on research. The global-scale plants engaged in the manufacture of Vitamin B3 and 3-Cyanopyridine at the SEZ makes Jubilant the largest producer of Vitamin B3 in India and the second largest globally.

The company is also setting up a manufacturing plant at the SEZ for Symtet, a crop science ingredient for one of the world's largest and safest low-cost insecticides through an environment-friendly process. This will make Jubilant the world's largest producer of the agro-chemical for insecticides through a green route. These facilities will generate exports of about Rs 1,000 crore at full capacity.

Jubilant Life Sciences records its operations in two functional groups to delineate the different focus points—the pharmaceutical and the life science segments of business. Signing contracts worth several hundred million dollars, it continues its quest for new and better drugs. It has accumulated fifty ANDA filings in the US, with twenty-five approved by September 2012, along with applications to drug regulators in Europe, Canada and the rest of the world.

The business strategy for the future is targeted at vertical integration for moving up the value chain; increasing penetration in key markets; innovation for new products and better margins; and, finally, focus on the Triple Bottom Line for economic, social and environmental performance.

Corporate social responsibility (CSR) is an integral part of how Jubilant conducts its business and the efforts are directed towards community development through focus on primary education, basic healthcare service and livelihood generation programmes centred on improving the employability of women and local youth. The company has been recognized with several awards, including the recent NDTV Profit Business Leadership Award 2012 for Corporate Social Responsibility presented by Dr Montek Singh Ahluwalia, deputy chairman, Planning Commission.

Home Delivery of Happiness

When I was living in Colombo, Sri Lanka, I experienced first-hand the advantages of Domino's over other pizza brands. 'It tastes much better, Mom,' claimed my teenage son, who was thrilled that the city now offered his favourite pizza through two outlets. 'And,' the final argument directed at a parsimonious parent, 'it's much cheaper!' With this proclamation, my son zeroed in on the two main strategies that Jubilant FoodWorks devised to target consumers like him—taste and cost.

Coming back to India, Domino's pizzas are no longer a metro phenomenon. Targeting 'massification' of pizza consumption, Jubilant went in for a multi-pronged ad campaign in small cities, reaching out to 118 cities through 552 stores by 31 December 2012. It uncovered a large new base of pizza-lovers, from Roorkee and Calicut to Sholapur and Sangli. Pizza for Indians is no longer just a new food item—it has come to embody the aspirations of millions of people for a global lifestyle, a chance to be part of modern Western culture. Most of all, it is about fun and friendship, to get together and share a pizza.

Jubilant FoodWorks, master franchise of Domino's Pizza in India, Bangladesh, Nepal and Sri Lanka, stepped out to make pizza a preferred option for food home delivery. Such a formal and extensive home delivery system had not been tried in India, where, typically, eating outside the home until recently was considered harmful for health in middle-class families and was usually not affordable. The jump in incomes after the economic reforms as well as busier lives changed mindsets, and it became acceptable to eat out on a regular basis. Even then, when families wanted to eat out, they would go to a restaurant or have street food. When outside food was needed at home, the neighbourhood dhaba would be called up.

The journey towards making pizzas popular was not easy. It began with the first store in Greater Kailash I, New Delhi, in 1996, aiming to create the taste for pizza as an alternative to fast food in the unorganized sector. Its 'Hungry kya?' ad typified the pizza as a quick snack option. This was followed up with the strategy of home delivery as practised in other countries.

Domino's India had to invent the home delivery model to begin with. Soon its motorcycles were well-recognized in cities, zipping around to deliver pizzas and other Domino's offerings within the stipulated '30 minutes or free'. It pioneered the organized cash-on-delivery system that online retailers have adopted with great success. It was truly a 'blue-ocean' strategy to sell pizzas in India, creating new tastes and new markets. The low price of just Rs 39 for a pizza enticed a new segment of consumers to try it out. 'Khushiyon ki home delivery' resonated with these new fans of pizza.

Jubilant FoodWorks Ltd went public in February 2010, receiving a tremendous response for its initial public offering. This was due to the strong growth potential seen by investors, who oversubscribed to the issue by almost thirty-one times and lifted its shares on the first day of listing. Since then, the company has delivered amazing value to its shareholders with continued fast-growing profits, new stores being opened at a rapid pace and plans for expansion that are on track. Again, Jubilant FoodWorks was the first company in the food industry to be listed in India.

In its first annual report, the company listed out its key strategies for organizational excellence. Its tie-up with one of the world's most recognizable brands from early days gave it not only high visibility, but also helped it gain the expertise and knowhow of the worldwide chain. The company set up a well-oiled supply chain with four regional hubs in the metro cities, which enabled quality control and timely delivery. Its marketing strategy was particularly effective, being targeted directly at creating high brand recall for quality and customer service among households.

Innovation in taste and new products were brought in to meet customers' high expectations. Costs were a key factor, as Jubilant aimed at supplying high quality at low and affordable price points. To maintain these prices, the company bought supplies from a limited number of carefully selected vendors, so that the whole chain was streamlined efficiently. Most of all, it emphasized employee training, and provided opportunities for its staff to grow, develop and move up the career ladder.

Lip-smacking new entrants to the menu continue to bring more and more customers into the pizza-eating fold—3-Cheese Pizza, Taco Indiana, Stuffed Garlic Bread, pasta, chicken wings, Twistyz, Potato Smackers and new toppings for Pizza Mania tempt consumers to return to the store again and again. Four of the five busiest Domino's Pizza stores worldwide are in India, and as many as 57.7 million pizzas were sold in 2011–12 alone.

For the opening of the 300th and 400th stores, Patrick Doyle, president and chief executive officer of Domino's Pizza Inc., travelled to India twice within fifteen months. Presumably tired of turning up in India every few months for a new milestone, he sent the executive vice president of Domino's Pizza International, Richard Allison, to celebrate the opening of the 500th store in August 2012. '... India operations have emerged as one of the largest and fastest growing,' he said.

After four years of 'Khushiyon ki home delivery', the brand repositioned itself for a deeper engagement with its customers with the new tagline, 'Yeh hai rishton ka time,' to promote family and other close relationships. The company is also the market leader with a 70 per cent plus share in the pizza home-delivery segment in India and a 62 per cent market share in the organized pizza market.

In February 2011, the Bhartia brothers went in for an alliance with Dunkin' Donuts, the leading international baked goods and coffee chain brand. This move envisioned capitalizing on the identification of a brand with the lifestyle of the youthful new consumer population of India. After careful development of the restaurant model and 'look', the flagship store was opened in Connaught Place, New Delhi. The brand name in India is 'Dunkin' Donuts & More' to signify the wide product range and the unique experiences that the restaurants offer.

For Diwali in 2012, the new chain innovated new tastes, mixing Indian with American tastes in interesting flavours such as coconut rasgulla, petal gulab jamun and motichoor laddu doughnuts. Jubilant FoodWorks was awarded the Emerging Company of the Year by the Economic Times Awards for Corporate Excellence, 2012. The prime minister, Dr Manmohan Singh, handed over the trophy.

Not Just Business

Sustainability is a mission for the Jubilant Bhartia Group, and its policies run the gamut of areas in environment, health and safety (EHS), climate change mitigation and green supply chain management.

Jubilant Organosys received the Golden Peacock Global Award for Excellence in Corporate Governance for 2006–07. Bestowed annually by the World Council for Corporate Governance, the UK, the award recognized Jubilant's disclosure, financial performance and contribution to society and the environment.

Jubilant also regularly receives awards for innovation management, energy conservation, environmental excellence, water management, manufacturing excellence and other areas, each of which affirms its strong commitment to ethical and responsible business practices.

As early as 2003, Jubilant took the landmark decision to compile a corporate sustainability report, one of the first such reports in India, in accordance with the Global Reporting Initiative guidelines. Covering economic, environmental and social performance in accordance with the Triple Bottom Line approach to sustainability, the report each year gains the A+ accreditation. It goes beyond the three pillars of sustainability to add governance to the equation.

Starlings at a bio-compost site, the black ibis, wagtails, cattle egrets, and other birds sighted at the company's plants—where they had not been seen earlier—are testimony to its management style. Responsible use of raw materials means that molasses account for over half the total used in products. As early as 1984, the company had gone in for a waste treatment plant that was then the largest in the country. This not only treated effluents, but also produced biogas and organic manure. Biogas consumption went up over five times in three years to 2011–12. Wastewater is recycled and reused, and reverse osmosis plants are established at all large units. Effluents get treated or disposed of in compliance with regulations, so that the company ends up with zero discharges.

To the great pride of its leaders, the company was one of four to be mentioned in the International Finance Corporation's publication *Market Movers: Lessons from a Frontier of Innovation*, as a case study for the above initiatives.[11] Citing liberalization in 1991 as a catalyst for Jubilant to 'rethink its business model', the report pointed out that the company's decision to use sugarcane waste, molasses, as its feedstock instead of crude-oil based feedstock protected it from market fluctuations and was environmentally friendly. EHS regulations are tough, but Jubilant goes beyond mandated standards, a defining feature that enables it to be a partner of choice for institutional investors. EHS cost considerations are factored into the products right from inception.

The Jubilant Bhartia Foundation is tasked with the social development efforts of the Group. In a typically global mindset fashion, the foundation aligns itself with the Millennium Development Goals adopted by the UN, which extend to literacy, maternal health, diseases and so on. It supports government primary rural education, working with 100 schools from sixty-five villages covering 13,500 students under its project 'Muskaan' (smile). Improving basic healthcare and livelihood generation through vocational training are also part of its comprehensive CSR agenda.

Also, dedicated to promoting social innovation in India, Jubilant Bhartia Foundation joined hands with the Schwab Foundation in the year 2010 to present the Social Entrepreneur of the Year award (SEOY). The award identifies and celebrates visionary social ventures that demonstrate large-scale transformative change. The organizations that do so are scaling or replicating their ideas across India and in other countries.

Working with all stakeholders, the foundation has strengthened a public–private–people–partnership or 4P model that integrates the government and communities into its efforts.

Global Leadership

With an estimated value of $3 billion and 30,000 employees all over the world, the Jubilant Bhartia Group offers many insights into the new model of Indian business. First, the Group sets no limits on itself. Rather, it ventures out into risky areas where high-entry barriers deter most businesses. It has identified such fields as huge opportunities where maximum value can be created.

Moreover, it is one of the few companies that has aligned itself to science, research and innovation in order to leverage the opportunities in high-growth sectors. Its management refuses to be afraid of scientific procedures and processes, employing many hundreds of top scientists to cross frontiers of knowledge. As a 'science active' company, it will remain at the cutting edge of new advances in science, ready to converge science with business.

5 PUTTING INDIA ON WHEELS

MARUTI SUZUKI INDIA LIMITED

There are companies that lead the race year after year, and there are companies that move in from behind to pole positions. But there are few companies that entirely change the race altogether.

Maruti Suzuki is one such Indian company that has steered its own course, leaving others to follow behind. That it was a government-owned company, set up by an Act of Parliament and subject to numerous rules and regulations, makes its success even more stunning. It pioneered an entirely new industry sector, reset rules of operations, conjured supply chains out of thin air and, at the same time, fulfilled the aspirations of millions of ordinary Indian citizens.

Maruti Udyog Ltd (MUL) was born of the dreams of Indira Gandhi after her son, Sanjay Gandhi, died while piloting a small plane in 1980. As prime minister, she wanted her son's idea of a 'people's car' to become a reality. MUL was set up as a government company in February 1981, to roll out 100,000 passenger cars and 40,000 light commercial vehicles. From the beginning, foreign technology and partnership was envisaged as part of the project.

This was an era when cars, viewed as luxury consumption items, were heavily taxed. Import duties on components were prohibitively expensive, foreign collaborations were not permitted and human resource capabilities for manufacturing were limited. In fact, only three car companies existed at the time, which were allowed to produce only three car models and were not permitted to import technology or develop new models.

Prices were fixed by the government, and for any capacity expansion, government permissions were required. Quality, safety and performance were hardly considerations in a market where anything produced could be sold because of a lack of options. In fact, customers had to wait for years after filing applications to purchase a car until their turn came up. The car, driven to the dealers from the factory, would arrive in a sorry condition and would immediately have to be taken to a workshop for repairs. Auto mechanics were wizards, being able to keep a car rattling on, long after its life would be considered over in any other country.

From the beginning, the premise of MUL was different from that of other public sector enterprises (PSEs). R.C. Bhargava's book, *The Maruti Story: How a Public Sector Company Put India on Wheels,*[1] outlines the out-of-the-box thinking that went into the first steps taken by the company. To begin with, a private sector expert, Sumant Moolgaokar, chairman of Tata Engineering and Locomotive Ltd (TELCO, now Tata Motors) was deputed as its non-executive chairman. Dr V. Krishnamurthy, who had been instrumental in revitalizing the PSE, Bharat Heavy Electricals Ltd (BHEL), was persuaded to come on board as vice-chairman and managing director. He brought in D.S. Gupta, a graduate of the Indian Institute of Management (IIM), Ahmedabad, as staff officer, and R.C. Bhargava from the Indian Administrative Service (IAS) as director, commercial.

Bhargava describes the next steps, 'Soon after the company was established and I had joined, a team consisting of Mr Krishnamurthy, D.S. Gupta, and myself from Maruti, and the late Mr Moolgaokar and V.S. Krishnan from TELCO went to Europe to look for partners and products...

'However, we had a UK-based consultant with us for most of the trip, as we needed technical help when looking at products and technology of different companies in Europe. We discussed with him the merits of cars with smaller engines against cars with larger engines, especially in terms of fuel efficiency and cost of operation. His advice was that smaller engines need not be more fuel efficient as compared to larger engines, and that in most situations, cars with engines above 1 litre were likely to be more economical. The argument was based on the premise that smaller engines may result in the power being inadequate for the weight of the car.

'Later, we found in Japan that they were also able to reduce the weight of the cars and these did not suffer in performance as compared to cars with bigger engines. We were of course aware that in the UK cars with engines below 1 litre were not available.'

In an unprecedented move, the government presented MUL with a target that would have been a stretch even for a private company, saying, 'Get a car on the road by December 1983,' which at the time was just thirty months away. Moreover, as many as 100,000 cars were to be produced each year, and the foreign partner was expected to buy back half the number in order to contribute to foreign exchange. Although the second condition was dropped later, the first was onerous enough at a time when car sales were just about 40,000 annually.

But first, MUL had to look for a suitable partner. This could hardly be considered an easy task, given that India had just recently turned multinational companies out and was not known to welcome foreign technology. And most overseas companies of the time were not producing small cars at costs that could be considered affordable by Indian standards.

After much to-and-fro, the only company with which a possible contract could be signed turned out to be Suzuki Motor Corporation (SMC) of Japan. It was by sheer chance that SMC got to learn about MUL's search for a foreign partner, since the original MUL letter requesting proposals had gone astray. An SMC manager read about MUL's predicament in a magazine during a flight back to his country from India, and took it up with the SMC board. Although SMC was already a market leader in small cars, its president, Osamu Suzuki, saw the potential tie-up with MUL as part of his ambition to expand the company.

Recalling the process, Bhargava adds with satisfaction, 'The delay in Suzuki entering the race to partner the government in the Maruti project, for reasons given in my book, probably worked in our favour, especially when Suzuki realized that its arch rival—Daihatsu—was walking away with the project. Our time for taking decisions was actually very limited due to the deadline for starting production and this was conveyed to Suzuki. As a result, Suzuki decided to partner the government without carrying out any due diligence about India, PSEs or the car industry... Suzuki, at that point of time, knew very little about India. I wonder if Suzuki would have partnered the government in this project if they had done a proper due diligence.'[2]

SMC's financial submissions and willingness to help in Maruti's quest for technology and quality carried the day and terms were negotiated. It also agreed to buy a 26 per cent stake in the new company. The Japanese were tough negotiators but equally difficult for the company was getting the requisite clearances from the Indian side. The Indian government—in the form of the Department of Heavy Industries, Planning Commission, Public Investment Board, Cabinet Committee for Economic Affairs and various ministries and departments—was fully involved in the decision-making and licensing process, overseeing each and every action of the new company. The final agreement papers, signed on 2 October 1982, Mahatma Gandhi's birth anniversary, had three signatories: Maruti, Suzuki and the Indian government.

For the first time with respect to a PSE, the contract included the objective of 'making profits'.

With just fourteen months to go before the deadline of rolling out the first car, the first years of the company's existence are a fascinating story by itself. The way Maruti went about setting up the factory, getting processes and systems in place and developing the initial supply chains downstream and upstream, is a saga of persistence, determination and sheer resolve. On 14 December 1983, right on target, Indira Gandhi recalled her son's dream and emotionally handed over the keys of the first Maruti 800 to the designated allottee.

The model went on to become the beloved icon of the Indian auto industry for the next twenty years. Maruti triggered a mindset revolution not only in the auto sector, but set an example for all of Indian industry, sparking a mentality of 'Yes, it can be done!' The company galvanized the stodgy Indian industry ecosystem and blazed a trail up and down the economy. Its impact transformed perceptions about moribund public sector enterprises and bureaucratic procedures. Process management, commitment to quality, team-building, cost control, stakeholder partnerships—all these and more were demonstrated through the success of Maruti's first cars.

'Maruti Udyog established new standards of quality, productivity, industrial relations and customer care in the automobile industry and the manufacturing sector at large. It not only came to dominate the Indian car market within a short period of time but also showed that India could manufacture and export a sophisticated engineering product to the demanding markets of western Europe. Importantly, all this was done by a PSE (public sector enterprise) at a time when the public sector was characterized by inefficiency and sloth...' Bhargava sums up in his book.[3]

MUL could achieve profits right from the beginning owing to the deposit that customers placed when booking a car. A few months after launch, it was already producing a hundred cars a day, far ahead of its two rivals, which belonged to the private sector. It also launched the Maruti van and the Gypsy. All three took the market by storm, generating tremendous interest among consumers starved of modern vehicles. By 1990–91, Maruti increased its sales volume to 110,031, far surpassing all other passenger cars at 67,408. Maruti made profits from the very first year, showing the pent-up demand for cars in India at the time.

But already the conditions were changing. More joint ventures were coming up, including in two-wheelers and auto components. Moreover, the Indian economy was trammelled by factors such as oil price hikes in the wake of the Gulf War, shrinking foreign exchange reserves, and the declining rupee. The government increased excise and customs duties on cars and imported parts, and rising prices of inputs like steel further added to final market prices. A new phase in India's auto industry was coming up, and Maruti would have to pull out all the stops to remain the market leader.

A Fresh Start

Fortunately, MUL had intrepid managers for whom meeting production targets was top priority, whatever the conditions. There would be no excuses and no scaling back. Bhargava took over as managing director in 1985 and also as chairman in 1990, remaining at the helm till his retirement in 1997. Dr Krishnamurthy gave up the post of non-executive chairman in 1990, but continued to take a keen interest in MUL as a member of the Planning Commission. 'We knew nothing [about making cars],' said Bhargava. 'But we had to convert that challenge into an opportunity.'[4]

SMC, too, was a challenging task master. After Bhargava persuaded the corporation that India, indeed, was a good market for small cars, Suzuki went all out to support the fledgling company, despite being fully aware that 'it is difficult to have a good operation in India'[5]. SMC trained hundreds of

MUL managers and technicians over the years, teaching them the methods of quality control and processes that the Japanese had perfected.

'Before we could manufacture cars we had to learn lessons in shopfloor cleanliness. We were ready to assemble cars in October 1983,' recalls Bhargava.[6] 'But the Suzuki engineers said "No." The director of production, A. Shinohara, said the shopfloor was dirty and had to be cleaned. He picked up a bucket of water and a mop and started cleaning the factory floor himself. All of us followed. For a whole week, all that we did in the factory was clean the floors.'

With this solid grounding, the PSE that had taken the bull by the horn, went on to transform itself to align with the emerging contours of a new India. The first change that was set in motion was that the company would no longer be a PSE.

To know the scale of the transformation, it is worth recalling the environment that PSEs were functioning in at the time. At the time of Independence, the private sector itself acknowledged that it did not have the resources to undertake the vast task of industrialization of the nation, and expected the government to take charge. In the industrial policy announcements soon after 1947, the government demarcated seventeen industries for exclusive operation of the public sector and another twelve where the public sector would have the dominant role.

Under Jawaharlal Nehru's visionary 'commanding heights of the economy' aspiration, PSEs of huge scale and impact were set up in critical areas such as steel, irrigation, capital goods and mining. These laid a foundation for manufacturing industries and also created a demand for goods and services from the private sector. Later, struggling private sector companies in areas across engineering, textiles, tea and other non-core industries were also taken over to avoid job losses. But over the years, the functioning of these iconic enterprises was severely constrained by rules and regulations, making them archaic in a changing world.

As companies owned by the government, any business decisions required much moving of files up and down the functionary ladder, and the PSE enjoyed little autonomy in devising its own strategies. Bureaucrats in charge of the PSE came to their jobs with little or no experience and were subject to transfers any time. From investments to pricing, to hiring decisions, the government—through the relevant ministry—intervened in all matters. Secure in their jobs, PSE managers—who were often the best in their field, given that private sector jobs did not carry as much prestige or perks—did not favour taking risks. Compliance with extra-business regulations, such as committees set up to examine PSE workings, also needed to be ensured. Thus, paperwork and red-tape were the defining characteristics of the PSE, which, over time, stagnated despite having access to adequate funds and markets.

The 1991 reforms exposed the public sector to competition as well. The 1991 industrial policy statement pointed to the 'serious problems' in public enterprises, including lack of growth in productivity, poor project management, bloated staff strength and paucity of technology. 'The result is that many of the public enterprises have become a burden rather than being an asset to the government,' lamented the statement.

The reservation of certain industries for the public sector was thus lifted, and the private sector was allowed to enter these areas. The list of reserved sectors came down to eight, and in the following years, more sectors were de-reserved. Sick PSEs were to be restructured; the government's shareholding was to be diluted; and boards were to be given greater powers with more autonomy and accountability.

For MUL, one of the best performing PSEs, this was the time to act fast and retool to meet the expected surge in global competition. To begin with, the government felt that reducing its stake and bringing in more equity from the overseas partner would adequately demonstrate to the world that India was serious about these policy announcements.

Thus, SMC was approached to increase its shareholding and it readily agreed to become equal partners with the government. In June 1992, after SMC bought 2.2 million shares, MUL ceased to be a PSE. It was no longer subject to public sector rules regarding hiring from employment exchanges, scrutiny by parliamentary committees and audits by the Comptroller and Auditor General (CAG), award of contracts, and other basic operational requirements. From then on, its journey continued in the private sector, although the government remained half the shareholder.

As Bhargava outlines in his book, this created somewhat of a confused identity of the government in the company. The government was not used to being an equal partner, and could not clearly distinguish its role as a shareholder, which entailed looking at the best interests of the company, from that of sovereign entity, which expected its decisions to be implemented without question.

It was difficult for MUL to renew its licence, expand capacity or obtain financing without the concurrence of the ministry, which was not often forthcoming or was delayed inordinately. Although the Board of Directors included government representatives, they tended to take the line of the Department of Heavy Industries. Regarding financing, the government was in no position in the early 1990s to offer fresh resources despite a long waiting period for the new Zen model. Thus, the second plant at Gurgaon came up through a loan raised in Japan, taking the annual production capacity to 278,000.

When the third plant was decided upon in 1995, the government again wanted its preference for location to be acceded to, even though it did not make business sense to have a new plant in southern India. A committee was set up to examine the issue, taking over a year to deliver its report. The new plant finally came up in Gurgaon, as the management had decided, in 1999. Financing again emerged as an issue and once again, the decision to invest was delayed and MUL at last opted for a more expensive debt rather than equity.

Several other issues were also handled similarly, leading to miscommunication between the two equal partners for a time, especially regarding the appointment of Bhargava's successor. Later on, resolving the pending issues with Maruti was considered important by the government, and Jagdish Khattar, who had the support of SMC, was appointed as managing director in 1999.

In 2001, the government decided to exit the company. This was to be conducted in two stages, with a rights issue and initial public offering, and the next round in 2007 with a complete exit. SMC would pay a premium to the government for gaining management control of the company as its equity went up. Thus, the following year, Osamu Suzuki presented a cheque for Rs 1,000 crore to the minister for heavy industries and took over the management of the company. The government's stake went down to 45.4 per cent and in 2003, it further offloaded 27.5 per cent of its share. The initial public offering (IPO) was oversubscribed ten times, and as share prices rose, the government was encouraged to reduce its stake further.

Finally, in May 2007, the government yielded its last remaining stake, twenty-six years after establishing the company. MUL became Maruti Suzuki India Ltd (MSIL). That same year, Maruti Suzuki sold more cars than its parent company, SMC. A year later, Jagdish Khattar retired as managing director of Maruti, and Shinzo Nakanishi took his place, the first Japanese to hold the post.

Even though the circumstances had completely transformed since 1981, Maruti was still the market leader in passenger cars in the country, selling two of every five cars. Through the years, it coped with the entry of major automakers, including competitors in its own low-cost model area, by relentlessly bringing out new versions in different price segments, from the Alto to the Swift, matching quality expectations and consumer satisfaction demands of a new generation of buyers. 'Maruti continued to increase the value of its products, both by reducing costs and adding to their content,' says Bhargava. The Maruti models remain the darling of the markets till date.

New Challenges

The differences between the two shareholders could not have come at a worse time. Car production was completely delicensed in 1994, and foreign companies, including the huge multinational companies dominating international markets, were allowed to bring in 100 per cent FDI. Auto components industries came under the automatic approval list for foreign technology and were permitted FDI up to 51 per cent. A scramble for tie-ups between Indian and foreign companies began as everyone wanted to cash in on the excellent profits being made by MUL, which at the time had close to 80 per cent of the market share. Daewoo, Peugeot, General Motors, Honda Motors and Ford set up joint ventures with various Indian partners to manufacture cars.

The impact of the delicensing of industry led to a surge in industrial production and economic growth, encouraging the government to make further changes in policy. FDI worth $50 million could be brought in over a period of four years, and seven years were allowed for a company to match its foreign exchange outflow with inflow. Cars as well as components could be exported. A relaxed period of seven years was permitted to reach a domestic production of up to 70 per cent of the vehicle.

But by 1998, India was again in the throes of an economic slowdown. Passenger car sales grew by just 4 per cent in 1997–

98. Even then, Maruti expanded its sales by 8 per cent, with its market share at almost 83 per cent. But the next year, sales of both the overall car market and Maruti contracted by 5 per cent. For Maruti, this was the first time sales had gone the other way, and the company wanted to quickly get new models off the ground. Further, it also had to contend with the new emission norms of Euro-I that were to be instituted in metro cities by 2001, and in Delhi by 1999.

Regarding the environmental compliance, Maruti had the earlier experience in meeting European emission norms for its exports in 1991, and this enabled its engineers to modify the carburettor of the Maruti 800 to required standards that passed the various emission checks. It also developed fuel injection systems internally for the Zen and the Esteem. 'This was a real feather in the cap of our engineers,' recalls Bhargava.

Maruti decided to go in for the Wagon-R hatchback, which became a huge hit, and the Baleno saloon, which gave it a presence in the upper-income bracket, and also made consumer-oriented changes in existing popular models. In 1999–2000, it touched a new high in sales with 3.85 lakh units, and became the largest car company in Asia after Japanese and Korean firms.

The Human Resource Aspect

From the beginning, Maruti had adopted the Japanese way of doing business, which involved a partnership approach with all stakeholders, including workers. Unlike other PSEs, Maruti operated on strict guidelines for recruitment of workers in terms of qualifications and number of posts. Commitment to the company and building trust were the objectives, as in the Japanese way. Training and patience were stressed rather than disciplinary action.

The company sent selected recruits to Japan for training with the Association of Overseas Technical Scholarships to learn about quality and productivity. Besides, it was important for trainees to adapt to an entirely new work culture that stressed continuous improvement and participation from each employee. Bhargava says that in the early years, sending staff to Japan entailed permission from the government for foreign exchange, and bureaucrats often failed to see that this was a necessity rather than a 'junket'. The mindset change had to take place among workers, executives and the ministries.

A story from Bhargava's book illustrates the difference in work culture that the two sides had to overcome. 'Dust is a perennial problem in Delhi... The Japanese, who didn't want a speck of dust on the shop floor, found the doors did not fit properly and would not keep the dust out. That amused many of the Maruti personnel, who wondered how one could avoid dust in India. The solution was to instal air washers and to keep the air pressure inside the factory more than the pressure outside so dust would not come in... Caps had to be worn inside the shop floor so that dust and hair would not fall inside. These were all new practices and a good lesson in not assuming that a problem had no solution.'

Productivity was the key to the success of Japanese industry, realized Krishnamurthy and Bhargava, and with the help of SMC, they set about inculcating excellence in the system. Each minute of a worker's shift was to be accounted for, beginning not when the employee entered the gate but when he was ready and positioned at his station. Suzuki even gifted time clocks to the factory to ensure punctuality. For people used to relaxed work cultures in PSEs, or for people recruited from villages, this insistence on time and attendance was unprecedented and a substantial amount of education and incentives were needed to ensure compliance.

As Bhargava puts it, '[The] productivity, quality, etc. of Maruti is largely because of Japanese experience, Japanese systems, and their management culture. The whole purpose of Japanese management is to create conditions where every individual in the company feels he has to contribute something to it. He identifies himself with the company. He feels proud of belonging to the company.'[7]

The company leaders wanted to create a team spirit right from the beginning and knew that this could be done if workers had respect for managers. A universal uniform was developed for the company, light grey trousers and a blue shirt with the Maruti logo, made from the same material for all levels of employees. As Maruti's performance improved, the staff started taking pride in this uniform.

Another way to foster team spirit was to have a common canteen with the same food and the same queue for self-service for employees and the management. Toilets, too, were the same, leading to greater cleanliness all around. Transparency was also ensured through open offices. The message that went out to workers was that they were important for the success of the company. The union was involved in all these decisions and senior managers met regularly with the union for continuing communication and education.

Even then, agitations could not be avoided. The Maruti worker strikes in 2000 arose from the need to devise a new incentive scheme related to productivity. The strike continued for three months with more than half the workers not attending work. The company hired temporary workers and kept the production lines running. It was January 2001 before the striking workers returned to duty after signing the undertaking. And for the first time in the company's history, a workers' agitation led to financial losses.

Ten years later, in 2011, the company again suffered from a prolonged worker agitation, this time at its highly automated Manesar plant. Partly, this may have been due to the after-effects of the global financial crisis during which production had slowed down. Thereafter, recovery meant a rise in demand, while capacities were still limited. The demand for a new union led to several strikes within five months and the company had to suspend production of certain models, just before the Diwali season. The strike ended after prolonged negotiations with the union with the help of the Haryana government, but resulted in a loss of Rs 1,600 crore in revenues.

Creating the Supply Chain

The short deadline to production and the lack of facilities meant that, to begin with, the Maruti vehicles were almost completely imported in the form of semi-knocked-down kits. They had to be assembled in the new factory, and engineers worked on the first car the whole night before the engine came to life. Only a few auto component firms existed at the time, and often did not meet the stringent quality and safety requirements of the Japanese partner. Indian companies were also not particularly keen on setting up ancillaries as Maruti was the single customer for components.

But to limit the foreign exchange outflow, Maruti had a commitment to increase local components to 95 per cent within five years, which was a massive task. To achieve this end, it set in place a phased manufacturing programme for indigenisation.

Despite the lack of manufacturers in India, Maruti decided to opt for outsourcing parts rather than producing them in-house, as was the practice in the other vehicle-making factories. This meant including vendors as partners in the project and developing a relationship of trust and respect.

For each part, two vendors were selected to supply products. In order to match the requirements for Maruti, vendors had to adapt to the Japanese way of production. As in Maruti, this involved a complete shift in the mindset of entrepreneurs. Quality, technology, and more important, sticking to deadlines—all these had to be learned. MUL was working to Just-in-Time methods, which meant that each component had to be available with the right quality specifications at the right place at just the right time. For a culture which considered a few days here and there as hardly of much importance, this was bewildering, to say the least.

Apart from that, the whole environment in India at the time was not conducive to smooth, efficient and timely supply chains. Rainfall would block roads, containers could not be unloaded from ships on time, bank loans were delayed and government clearances took their own time. It was no wonder that the car companies before Maruti preferred to produce most of their own components to make the 40,000 or so cars of the time.

The initial scepticism was allayed by the excellent performance of Maruti vehicles and finally, it was realized that the company was there to stay, and that it would have the volumes to sustain component-makers. But even then, there were restrictions to be overcome. The reservation of certain sectors for small-scale industry prohibited the high investment required and much persuasion was required for de-reserving critical auto parts. Maruti also had to help the vendors with finding partners, getting licences, arranging finance and providing them with technical assistance. Senior managers of MUL were seen walking the halls of banks, trying to tie up finance for vendor companies.

It took time before auto component firms tied up with MUL, but their success was amazing. Some of them went on to become large players in the global auto parts market, supplying original equipment to major auto-makers. Bharat Forge, Sona Koyo, Amtek Auto and others went on to become the leaders of India's modern automotive component industry, the face of a new India. In later years, MUL formed joint ventures to produce certain parts, going in for stakeholding in the true Japanese model. Most of the suppliers were based within a 100-kilometre radius to reduce travel time, forming an automotive cluster that became the model for future car and ancillary plants.

Despite all this handholding, when liberalization swept the

operational scene, MUL needed a new direction for meeting the competition. Competitiveness of vendors became a matter of the highest importance, and Maruti took the lead, with CII, to start a process of shared learning for imparting quality concepts to selected vendors. Dr Krishan Kumar, who had taken over in the engineering department, headed the initiative. Again the help of the Japanese institutions was invaluable.

The shared learning programme, where ten to twelve small companies came together, was meant to lower costs and reduce time as the smaller companies could not afford the costs of individual consultations. It was obvious that the weakest link in the supplier chain determined the final quality of the product, and vendors had to be aware that they had a larger stake in quality.

MUL began with explaining the elements of ISO, preparing a small quality manual for the use of suppliers. ISO 9000 was the first step in the quality journey. Dr Kumar compared the method to fighting a fire—first, the fire itself had to be extinguished, then its causes had to be investigated, and finally, methods for avoiding it had to be developed. Similarly, defectives had to be segregated, the causes identified, and then rectification had to take place. In the first phase, from 1987 to 1992, standardization and avoidance of errors were stressed.

In the next phase, two clusters for group learning were formed, depending on the level of interest of vendors to attain quality benchmarks. Professor Y. Tsuda from Japan was tapped to lead the teaching in 1998. The quality concepts started with 'exactness' in measurements, analysis, etc. According to Dr Kumar, it took almost two years for MUL, CII and the vendor companies to understand this concept. Production was all about statistics and analysis rather than relying on the experience of the worker or supervisor.

The concept of learning 'daily work management' took another two years. Finally, business plans for setting targets were detailed. The last stage for companies was learning the process of policymaking for the next three to five years. According to Bhargava, the Japanese asked the crucial question of 'why'—why defects occurred and why improvements could not be made. The cluster learning format was so successful that CII went on to make this a regular practice for boosting the competitiveness of SME companies through its AVANTHA Centre of Excellence for Competitiveness of SME, bringing quality concepts to over 2,000 small companies.

At all vendor conferences, MUL stressed the importance of quality and vendors were encouraged to come forward with their problems so that high standards of the vehicles could be maintained. For example, truck unloading was identified as a problem as it took too long. This factor was solved by setting up specific unloading points for different parts, which substantially cut down the time in a queue for delivery. Since 1,200–1,300 components had to be sourced, ensuring quality supplies at the right time was a superb task of management. Maruti engineers often spent entire days in the factories of producers, ensuring that work was done correctly.

It is to the company's credit that its efforts could create an entirely new ecosystem for the automotive industry, one that was efficient and matched global standards of quality. It is to their credit that many of the vendors that started on the quality journey with MUL went on to become best-in-class producers, competing for the prestigious quality award, the Deming Prize, and the Total Productivity Maintenance awards given by Japanese institutions.

Working with vendors remains one of the key strengths of the company. In 2010–11, when MSIL had calculated that growth would remain subdued in the event of the global economic crisis, it was surprised by a huge upsurge in demand. Although vendors had planned production later in their calendars, Maruti supply teams worked closely with them to advance their schedules.

Under high pressure, the suppliers nevertheless rose to the occasion and helped MSIL produce an additional 250,000 cars without new capacity creation.

Bhargava explains, 'We understood that the strength of the dealer network was critical for beating the competition in the post-1991 days. Many steps were taken to improve dealer profitability, since without that dealers would be unable to expand and improve their facilities. Dealers were helped to improve their customer relations, and extensive use was made of information technology. The sales and service network continued to expand and reach areas not earlier serviced.'

Fast Forward

In February 2012, the company achieved the milestone of 10 million cars sold. This was just six years after it reached the 5-million mark. In its long line of models over the years, the Alto sold 1.9 million units, the Omni 1.4 million, the Wagon R 1.1 million and the Swift 0.7 million. But these were trumped by the faithful old warhorse, Maruti 800, which sold 2.63 million cars since it first rolled out of the Gurgaon factory in 1984 to take the entire nation by storm.

Maruti continues to go from strength to strength. In 2012 alone, it revamped the A-Star and launched its life utility vehicle, the Ertiga, designed by Japanese and Indian engineers. At the 2012 Auto Expo, it unveiled a compact SUV, the XA Alpha, for young urban buyers. Earlier, in the 2010 edition of the Auto Expo, MSIL had brought out its luxury vehicle Kizashi, entering the high-end market for the first time since the 'people's car' was developed. The company offers fifteen models with new ones constantly coming onstream. The Maruti 800 remains in production, although it is not available in thirteen cities due to environmental regulations.

The Manesar plant commenced its second line, and the third line will be ready shortly. Maruti Suzuki is spending Rs 4,000 crore on setting up a plant in Mehsana, Gujarat, to expand its capacity to 2 million cars, with an emphasis on exports. The company is preparing to retain Maruti Suzuki's lead position as India heads into a market of 4 million passenger vehicles by 2015–16.

Road safety has also been high on the agenda for Maruti. It has established driving training facilities (IDTR) in six locations in the country, including driving simulators, training tracks and training vehicles. Under a public–private partnership model, the IDTR are large institutions built with the help of state governments. They also run 200 Maruti Suzuki Driving Schools, the courses including training for commercial drivers and learners and for specialized drivers such as police staff. Maruti's National Road Safety Mission has trained over 5 lakh drivers, of which 140,000 were sponsored by MSIL.

Fuel efficiency and environmental considerations have been constant features of MSIL since the beginning. When Maruti conducted a survey, the first ever by a public sector company, in 1981, it was evident that consumers wanted cars with maximum mileage per litre. Even though fuel efficiency was not high on the radar of car-makers of the day, Maruti stressed the importance of performance and this was one reason why the company looked at Japan for a joint venture. During the promotion of the 800 model, its fuel efficiency was one of major characteristics highlighted. Till date, fuel efficiency continues to be a key factor in purchase decisions of families, as Maruti had forecast thirty years ago.

When Delhi introduced Euro I norms two years ahead of the rest of the country, Maruti engineers scrambled to meet the tight deadline. They succeeded in re-engineering the carburetor to match environmental requirements instead of switching to multi-point fuel injection systems, which would have put the cars off the road—a feat which earned them the respect of Suzuki engineers.

MSIL engineers continued to break the mould by driving up fuel efficiencies with lower emissions. The new Swift and Swift Dzire reduced emissions by 4–5 per cent per kilometre, a significant saving where the carbon footprint is concerned. Aerodynamics and the weight of the models were aligned to boost efficiency. Ertiga offers as much as 20.77 kilometres per litre, a record for multi-utility vehicles. MSIL's K-series engines are lighter to ensure higher fuel efficiencies.

Even in its manufacturing processes, the company is constantly looking for innovation to reduce its carbon emissions. For example, the Manesar B plant is the first car factory ensuring 100 per cent of Light Emitting Diodes (LED). Its hazardous wastes like mercury, lead and cadmium have been almost completely eliminated from most of its models, much before 'End of Vehicle Life' norms came into India. MSIL follows SMC's philosophy of 'Smaller, Fewer, Lighter, Shorter and Neater'. The company continues to work with the government for environment-friendly policies and to promote electric and hybrid vehicles.

MSIL believes that India's car market will double in the next five years, and has set in place the basis for retaining its market share as well as expanding exports of its small cars. The company's Gujarat plant is strategized to take advantage of port facilities. India's rural markets are also considered a major opportunity for business, and one-fifth of MSIL's sales now happen in small towns and villages. It has set up new service and sales centres to tap these markets.

More important, MSIL has made product design the centrepiece of its strategy for the coming years—integrated car development was being carried out in Japan till recently. In April 2012, the company started building its R&D centre in Rohtak, Haryana, spread over an area of 600 acres and entailing an investment of Rs 2,400 crore. It is envisaged as a state-of-the-art facility that will design, develop and launch cars attuned to the expectations of the Indian consumer.

'India is set to become one of the top automobile markets of the world. This may become evident as early as the next Delhi Auto Expo [in January 2014]. Maruti Suzuki will lead India's automobile growth and evolution by strengthening its compact car portfolio, entering new segments and creating new product categories across fuel options,' said S. Nakanishi at the Auto Expo 2012.[8]

India is now the second fastest growing car market in the world, driven by rising incomes and export growth. Significant cost advantages, a large talent pool and facilitative policies have led to the entry of all major car producers into the Indian scene. From just 600,000 units in 1992, production of all vehicles, including cars, two-wheelers and trucks, zoomed to 11 million units in 2007 and 18 million units in 2010, including 3 million cars. It is the world's largest producer of tractors, second largest manufacturer of two-wheelers and Asia's fourth largest passenger car market. India has carved a special niche for itself in the small cars market too, and is fast scaling up exports.

Similarly, the component industry supplies domestic and overseas vehicle manufacturers as original equipment manufacturers (OEMs) and lower tier suppliers of high repute. Investments and exports are growing rapidly, and the country is fast emerging as a global R&D hub.

Since its inception, Maruti developed an entirely new work culture, a culture that was totally different from the usual public sector environment. It not only created the entire auto industry in India, but tapped into the aspirations of a new class of consumers, meeting their needs for transport in a manner that completely satisfied buyers. The confidence that it created in the minds of drivers is the basis for its continued domination of the car market, something that it treasures and nurtures constantly with its continuous innovation in quality.

Equally important, Maruti for the first time allowed Indian manufacturers to dream big, to understand that there were no limitations on what they could achieve and to see the world as their market. Apart from setting up the foundations of the Indian auto industry, Maruti built the confidence of stakeholders in the Indian economy. If a public sector company, given the myriad constraints of operation, could be so successful, there could be nothing to stop Indian entrepreneurs from taking on the world.

As Nakanishi said at the Auto Expo 2010, 'About three decades ago, a group of wise and visionary people broke the boundaries of mind and geography, and laid the foundation for Maruti. It was a defining moment, not just for one company, but for an economy and a nation.'[9]

6 THE POWER OF SMALL

NIVO CONTROLS

It is with the small enterprise that it all begins. An idea takes root, an entrepreneur is born, and with careful nurturing, an enterprise grows into a global giant. The Small and Medium Enterprises (SME) sector is the vibrant, pulsating base of an economy, the hotspot for industry, the seedbed of innovation.

In India's liberalization journey, the small enterprise's passage was the most difficult. Buffeted from all sides, making do with limited resources, and struggling to cope in an environment where flux was the only constant, the small enterprise faced continuous challenges. Amazingly, the sector as a whole has consistently outperformed industry at large. The experience of Nivo Controls shows how SMEs adapted to changed circumstances and came out winners.

Praveen Toshniwal grew up in Mumbai, but moved to Indore after completing a BTech in electrical engineering from IIT Delhi in 1975. Entering business directly after graduating, he bolstered his managerial expertise with several development programmes in the IIMs.

Here he relates his experiences as an SME entrepreneur in his own words.

The Nivo Story

In the 1960s, there were very few manufacturers of process control instruments in India and only simple instruments were being manufactured. The process control instrument industry's requirement for modern and sophisticated instruments was being met through imports, but importing itself was not easy.

An import licence was required to import almost everything, but the process to obtain the licence was time-consuming and exhausting. Further, not all items were allowed to be imported against a licence and those that were allowed were levied a very high import duty. For process control instruments, this was often in excess of 100 per cent of their value.

Importing spares was equally difficult and expensive. Moreover, an Indian company representing a foreign company could not import equipment or spares for providing after-sales services to the user because all imports were allowed to end-users only. Under these conditions, the process of importing goods and machines and maintaining them during their time of use was extremely difficult and expensive because of the process involved, the import duty levied and the need to get services done during the warranty period and the lifetime of the equipment.

The Toshniwal family entered the instrumentation business in 1948. The business began by importing instruments. We introduced products made by foreign manufacturers to the Indian industries. We provided them support before sales to select the right product for their needs, and assistance in commissioning and repairs during the warranty period and lifetime of the product when needed. In 1959, we established our first manufacturing company to bring out simple products required by the Indian industries. Over the years, more products needed by Indian industry and educational and research institutions were identified for manufacturing in India from the range of products manufactured by the companies we represented. In this manner, we made products, both imported and manufactured indigenously, available to the Indian customers and also provided technical support during the products' lifetime.

At the beginning of the 1970s, we identified the need for instruments to measure the 'level' in industrial processes, including processes in cement plants, power plants, steel plants and various chemical plants. The instruments being produced in India were not of very reliable quality and there was also a need for more types of products and newer technology. We were already in contact with a company that manufactured such products. This company was also willing to license the technology to manufacture some of their products in India. Manufacturing the products did not require large investments and we could start as a small-scale industry.

Establishing a large manufacturing plant required an industrial licence, which came with its own conditions regarding the location, permitted production volume and many others, making the process lengthy and time-consuming. Starting a small-scale industry was much easier and faster.

The import of technology was not an easy process either. First, an application had to be made to the government for permission to license technology. After getting this permission, approval was needed from the RBI to obtain foreign currency to pay for the technology. The entire process could take a long time, stretching to one to two years.

Many foreign companies were not willing to transfer technology to Indian companies. The conditions under which the government granted permission to Indian companies to obtain technology were very stringent and often not acceptable to foreign companies. The Indian economy was quite small and so also the Indian market for industrial equipment, especially instruments. Hence, foreign companies were not very interested in entering the Indian market, much less to transfer technology. Additionally, there was a perceived risk, sometimes genuinely so, of the products being copied by other Indian companies.

We obtained permission to import technology and started manufacturing a small range of level measuring instruments in

1978. Although the range of products manufactured was small, we also offered customers products from our foreign partners. In this way, we were able to offer a wide range of products as a single source to our customers.

Some of the products manufactured by us were already available in India but many users were not happy with their performance or reliability. Along with the technology to manufacture, we also received training and knowhow for designing and selecting products for the customer's specific application. To gain the confidence of our customers we had to offer, at times, our products for trials free of charge to demonstrate the performance and reliability of what we offered. If the customer's need was not adequately met by one of the products that we manufactured in India, we would offer another from the range of our technology partner. Gradually, in this way, we became a reliable and, equally important, knowledge partner of Indian industry to fulfil its need for level measuring instruments.

The business grew, and in 1984, we updated the technology for the products from our collaborator and additionally, obtained the technology for magnetic flow meters and tank gauging systems. This technology came for a fee and a 40 per cent equity stake for our collaborators; Nivo became a joint venture. At that time, 40 per cent was the maximum equity the government permitted a foreign company to hold in an Indian company.

In 1991, when the country encountered its economic crisis and was compelled to liberalize its economic policy, our business was amongst the most affected. Our industry was considered as 'high-tech'; consequently, the products that we manufactured were opened up for import without an import licence under the liberalized trade policy. The import duty was also drastically reduced from more than 100 per cent before liberalization to 25 per cent in 1996. This was further brought down to nil a few years later. Our company had no protection against imports.

Under the liberalized regime, foreign companies were permitted higher equity in joint ventures, up to 74 per cent in our industry, and soon were also permitted to open branch offices in India to promote business directly.

As a result of these changes, products that we manufactured could be imported very easily and at considerably lower costs. New technology came in. We had last received technology in 1984, and we, too, felt the need to upgrade technology and widen the product range. Our collaborators insisted on a higher stake in our company as a condition for the transfer of new technology. Not able to reach an agreement on the terms for the higher stake for our collaborators, we mutually decided to part ways. Our partners decided to establish a branch office to market their products directly. We bought back their equity and Nivo Controls became, once more, a fully family-owned company.

Perceiving a threat from international companies offering products with newer technology and better quality, we started to search for a new partner for technology and products. This was the time when Indian customers, who had been denied easy access to new products and technology for many years, had a strong preference for imported products. This was a serious handicap for an 'indigenous' company.

For many years, I had made a practice of visiting international exhibitions for instrumentation not only to keep updated about technology and industry, but to use the opportunity to meet and get to know the competition. At the time we decided to part ways with our collaborators, a major international exhibition for instruments was coming up in Frankfurt. I sought appointments and decided to meet the competitors at the exhibition or in their factories. Being dependent for many years on our foreign partners for technology, we lacked the confidence in our ability to stand on our own feet. We had invested in an R&D set-up and even received recognition for this from the Government of India in 1987, but our ability had never been put to test.

Our confidence in ourselves was strengthened by one of the international companies we met in our search for new partners. We were discussing collaboration for technical know-how with this company, showing them the catalogue for the products that we had been manufacturing, and requesting for technology to upgrade our product range and for additional products. The CEO of that company observed, 'Why do you want technology from us? You are already manufacturing products which may not be of the latest technology, but these products work and meet the needs of your customer. What will you gain from us?'

This strengthened our confidence in ourselves and also made us decide to evaluate and to build on our strengths. We concluded that to be successful we did not need the latest technology for our products, but technology that worked and served the needs of our customers. Our products had to be of good quality and reliable. If our products had this and were priced below those of the international companies, we could be successful. We decided to strengthen our R&D so that we could continuously upgrade the technology and adapt the products to our customers' needs. We also decided to improve our processes and systems to be able to deliver, consistently, products of reliable quality. We concluded that though we could not compete with international companies in technology we could compete with them successfully, provided we regularly upgraded the technology, never lagging very far behind, and offered quality products and better prices.

One of the first steps we took was to redesign our products so that they looked different from our collaborator's products, which we had been manufacturing for many years. We engaged a professional industrial designer from a leading technical institute to redesign our products and make the design more contemporary and international.

This was the time when ISO 9000 standards were becoming known in India. They had already become popular in Western countries. We decided to work towards achieving this standard and received a compliance certificate in 1996. We were amongst the early recipients of this in our industry. Compliance to this standard also helped us in our efforts to export our products.

The market for our products outside India was potentially many times larger than the Indian market; even a tiny share of this market would add considerably to our turnover. Knowing the prices of imported products in India, we believed that with our cost structure we would be able to offer our products at lower prices and be successful in foreign markets. We learnt quickly, however, that exporting from India the products that we manufactured was not as easy as we believed.

India was better known outside for its handicrafts, gems and jewellery, exotic and mystic culture and, more recently, software. Engineered products, and specially instrumentation 'Made in India', were not readily acceptable. ISO 9000 and a contemporary design helped but not enough to overcome the 'Made in India' disadvantage .

Finding a good distributor was not easy. The distributors with experience and knowledge of our products already carried products or preferred products manufactured by companies from Europe, US or Japan. The distributors willing to promote our products had little or no experience or knowledge of our products and needed extensive training and continuous support. Training and support over long distances was a large investment not feasible for a small company like ours.

We discovered very soon that the ISO 9001 certificate was not adequate for us to get an entry to the international markets. Our products also had to comply with the CE standards for Europe and the FM approval standard for the US markets. We worked and designed our products to comply with the CE directives for the European market. When we went back to Europe with these products, we learnt that a new requirement had come up in the meantime—Restrictions of Hazardous Substances

(RoHS). We came back to our laboratory to make our products RoHS-compliant. We were one of the first Indian companies to be audited and certified by DNV, the globally accepted certification body.

For the US market, our products had to meet the requirements of the FM standards. There was no certifying body in India which could issue an FM certificate. There was no test laboratory in India whose tests would be accepted by certifying bodies outside the country issuing the FM certificate. We decided to send our products to Canada to CSA for testing and certification. Apart from high costs involved, this being our first attempt, it took us around two years to get FM approval certification.

We received our first export order in 1998. Since then, we have been exporting to the US, Europe and countries in South and East Asia. Exporting our products has been a tremendous learning experience.

We learnt to be more sensitive to customers' needs and their concerns, and to respond quickly and effectively to address these. This learning came at a great cost. We had successfully received orders for one of our products from two countries in East Asia. Language was a challenge. When we received feedback from the customers expressing dissatisfaction with the performance of our product, we did not respond fast and adequately, attributing the problems to their poor understanding of the English language and cultural differences. When we did respond, it was too late. We lost the customers. We could not regain their confidence again. We learnt the hard way that in a ruthlessly competitive environment, there is no second chance.

We were marketing products of a leading international company. This was a small company well known for products with superior technology and extreme reliability, giving a trouble-free performance over many years. Though this sounds like a winning formula, it put us often at a disadvantage in the Indian scenario, where orders are decided on L1 or lowest-bid basis, without any weightage to better specifications, past performance or such other parameters. Once the product meets the tender specifications, and the company is not blacklisted due to its past performance, all offers are considered equal and price is the determining factor. The system does not recognize that better technology, more reliable quality and performance should be entitled for a premium, even if very small.

Under these circumstances, we often lost orders on price grounds. An in-depth analysis revealed that one instrument which we offered was very much over-specified compared to the specifications that were in the tenders and also much higher in prices compared to our competitors. We proposed and convinced the foreign company to allow us to develop a version of this instrument such that it met the specifications asked for in the tender, but was not over-specified—as their products were—and was more competitively priced. The company supported us in developing the instrument, with the result that we become more competitive and the business grew. Realizing that the instrument we had developed primarily for the Indian market also met the needs of many markets outside India, it started buying this product from us and we added to our exports. Our business grew in India and so did our exports for this product. The business ended when our foreign partner was acquired by a larger international company.

As India opened up its markets and integrated with the global economy, managing a small business became ever more exciting and challenging. The new business paradigm emerging from the changes brought unprecedented opportunities and threats, requiring continuous learning to understand and to adapt to the new reality. Whereas big businesses could seek and engage consultants and experts with international experience, these were beyond the reach of small businesses. In all this, CII provided a platform and a forum for businesses, both large and small, not only to learn from international practices, but also from sharing experiences with each other.

Today, businesses in India are far more integrated with and impacted by international businesses. International businesses, too, are far more integrated into the Indian economy. International companies came to India for the market here, but have learnt the advantages that manufacturing in India offers—that the learning from this market can also be applied successfully to markets in other countries. Products that are developed specifically for Indian customers also meet the needs of customers in many other countries. We experienced and benefited from this over a decade ago.

Small businesses have a huge potential to benefit from cooperating with one another. The trick lies in complementing and leveraging the strengths of each other. Every small business has its strengths, which makes it successful in its own markets. These may be closeness to the customers, the technology of their products or manufacturing competence; or two companies manufacturing complementary products—products that together make a more complete product basket serving the needs of the same customers.

We have been working with international companies from our very inception, initially as a technology licensee, manufacturing products with their knowhow. For over a decade, we have been exporting our products to the US, and also to Europe, South and East Asia; to companies that label our products and offer these as their own; to distributors who offer our products under our label as 'Made in India'; and to companies that buy critical components from us and add their own manufactured parts to make a complete product under their own label. We have also jointly developed products for an international company, initially for the Indian market, but which was successfully offered to customers in developed and developing countries across the world. We will continue to look for opportunities to work with more companies across the globe.

Large physical distances are no longer a barrier to communication, sharing of information and close cooperation. What is needed is the will to cooperate over long distances with other small businesses with complementary strengths. A company with good products and technology needs a company with closeness to customers or manufacturing competence or the other way round. The challenge is also for businesses with this will to find other, similar-minded businesses in faraway lands.

We had learnt early that working with large companies carried the risk that once the business grows sufficiently, it motivates the company to establish direct operations, taking away the business we had worked hard to develop. We also learnt that working with smaller companies carried a risk too, of losing business in case the company was merged or acquired by another one.

From our efforts to enter the European and US markets, we learnt how standards and compliance can work to effectively protect the indigenous industry in their country and how helplessly inadequate is our response and understanding, as a nation, about these practices.

We see the important role standards and compliances can play to make the indigenous industry competitive in the global arena. The absence of certification bodies and test laboratories in India, which can certify Indian products for acceptance in markets outside India, is a huge hurdle, especially for the small industries, to enter the foreign markets. Further, by not meting out similar treatment to the foreign companies selling products in the Indian market, our government has effectively given foreign companies easy access to the Indian market. In effect, the Indian indigenous industries are many times placed at a disadvantage against foreign competitors competing for business in our country.

Further, developing national standards that are harmonized with global standards, and supporting Indian industry to comply with these, will strengthen the competitiveness of Indian industry in the international market.

Being engineers and technocrats, and not hard-nosed businessmen, helped us pursue technical development without looking at short-term Returns on Investment (ROI). The satisfaction we derived from making technical advancements was often more fulfilling than short-term monetary gains.

We have never allowed financial incentives and subsidies offered by the government to determine our business decisions. This doesn't mean that we have not taken any advantage or benefited from such incentives. These benefits have always been for us 'something additional'.

Probably the period of dramatic changes that followed the liberalization of the Indian economy has passed, at least for most industries, but change there will be as the country progresses and integrates more closely with the global economy. In all this, small businesses have a bright future. By nature, small businesses are more agile and responsive, having, therefore, the ability to change quickly. What is required probably is a greater willingness to learn and to adapt.

The SME Backdrop

The experiences of Nivo Controls as related by Praveen Toshniwal amply illustrate the challenges faced by small Indian companies in general and specifically due to the new liberal environment. A look at the changes in SME policy over the reform period helps one understand other issues that such companies confronted and the risks they took to be successful in entrepreneurship.

No emerging economy can succeed on its development path without a robust and thriving SME sector. Supporting the sector is, therefore, a major policy priority for governments. SMEs contribute to the dynamism and creativity of the industrial economy. In many sectors across the globe, such as textiles, construction or real estate, 70–80 per cent of employment is in small enterprises.

The Indian industry landscape, too, is dominated by a massive base of small production and service units. Large enterprises are supported by a vendor base of millions of small businesses, going down from tiers one and two to a vast diffused segment of unorganized units that supply a huge range of goods and services up and down the value chain.

So what exactly is a small enterprise in India? Indian policy statements since Independence define SMEs in terms of how much is invested in their plant and machinery. Small-scale industry (SSI), as SMEs were then known, covered units below a certain threshold of investment. There were also sub-categories, such as ancillary, tiny and export-oriented enterprises. Till as late as 1991, a unit would qualify under SSI if its investments were less than Rs 60 lakh or as 'tiny' with less than Rs 5 lakh. In 1997, the SSI investment limit was raised to Rs 30 lakh, but again came down to Rs 10 lakh two years later.[1]

In 2006, the Micro, Small and Medium Enterprises Development (MSMED) Act was passed by Parliament, changing the definition of the firms included in the sector and instituting separate categories for enterprises within the overall definition. For the first time, the services' sector firms were also included in the definition. A micro-manufacturing enterprise would not have more than Rs 25 lakh of investment in plant and machinery, while a small enterprise would have investments of Rs 25 lakh to Rs 5 crore. A new category of 'medium' was created, with plant and machinery worth between Rs 5 crore and Rs 10 crore.

India's 30 million MSMEs provide employment to about 70 million people. These ventures are producing over 6,000 products, with a rate of growth higher than that of the industry as a whole. They contribute 8 per cent of the country's GDP, 45 per cent of its manufacturing GDP and 40 per cent of its exports.[2] The nature of these MSMEs ranges from village and rural industries, handicrafts and handlooms, food processing and manufacturing to the cutting edge of technology and innovation. Indeed, the heterogeneous nature of the sector imparts it vitality and resilience, which has helped to protect the Indian economy under changing global economic conditions.

Right from Independence, the value of the SSI sector was recognized and policies were set in place to support the sector. In fact, the 1977 Industrial Policy Statement went so far as to stress that 'whatever can be produced by small, cottage industries must only be so produced'.[3]

But the most important policy, which had a far-reaching impact on the SSI sector and for the industry as a whole, was that of reservation of certain products for exclusive manufacture by SSI units. From forty-seven items reserved for the sector in 1967, the list expanded to over 800, including items such as ice cream and biscuits, readymade garments and toys. The idea was to promote growth of the SSI sector and employment; in actual fact, the reservation policy meant that economies of scale were not available and large enterprises were debarred, resulting in a lack of competitiveness across sectors.

Liberalization brought a shift in the policy for SSI through a special statement directed at the sector. Most important was the setting up of the Expert Committee on Small Enterprises, chaired by civil servant Abid Hussain, to recommend policies for the promotion of SSI. In its 1997 report, it pointed out the deficiencies of pre-liberalization policies: 'The fundamental difficulty with reservation as an instrument of policy is that it does not discriminate between production units on the basis of their efficiency—current or potential.... The basic accent of India's policy for small-scale industries has been defensive, aiming to insulate the small-scale sector from the dynamics of competitive growth. In the world of today, such insulation is not practicable.'[4] After thirty years, the reservation policy was gradually dismantled. Given the political implications of this reform, the process of change was slow and as of 2010, some twenty items were still reserved for exclusive manufacture by MSMEs, including chutneys and bread.

Additionally, after liberalization, import tariffs were brought down, which meant that while goods from overseas could enter the market, Indian companies other than SSIs could not engage in the sector. Finally, due to the incentive structure for SSIs, units were discouraged from expanding since it would result in a huge jump in applicable taxes. This led to a distorted industrial system.

It was only in 1999 that a ministry was created for 'small scale industries and agro and rural industries'. This became the MSME ministry after the MSME Development Act came into force in 2006. In April 2001, under the World Trade Organization (WTO) regulations, India was obligated to remove quantitative restrictions on imports, which led to anomalies for the SSI sector. A hue and cry ensued, charging that Indian SSIs would be swamped by imports and would implode. As with many other such fears about market liberalization, this did not happen, and the SSI sector continued to thrive and grow after imports were liberalized.

The support structure for MSMEs today is strong, with the presence of diverse institutions to meet needs of small enterprises across the spectrum. The National Board for MSME coordinates efforts and advises the government; three National Entrepreneurship Development Institutes provide training and research to new entrepreneurs; and the Small Industries Development Bank of India (SIDBI) targets financing for the sector and has dedicated funds for venture capital in new enterprises. A new form of enterprise, the limited liability partnership, which combines the advantages of partnership firms and companies, has been permitted and FDI regulations regarding the sector have been liberalized. Recently, a stock exchange for MSMEs has also been set up to allow equity trade.

It is a measure of the progress made by the economic liberalization process that the Twelfth Plan working group set up to suggest policies for the MSME sector concentrated on issues of immediate concern to small units, such as finance, infrastructure, technology, marketing and procurement, and skill development and training. '...the MSME sector of India is today at the gateway of global growth on the strength of competitive and quality product range,' said the report,[5] while stressing, 'However, facilitation from the Government is required to minimise the transaction costs of technology upgradation, market penetration, modernisation of infrastructure etc.' This approach marks a mindset shift in the way promotion of the sector was conducted—from protection to competition, supported by institutional and policy infrastructure.

The rapid pace of globalization threw up fresh challenges for small enterprises in India. Variations in tariffs, rates of interest, inflation and exchange rates impact them in larger measure, while global prices and output environments also affect them deeply. Thus, they are increasingly vulnerable to external developments. At the same time, globalization brought bigger markets and more opportunity for technological progress.

Over the last decade, the nature of the Indian MSME sector has changed somewhat. Technology-led enterprises and services sector enterprises are growing in number, as is seen in the proliferation of these units in urban areas. More of these units are looking at overseas opportunities and venturing out, despite their small size and limited resources, while quality and standards are improving in many sectors. Units run by professional managers and technocrats co-exist with tiny, unorganized units.

There are several reasons for the emergence of India's SME sector as a dynamic and vibrant entity in tune with global trends. One, as large companies reconfigured themselves to attain global standards, they helped put in place a support structure of SME ancillaries. Vendor development programmes by large companies, such as Maruti Suzuki, as noted in the previous chapter, brought an increasing number of lower-tier suppliers into the ambit of quality and competitiveness. Two, the entry of foreign manufacturing and IT firms spurred tie-ups with smaller enterprises in India. These enterprises had to conform to global standards and thus a culture of quality spread into the Indian manufacturing ecosystem.

Three, policies also encouraged technology upgradation and adaptation. MSMEs that were able to take advantage of these schemes could modernize themselves according to the requirements of the global industry. Four, India's promise has attracted many technical and professional persons who had gone overseas and are now returning to India with enough money, experience and ambition to do something on their own. Five, domestic entrepreneurs with a greater appetite for risk are themselves keen on becoming a part of a new globalized India, and are changing outmoded ways of doing business. They are entering new market segments, using new technologies and availing of new opportunities.

India's SME sector is now an incubator of entrepreneurship, creativity and innovation. But for it to be a leader in manufacturing, employment and inclusive growth in accordance with its potential, a lot more policy support will be needed.

7 NEXT-GEN LEGACY
RP–SANJIV GOENKA GROUP

There is a fair chance that a well-established corporate Group, which traces its origin to 1820, would stick to a time-tested approach to business. However, almost two centuries later, the Goenka-owned RP–Sanjiv Goenka Group continues to reinvent itself. The Group acquired a new identity in 2011, and adopted a refreshed strategy to accelerate growth through prudent investments, both in existing and new business verticals.

The Origins

Entrepreneurship and business acumen are ingrained in the DNA of the Goenka family, which made Calcutta its home way back in 1820. Scions of the family successfully conducted business through challenging times that spanned British rule, the monopoly of the East India Company, the freedom struggle, Nehruvian socialism and the licence raj. The economic liberalization in 1991 presented an opportunity to rethink and reorganize the business.

Over the years, the Goenkas went through several corporate realignments. Until 2010, Sanjiv Goenka, son of late Rama Prasad Goenka, was vice-chairman of RPG Enterprises. That year, R.P. Goenka divided the portfolio of the businesses of RPG Enterprises, a Group that he established in 1979, between Sanjiv, the younger son, and his elder brother, Harsh Vardhan.

In July 2011, Sanjiv Goenka consolidated his business under

the RP–Sanjiv Goenka (RPSG) Group brand. The RPSG Group comprised a range of businesses—power, retail, carbon black, media and entertainment—aggregating revenues worth Rs 13,800 crore. An integral part of the Group is CESC Ltd, Kolkata (the erstwhile Calcutta Electric Supply Corporation), which supplies power to 26 lakh customers in that city. More than half of CESC's coal comes from its captive coal mines near Asansol, which is operated by Integrated Coal Mining Ltd (ICML).

Apart from CESC, which is India's fourth largest private power company, the Group has a leadership position in a few other business sectors. There are more than ten companies in the Group, of which five are listed in the stock exchanges. Phillips Carbon Black Ltd (PCBL) is the second fastest-growing carbon black company in the world and the largest producer in India. Spencer's Retail, a subsidiary of CESC Ltd, is a pioneer in organized food and multi-brand retail in the country. Saregama India Ltd has the largest archive of Indian music, while Open Media Network publishes the avant-garde current affairs magazine, *OPEN*.

The Group recently acquired Firstsource Solutions Ltd (FSL), marking its entry in the Business Process Outsourcing (BPO) sector. RPSG had been scouting for high-growth diversification options for some time and McKinsey and Company was appointed to advise on suitable investment alternatives. While McKinsey had suggested some sectors, Sanjiv Goenka sensed that FSL was a promising opportunity. Ranked by the National Association of Software and Services Companies (NASSCOM) as India's fifth largest pure-play BPO company, FSL has forty-eight delivery centres in India, Sri Lanka, the Philippines, Ireland and the US, and employs over 32,000 people.

RPSG's plantation business with 6,215 hectares of rubber and tea estates is located in south India. The Group is also developing eastern India's first luxury mall in Kolkata.

The Evolution

It was in 1820 that Ramdutt Goenka came to Calcutta from his native Rajasthan looking for opportunities with the East India Company. With time, the Goenkas' business expanded to banking, textiles, jute and tea.

The contributions of the fourth-generation Goenkas—Hariram and Badridas—were significant and both brothers were knighted. Sir Badridas Goenka was the first Indian to be appointed chairman of the Imperial Bank of India, the forerunner of the Reserve Bank of India (RBI) and the State Bank of India (SBI). His son, Keshav Prasad Goenka, expanded his enterprise in Independent India by acquiring a couple of managing agencies involved in tea, textiles and jute.

Dr Rama Prasad Goenka, Keshav Prasad's eldest son, established RPG Enterprises in 1979 after a division of assets among Keshav Prasad's three sons.

Often described as India's 'takeover specialist', R.P. Goenka embarked on a highly accelerated entrepreneurial adventure. Through the 1980s, Goenka targeted and acquired one large company after another. CEAT Tyres of India was taken over in 1981, followed by KEC International (formerly Kamani Engineering Corporation) in 1982, Searle India in 1983, the Gramophone Company of India (later renamed Saregama) in 1986 and HML (Harrisons Malayalam) in 1988. The next year was particularly busy with the acquisition of the more than hundred-year-old south India-based retailer Spencer's, Raychem RPG, which specialized in electrical manufacturing, the IT firm Zensar, and finally, CESC.

As early as 1985, R.P. Goenka had unexpectedly announced that he would retire in 1990. Since then, his two sons, Harsh Vardhan and Sanjiv, held the reins of the Group, with R.P. Goenka as chairman emeritus. Harsh, who was based in Mumbai, managed CEAT, KEC and other firms in western India, while Sanjiv looked after CESC and PCBL, among other businesses.

Sanjiv distinguished himself in business as the deputy managing director of Dunlop at the young age of twenty-three. During this stint, he earned respect for growing the company. In 1989, Sanjiv started the process of acquiring CESC.

This acquisition was not an easy decision at the time. Dating back to 1899, the power company was a relic of the Raj era. In 1899, CESC had commissioned India's first thermal power plant, consisting of three boilers of 500 horsepower. At the time, it pioneered the supply of electricity to Calcutta, then the second city of the empire, just eleven years after London had been electrified. Ninety years on, it was suffering from a serious power shortage.

'Yes, CESC was small. It was inefficient,' says Sanjiv. 'But it's been a very interesting journey, filled with lots of challenges...'[1]

When CESC became part of the Group, it was in charge of supplying power to 567 square kilometres of Kolkata. That's when the economic reforms were announced.

The Early Years

The advent of liberalization left the Group flummoxed. Over the years of its existence, the Group had relied on the wisdom of R.P. Goenka, who aggressively pursued inorganic growth. Not all the companies that he picked for acquisition, relying solely on his 'gut instinct', were great choices, and some had to be sold off later. Twelve years after R.P. Goenka had set out on his own, his Group included companies across diverse fields. But there were gaps in developing synergies or converging strategies. Technology was not always high on the agenda. A managerial restructuring was called for.

In 1991, the Group made a conscious departure from the traditional Indian way of doing business, relying solely on instinct. The consultancy firm, McKinsey, was brought in for the first time to analyse and redress the situation. It advised them to stick to its core businesses, and divest those that did not fit into their strategy. Post-1991, some companies that were not so profitable were sold off. Though Noida Power was acquired in 1992, the 1990s were a far cry from the takeover spree that characterized the 1980s. In the next few years, the Group consolidated its businesses, and ventured into retail, IT, telecom and life sciences.

At this time, CESC was taking up a lot of Sanjiv's energy. Trade unions had been opposed to the power company's change in ownership, and it took all of Sanjiv's considerable charisma to develop a healthy relationship with workers. He also found that the plant load factor (PLF) of the CESC facility, which should have been at least 80 per cent, and preferably 90 per cent, was actually just over 50 per cent. It was no wonder then that Kolkata was prone to load-shedding. CESC's 9 lakh customers at that time were an unhappy lot, often suffering from as many as ten hours of power cuts in a day.

With customary confidence, Sanjiv recalls, 'We welcomed the new economic policy announcements as they opened up a host of opportunities for business expansion in India. Learning to operate in the newly liberalized economy brought its own challenges and the Group hailed the reforms with cautious optimism. The abolishment of the licence raj was very welcome. The removal of the mandatory convertible clause for obtaining loans from banks was one of relief and, as a result, we raised GDRs worth $90 million around that time. The power ministry also stepped in with a host of incentives to encourage private investment in generation. CESC made good the opportunity and soon set up a new generating unit in 1996–97 to double its existing capacity, with one of the largest private sector investments in the power sector at that point in time.'

The first requirement was to raise the efficiency of the power-generating units. Sanjiv gave his engineers the task to set a new target, which they could then work towards. But setting targets proved to be a new concept. After deliberating for some time, they returned with an 'ambitious' plan—to increase the PLF by as much as 10 per cent! Sanjiv was disappointed but did not lose heart.

'The idea was to be customer-centric, anticipate customer requirements and gear ourselves to perform up to expectations to focus on efficiencies and to focus on costs and to increase margins,' says Sanjiv with emphasis.

He adds, 'The rapid reforms in the national economic environment called for comparable reforms within the organization; we needed to understand that the economy was now open to competition, and as an organization this called for a change in mindset. We had to poise ourselves to react quickly and effectively to changes around us. And in the way of doing business too. As a business leader, I had to ensure that the businesses were run by a carefully chosen, good team of people, and that I was hands-on only in a crisis.'

Sanjiv felt it would take a long while before the aspirational 90 per cent target could be met. Over the next six months, he interacted continuously and patiently with managers, sharing with them his vision for making CESC a leading power supplier. Efficiency was the key. 'Reinventing attitudes, managing systems and processes,' according to him, were the areas where innovation would help.[2]

At the time the Group took over the reins of CESC, its assets were worth about Rs 330 crore and it had a capacity of 2,445 million units (MUs). The generating plant at New Cossipore dated back to 1949, and the plant at Titagarh had come up in 1983. CESC set up its third plant of 135 MW capacity, the Southern Generating Station, under the Group in 1990. With this third plant, Kolkata households were partially relieved from prolonged power cuts.

It was a long haul to efficiency. But with continuous improvements in systems, processes and attitudes, CESC soon reported its highest profit ever. In what is a testimony to Sanjiv's management skills, many of the same engineers who had once set low targets changed their practices and enthusiastically came on board to meet the new targets. Today, CESC's four generating units have a combined PLF of about 90 per cent.

After crossing this first hurdle, funds were needed for the next phase of expansion. In 1994, the company went in for Global Depository Receipts (GDRs) by selling over 8 million shares to the tune of $90 million to an international bank. This, plus a later bond issue, went towards the construction of the first phase of the 2 x 250 MW Budge Budge Power Station. The new unit came up in 1997. But this was still not enough to meet the fund requirements, and the following year, CESC had to persuade the West Bengal government to raise electricity tariffs by as much as 20 per cent.

Sanjiv sums up this entire process with pride, 'Our key success was in establishing a performance-driven culture at CESC. At the time we took over CESC, Kolkata suffered from average power cuts of eight hours every day, whereas today there is practically none; this has been achieved largely through achieving operating efficiencies, meeting international benchmarks. Transmission and distribution (T & D) losses that were as high as 23 per cent in the 1990s have been brought down to sub-12 per cent levels. The PLF has increased from 63 per cent to 95 per cent. And as a result, today, all three generating stations are among the top ten in the country!'

In the meantime, as part of the reforms process, the entire regulatory environment for the power sector was changing.

The Story of Electricity

The evolution of the power sector in India is a fascinating tale that epitomizes the challenges arising in India's reform journey. When the Industrial Policy Resolution came into force in 1948, electricity fell in the domain of the government. It was also in the Concurrent List of the Constitution, which meant that both the centre and the states could make laws on the sector. Lack of competition and the potential for amassing largesse triumphed over commercial considerations, and electricity became a political tool. Cheap power was provided to some segments by cross-subsidizing the charges and imposing elevated tariffs on others.

By the end of the 1980s, the State Electricity Boards (SEBs) were in a complete financial mess, power cuts were endemic across the country and power stations performed at dismal efficiencies, with the PLF as low as 40 per cent in some cases.[3] Consequently, the financial ills were deeply entrenched and there was little impact of the government's initiative of mandating commercial viability.

Recognizing that an efficient power supply was central to industrial growth, power was one of the first sectors to be taken up as part of the overall economic reforms process. An amendment to the Electricity Supply Act 1948 as early as 1991 allowed the private sector to enter the power-generation industry. For a nation used to the government taking charge of public services, this was like Arnold Schwarzenegger giving way to Mickey Mouse! Further, demonstrating the complete mindset change, 100 per cent foreign investment, too, was permitted.

The Electricity Regulatory Commission Act, 1998, brought in the Central Electricity Regulatory Commission and state regulatory commissions to determine tariffs. But the Act was not effective enough since most of the generation capacity, along with the monopoly over transmission and distribution, remained with the public sector.

Power sector reforms received a massive boost with the Electricity Act of 2003, which was a comprehensive overhaul of the sector. The basic intention was to create competition, by privatizing distribution and restructuring SEBs, as well as to address environmental issues, among a slew of other measures. Tariff reform and open access, allowing users and suppliers to select each other, were central to the Act.

Since the Act came into force, results have been mixed. On one hand, subsidies continued to overload the sector and on the other, private generation increased rapidly. As of 2010–11, the capacity of the private sector accounted for over 41,000 MW of India's total generation capacity of 181,000 MW.[4] Sixteen private sector companies are also active in the distribution sector, including CESC. The average PLF had gone up substantially, to well over 77 per cent in thermal plants as of 2008–09, while state government-operated power plants continued to have a much lower PLF.[5]

CESC, as one of the oldest private utilities, had to meet the many changes arising from the constant shifts in the power environment.

'The most impending challenge that the company faced was its stressed financials and cash flows,' says Sanjiv ruefully. 'The gearing ratio soared to over 5, which was beyond acceptable norms. This called for an immediate restructuring process which was necessary for maintaining the confidence of its stakeholders.... With the Indian economy being open to private sector and foreign investments, competition increased manifold. It was imperative to not only survive, but also beat peers and establish efficiency, both operationally and financially.'

Financial Re-engineering

The 1998 Regulatory Commission legislation transferred the authority to raise tariffs from the state government to regulatory commissions. The West Bengal Electricity Regulatory Commission started operations in 2000, but this was an entirely new domain for any state, and there was scant understanding of the requirements of power utilities. Moreover, the Act itself was incomplete and did not address all the issues regarding regulation.

At the time of these changes, CESC had consolidated its

operations to stabilize the power situation in Kolkata. It had almost doubled its generation capacity after the two Budge Budge units went onstream, and had significantly strengthened its distribution network. 'The government encouraged CESC to pursue growth, specially to make Kolkata a power-cut-free city,' says Sanjiv. 'But with low tariffs, CESC started experiencing somewhat stressed financials and cash flows.'

CESC's expansion was funded by nearly twenty domestic institutions and four multilateral finance agencies, including the International Finance Corporation (IFC), Asian Development Bank (ADB) and Actis. The floating rate notes issued by CESC exposed it to foreign currency money markets. Gearing, that is, the proportion of debt to equity, deteriorated to over 5, which was beyond the contractual obligation as well as prudent norms, and interest rates were also on the higher side. The lenders were now keen to offload their facilities, and matters came to such a head that even legal action was contemplated for quick recovery, in case the regulations changed again.

Sanjiv notes, 'This was the biggest challenge the company had ever faced in its hundred-year history. The first thing the company did was to initiate a credible process of debt restructuring for maintaining the trust and confidence of lenders, especially the international lending community.'

The lenders brought in a number of agencies, such as Ernst & Young, J.P. Morgan and others, to critically examine CESC's business plans. Amid this confusion, Sanjiv took the bold step of injecting more funds and expanding his shareholding. This was to demonstrate to the lenders that the promoters were committed to the interests of the company and determined to stay invested for the long haul.

It needed a great deal of persuasion to convince the agencies that the new tariff system, which was beyond the company's control, had led to its financial problems. Sanjiv undertook this task with fervour. He intervened personally on many issues on a day-to-day basis, maintaining regular communication with the lenders.

Finally convinced, not only did the lenders agree to keep their funds in the company intact, they also decided to give CESC more loans when needed. These additional resources were used to restore financial health, as well as increase the efficiency of the company. CESC drove productivity growth in power-generation, brought down transmission and distribution losses, and rationalized its employee base. In all of these areas, the lenders were directly involved in the changes.

Once these steps were successfully implemented, demonstrating once again that the top management was taking its job with all seriousness, the lender community was requested to bring down the interest rates by an average of 2 per cent, extend repayment period by two years, and waive penalty charges.

The company's stand was finally vindicated when the Supreme Court passed a judgment in its favour, ruling that tariffs were indeed unfairly determined. It awarded the recovery of arrears of over Rs 500 crore relating to a two-year period.

After this ruling, most of the lenders fell in line and agreed to the company's request for loan restructuring. It was more difficult to persuade the foreign lenders, an exercise that took several months more. CESC repaid loans of those lenders, who were reluctant about the terms, with the concurrence of the other lenders. Throughout the procedure, IFC, ADB and the Indian lenders supported the scheme. 'It took almost two years to carry out the exercise and complete the process, including the job of convincing the foreign lenders,' said Sanjiv.

It was another two years by the time CESC could conform to the terms of the financial restructuring and free itself of the restrictive stipulations. The ratio of debt to equity came down, and interest costs were reduced. Most importantly, it could then enter the international equity market for the second time through another issuance of GDR, which met with overwhelming success.

CESC's debt-restructuring exercise is counted among the notable success stories in the industry and became a model for many to follow. Today, CESC is recognized as one of India's best-run power utilities. Its three units perform at a PLF of 90 per cent, and it is continually adding to its infrastructure for better service delivery. In 2011–12, according to its annual report, CESC commissioned four new distribution stations and expanded its underground cable network, among other initiatives. Two greenfield power plants are coming up at Chandrapur (2 x 300 MW) in Maharashtra, and two more (2 x 300 MW) at Haldia. In addition, the Group is now venturing into renewable sources of energy, with solar, wind and hydro-power projects in various parts of India.

The Kolkata Challenge

As an integrated power company serving the majority of its customers in Kolkata, CESC has to continually upgrade its generation to meet rising needs, as well as ensure uninterrupted distribution. With Kolkata having been inured to power cuts for years, ensuring an uninterrupted supply is certainly laudable.

Once CESC had achieved commendable efficiency in generation, Sanjiv collaborated with Singapore Power to help the company reach international industry benchmarks in distribution. There has been a complete overhaul of the distribution network in the last five years; CESC has moved to Smart Grid, as a result of which it can ensure a higher level of distribution efficiency through automated mechanisms.

CESC took on the challenge to meet international distribution standards with determination. All the gaps in distribution were identified and addressed one by one. Gas-insulated substations helped to reduce breakdowns. Automated meter-reading facilities were installed, along with supervisory controls and data acquisition systems to monitor load on a continuous basis. Extra capacity was also added. The increased number of distribution pillar boxes meant that faults were ring-fenced and restoration was faster. Regular maintenance was part of the routine. Finally, customer services and response were ensured through better organization and processes—and a dedicated team.

The average power cut per day in 2011–12? Just two minutes!

In July 2012, a massive triple grid failure plunged north, east and northeast India into darkness, raising a widespread hue and cry about the country's power situation. But Kolkata remained immune to the crisis. Seconds before the failure hit the state grid, sensors at the CESC connection point rang the alarm bells. A call went out to Sanjiv on the hotline, asking permission to isolate CESC from the grid—Sanjiv immediately responded in the affirmative and the connection was isolated.

'If the CESC network had failed to isolate itself, it could have been a disaster. But since CESC stations were running to full capacity, they could lend a helping hand to the state grid for restoration of other generation stations. Simultaneously, all essential supplies within the CESC licensed area were not interrupted,' Sanjiv later told the *Economic Times*.[6]

Another notable success for the company was its voluntary retirement scheme (VRS). In 2003, CESC rolled out this scheme for its employees as part of an initiative to reduce costs, and around 4,000 employees opted for it. Sanjiv was instrumental in convincing the pro-labour Left Front government in the state at the time that this was a necessary step and he was proved right later on.

Sanjiv has big plans for the next decade. As world energy demand expands, with China and India leading new consumption, the country confronts challenges relating to availability of coal, rising prices and continued losses by distribution companies. Despite this scenario, CESC plans to add as much as 7,000 MW to its total generation capacity, pumping in Rs 35,000 crore for thermal, hydel and solar power.

Division of Businesses

The turnaround of CESC is just one of the chapters in the story of the Group. The twenty years post-liberalization proved to be extremely productive under the management of Harsh and Sanjiv Goenka and the overall direction provided by their father.

In 2010, when R.P. Goenka decided to split the business, it was a $3.4-billion entity. Power and infrastructure were its two biggest sectors, each contributing close to a billion dollars in revenue. CEAT, the tyre-manufacturing company, came in third, while the carbon black, retail, specialty and information technology arms together accounted for $200 million–$300 million worth of revenues.

The aim was to have an easy transition of the business to the next generation. After witnessing earlier splits in his father's and his own generations, R.P. Goenka wanted to ensure a non-disruptive and healthier settlement as he turned eighty. Bringing together stalwarts of the Group, he devised a new holding structure for the investment companies promoting different companies. The division of businesses between the two sons turned out to be very smooth and amicable.

In Harsh's domain were the tyre, infrastructure, IT and specialty firms, as well as some other companies. CEAT operates three manufacturing units in India and is the fourth largest tyre producer in the country for passenger cars and commercial vehicles. It is also the largest exporter of tyres from the country.

KEC International is an engineering, procurement and construction (EPC) giant that manufactures transmission equipment, power systems, cables, rural electrification and railway infrastructure, among other things. The company has a significant international presence across the West Asia, Africa, Central Asia and other regions.

The plantations at Harrisons Malayalam—35,000 acres

spread across twenty estates, growing rubber, tea and coffee, cocoa, cardamom, pepper, arecanut and other spices—have been divided between the two groups. For example, ten rubber estates in Mooply Valley, Ranni Valley and Venture Valley produce some 8.5 million kilograms of latex and process another 1.5 million kilograms, making it India's largest rubber producer.

While Harsh continues with the RPG Enterprises brand name, Sanjiv carved out a new identity, the RP–Sanjiv Goenka Group brand. 'My father was closely involved in the process,' Sanjiv emphasized during a media briefing in July 2011 to announce the Group's identity. 'My brother Harsh runs one group of companies, and I run another. So it was my decision to have a new corporate identity for my companies, distinct from RPG. The idea was to give a clear focus on what my corporate Group represents, in order to avoid any potential confusion.'[7]

The two entities often deal with each other. For example, KEC International was contracted to install a transmission cable for CESC's upcoming Haldia unit, and CEAT buys carbon black from Sanjiv's PCBL. This is a continuation of how various companies in the undivided group work with each other, competing with other companies for orders and offering the same prices to each other as to other clients.

Both the branches have flourished after the division, which took place amicably, much to the surprise of industry watchers. After the division, the RP–Sanjiv Goenka Group grew its operational profitability by almost 50 per cent. The revenues soared from Rs 8,000 crore in July 2011—when the RPSG Group came into existence—to Rs 13,800 crore in 2013.

Within the first year of its incorporation, the RPSG Group's expansion initiatives included about Rs 10,000 crore in new projects. The Group is, however, committed to aggressive rather than indiscriminate growth, and has a 'calibrated' game plan.

BLACK IS THE COLOUR

'All businesses are close to my heart, but going by potential, power and carbon black take more of my time,' commented Sanjiv.[8]

Carbon black is a pigment sourced from petroleum products, and is most widely used in making tyres since it conducts heat away from the points of friction. PCBL, a company set up in 1960 in collaboration with a US company, started production with 14,000 metric tonnes (MT) of carbon black at Durgapur. When Sanjiv took charge of the company following the recent division, PCBL had a capacity of 410,000 MT per annum and was India's largest carbon black exporter in 2012.

During the first flush of liberalization, PCBL had expanded by acquiring two companies, Gujarat Carbon and Carbon & Chemicals, in 1996 and 1997, respectively. The objective was just to expand capacity. PCBL was concentrated in eastern India, while the two acquisitions provided a strong footprint in western and southern India. Both companies were not doing well and were plagued by operational difficulties and it was PCBL that led their turnaround. By 2010, the capacity of these units had been enhanced from 30,000 MT to 270,000 MT.

The late 1990s was a period of consolidation for PCBL. Since 2009, PCBL has again been in expansion mode, setting up production and power-generation plants at Mundra and Durgapur. Thanks to state-of-the-art manufacturing facilities, PCBL has built up a customer base spanning twenty countries, and supplies its products to top tyre manufacturers in India and overseas. It has invested heavily in R&D, developing indigenous technologies and imbibing best practices through its association with leading global companies.

Interestingly, PCBL uses waste gases from the carbon black manufacturing process to operate captive power plants in each of its units. PCBL is the first carbon black company in the world to receive carbon credits from the United Nations Framework Convention on Climate Change (UNFCC), the UN agency for climate change, for its 12 MW captive power plant at Palej. The success of the Palej unit has led to more such plants, which, as of 2012, generated an aggregate capacity of 76 MW of power. In an environment-friendly move, some 5,000 trees have been planted around the Durgapur plant to absorb carbon black particles and minimize pollution.

Since the creation of the RP–Sanjiv Goenka Group, PCBL has had aggressive growth plans, aspiring to be among the top three carbon black companies in the world. These plans include a new plant at Chennai and additional power-generation capacities. The goal is to drive a 50 per cent growth in capacity from the current 410,000 MT. In addition, the company, in a bid to drive backward integration, plans to manufacture products such as coal tar pitch, creosote oil and naphthalene.

PCBL has received several awards for its environmental practices and pollution-control efforts. Its manufacturing facilities recycle waste and have adopted zero discharge measures, apart from sustainable practices like rainwater harvesting. The company works with the local communities on afforestation, waste water management and zero emissions. It has also been recognized for being an excellent supplier and exporter of its products.

The Sound of Music

Few people in India are unaware of the Saregama brand. But many may not know that the company is the same as the HMV (His Master's Voice) of yesteryear, a company that endeared itself to music lovers with its numerous gramophone records. Gauhar Jan, Hindustani classical singer, recorded the first song in India under the HMV label as far back as 1902. Since then, HMV has been among the most recognized brands in Indian business. Its archive consists of over half the music ever recorded in India.

This includes songs in twenty-six different languages by 23,000 artistes, extending to more than 25,000 hours. Its association with the Group began in 1988.

Enjoying traditional links with most of the outstanding and successful film banners, Saregama can lay claim to recording music created by almost all top musicians across an astounding range of genres of music, including greats such as Pandit Ravi Shankar, Mohammad Rafi, M.S. Subbulakshmi, and many others. The company was also among the first to enter new media. Sanjiv ensured that, in line with technological advances and the huge growth in the telecom market, the entire Saregama catalogue was digitized. By 2004, when a media explosion took place in India, close on the heels of the growth in mobile telephony, Saregama went into sales of digital content, including those made through the Internet and mobile phones. In fact, Saregama has a large share of the ringtone market, one of the most popular forms of music distribution today.

Saregama's foray into television is interesting—originating in eastern India, it has evolved to become one the largest content-providers for south India, encompassing four different languages. *Athipookal*, the Tamil drama, was a complicated story with twists and turns that were a hit with TV watchers. *My Dear Bootham*, *Velan*, *Soolam* and *Raja Rajeshwari* were other popular serials, while *Prayaschit: Gunahon Ke Zakhm* was a reality TV show in Hindi. The company also produced the Hindi film *Jhhootha hi Sahi*, with music by Oscar-winner A.R. Rahman.

The Tale of Retail

As far back as 1863, the first Spencer's store was set up in Madras. Today, Spencer's retail business is geographically dispersed, with stores of various sizes in twelve states across the country.

Spencer's entered the fresh supplies business in 1920, becoming possibly the first grocery store in the country. It also ventured into the supermarket format when it became part of FoodWorld, which was run by Dairy Farm International Holdings Ltd. In 1989, the Goenkas acquired a majority interest in Spencer's, which had revenues of about $21 million at the time.

Sanjiv observes, 'In the retail sphere, the Group pioneered organized retailing in India in 1995. It signed a joint venture with Dairy Farm International, and opened supermarkets under FoodWorld, and later Health & Glow, all brand names.'

Under a joint venture and technical assistance agreement with Dairy Farm, Spencer's continued to run the FoodWorld stores, but Sanjiv was keen to expand into hypermarkets as well. Organized retail in India in the mid-1990s was an entirely new field, and supply chains were practically non-existent, so to conceive of a hypermarket at that stage was a pioneering move. Between 1995 and 2000, Spencer's Retail operated the supermarkets under the FoodWorld brand and drug stores under the Health & Glow brand, as well as hypermarkets.

Dairy Farm, however, was not too keen to expand in the hypermarket format. A large multinational company, with operations in China, Singapore, Indonesia and many other countries, it deemed the Indian retail market too underdeveloped and preferred to focus on the fast-growing markets of eastern Asia. After five years and negotiation with the Hong Kong-based company, Sanjiv took the decision to end the joint venture for hypermarkets. With that, Spencer's launched large-format stores under the brand name Giant.

While Spencer's continued with the partnership for another five years, eventually the two Groups parted ways in 2006. Dairy Farm continues to operate the supermarkets and the drug stores. But Spencer's embarked on its own journey of expansion, building up its portfolio by retaining forty-eight of the ninety-three FoodWorld supermarkets. In 2012, the company had a total of 158 stores—now under the Spencer's brand name—of which twenty-six were hypermarkets and called Spencer's Hyper. 'In view of the Group's aggressive expansion plans for large-format stores and the possibilities of an overseas expansion, Spencer's Hypermarket has been launched as a brand,' Sanjiv remarked at that time.[9]

The positioning of the stores was carefully crafted to target discerning middle-class consumers, who like to enjoy world cuisines from satay to sushi, fondue and wine. An upscale shopping experience is Spencer's stated aim, created through a welcoming entrance arch, modern design and cheerful ambience. The 150-plus stores cover a total area of almost 1 million square feet in different cities. The hypermarkets extend to at least 15,000 square feet of store space, and offer 70,000 items from home and fashion to gourmet food and electronics.

Sanjiv had more plans for Spencer's Retail. In 2006, he set up a joint venture with Cellucom, a mobile phone retailer from Dubai, for RPG Cellucom. But this venture was short-lived. In 2009, another partnership was negotiated with Au Bon Pain, a Boston-based café chain consisting of casual dining and bakery outlets, a venture that has met with greater success. Au Bon Pain currently has twenty-five cafés in Bengaluru and has a robust expansion plan in place under the leadership of Sanjiv's daughter, Avarna. Other tie-ups with major overseas fashion companies were made in 2010, bringing new designs to India. All these ventures are set for rapid expansion, as the Indian markets become more internationally attuned and conscious.

The organized retail sector is a complex and challenging business, which involves investment in supply chains that extend into many sectors such as agriculture, food processing and FMCG. With that in mind, Spencer's Retail has plans to expand further through an initial public offer once it turns profitable. As of 2012, Spencer's was a subsidiary of CESC.

The IT Plunge

In 2012, Sanjiv took a step into yet another market, the IT space, by taking over Firstsource. Speaking in an interview, Sanjiv said, '...we have been looking at entering a different segment of business and had appointed McKinsey to help us strategize and decide. Given that growth opportunities in the power sector are getting limited, and they are taking very long to materialize due to environmental and land issues, they recommended the BPO sector.'[10]

Sanjiv appointed McKinsey in early 2012 to advise on how RPSG could rapidly scale up in all sectors of operations. It currently looks unlikely that the power sector would yield fast and high returns in the near or medium term. This is despite the fact that there is so much unmet demand for power in India, where several hundred million people still do not have access to regular electricity supply. The power sector is heavily regulated by the government and is dependent on coal, which again is a sector characterized by strong controls. The sector, therefore, compares poorly with others that offer a higher growth potential.

In areas where the RP–Sanjiv Goenka Group operates, it has emerged as a frontrunner—be it CESC, which is one of the most efficient utilities, or Spencer's, which has high revenues per square foot, or PCBL, in the top ten among global carbon black companies, or Saregama, with the richest archive of Indian music.

The companies of the RPSG Group, even before the incorporation of its new brand identity, benefited tremendously from Sanjiv's astute guidance. But he attributes its success to certain principles, 'My business philosophy has simply been—be fair to people, be efficient, and be growth-oriented without thinking in isolation of cash flows.'[11]

Sanjiv has also demonstrated his leadership through his various industry associations and responsibilities. He has been the youngest-ever president of CII, chairman of the board of governors of IIT-Kharagpur, president and honorary life fellow of the AIMA (All India Management Association), and member of the Prime Minister's Council on Trade and Industry. He was honoured with the coveted '2013 Indian Business Leader of the Year' award at the 2013 Global India Business Meeting in the UK. Along with essaying a leading role in the top echelons of management, he also finds time to indulge in his many passions, like food, music, art and cinema.

Sanjiv, who calls his father his most admired business leader, is acutely aware of the legacy he will build for the next generation. 'In five years, our target is to take the Group's revenues to Rs 25,000 crore and assets to Rs 50,000 crore,' he says with quiet determination. 'There is a Rs 35,000-crore capital expenditure plan.'[12] CESC will continue to be the highest priority, the goal being to enter the ranks of the top five private power companies in India.

Sanjiv's son Shashwat, a triple business major from Wharton Business School, is clearly being groomed to manage the future of the Group. After passing out from Wharton, he worked with McKinsey on the business transformation exercise for the first five to six months. He is now gaining hands-on experience in retail. He was also part of the core team that worked on the landmark Firstsource acquisition and is a non-executive director on the FSL board.

As Shashwat enters the business, Sanjiv hopes that the formidable legacy, which he inherited from his forefathers and helped nurture, will only grow over the generations to come. His advice to entrepreneurs is simple, 'Believe in yourself, work with passion, work with transparency and communicate all positives and negatives to all stakeholders.'

8 A TEMPLE OF MODERN INDIA

SAIL

Soon after Independence, Jawaharlal Nehru activated the formidable vision of developing a strong industrial base. He termed the large public projects that started coming up in the first decade of nationhood as 'temples of modern India'. Regularly visiting project sites all over the country, he imbued the task with his customary passion, galvanizing managers, engineers and workers alike to devote themselves to the task with utmost effort and nationalistic fervour. Steel was one of the first industries on the government's policy radar, since it was considered the foundation of all other modern industrial activity.

The landmark Industrial Policy Resolution (IPR) of 1956 spelled out the architecture of the mixed socialist economy that India was to espouse for the next thirty-five years. Seventeen industry sectors, considered of strategic importance to national economic growth, were reserved for the exclusive responsibility of the state under Schedule-A of the IPR. The existing private companies in these demarcated sectors would continue to operate—under a heavily controlled regime—but any future growth would come from government initiatives. The government would own, build, operate, promote and regulate companies in these areas. Iron and steel were part of the reserved sectors.

Hindustan Steel Private Ltd (HSP) was set up in January 1954 to manage a new steel plant at Rourkela, which was coming up with German collaboration. The Ministry of Iron and Steel supervised the initial stages of the new steel facilities at Bhilai and Durgapur, but in 1957 handed over their management also to HSP. The first million-ton capacities of Bhilai and Rourkela were completed by December 1961, while Durgapur went onstream a month later. But more coordination was required to synchronize the vast amounts of raw materials and final products that flowed in and out of these mega plants. Thus, in 1973, the Steel Authority of India Ltd (SAIL) was instituted as a holding company to bring these three plants as also those at Bokaro and Burnpur under a single entity.

Five years later, it was felt that more efficient management was required for better operations of the iron and steel sector. The Public Sector Iron & Steel Companies (Restructuring) and Miscellaneous Provisions Act was passed, and SAIL was restructured to become the operational company in charge of four integrated steel plants, and alloy and special steel plants. Through the years, it took over various other steel companies, emerging as the steel behemoth of the country.

I have a special connection with the steel vision of India. As Jawaharlal Nehru cut the ribbon to inaugurate the Rail and Structural Mill at Bhilai Steel Plant in October 1960, the tall bespectacled man smiling over his right shoulder was Nirmal Chandra Shrivastava, my grandfather. He was an Indian Civil Service (ICS) officer handpicked to lead the construction of the plant. My grandmother, at the age of ninety-five, still remembers the Russian sentences she learnt to interact with the families of Russian engineers who were assisting the Indian government in building the steel factory!

Public sector enterprises (PSEs) emerged from independent India's desire to be self-sufficient, aiming not to depend on imports for essential goods nor on foreign enterprises for industrial growth. This was a natural corollary to the colonial nature of overseas businesses at the time. India's first PSE was the Indian Telephone Industries Ltd, and through the years, the government as a matter of policy ventured into different sectors through PSEs.

In some sectors such as mining and banking, nationalization led to the takeover of companies by the public sector. In other sectors, the state's intention of reserving this exclusive domain for itself meant that new companies were all PSEs. Often, loss-making or troubled companies in the private sector, including many old British managing agencies whose owners and managers had returned to the UK, were also taken over by the government. The PSEs played an important role in laying the foundations of industry in India, contributing to the creation of jobs, development of the private sector industry and economic growth.

At the time of liberalization in 1991, there were some 244 PSEs under the central government and many more under state governments, operating across a vast range of sectors from steel, aircraft and heavy machinery to textiles, automotives, and even bread.

Right from the beginning, the integrated steel plants of SAIL were built to cater to the entire range of products required for diverse end-users such as the construction, power, railways, automotive and engineering industries. In its massive factories, SAIL churns out bars and wire rods, coils and sheets, pipes, rails and wagon wheels and other products from coke ovens, blast furnaces and hot and cold mills.

The company also owns mining facilities, its repertoire including seven iron ore mines, five limestone mines and four dolomite mines supplying its plants. In fact, it is the second largest mining company and largest iron ore mining company in India. It has built up its own direct marketing network, rather than working through agents, enabling it to have better control on quality. SAIL called itself 'a supermarket for steel'.

But in the mid-1980s, SAIL was dragged down in the quagmire of recession, experiencing losses and a fast-deteriorating staff morale. The rest of the world had moved to newer technologies, including basic oxygen furnaces and continuous casting. But under the system of administered prices and government regulation of what and how much to produce, the Indian steel companies just could not earn the extra money required for investing in modernization or upgradation. Finding themselves ill-prepared and uncompetitive, the employees, too, had lost enthusiasm.

SAIL instituted a new strategy in 1986, called 'Priorities for Action', which depended on making its workers more productive. This plan proved to be quite successful, and the company could make profits for the next decade or so. In fact, in 1987–88, it stopped taking funds from the government for its operations and utilized its own internally generated finances, paying out its first dividend in 1991–92. It also signed a Memorandum of Understanding with the government, delineating targets, roles and responsibilities of both sides, which serves as its guiding policy to date.

And then came the hurricane of reforms.

The Impact of Liberalization: The Initial Years

Steel, being one of the most heavily regulated sectors of the Indian economy, was—naturally—among the industries most impacted by the new framework of liberalization that descended on Indian industry abruptly and without notice.

The industrial policy, announced on 24 July 1991, completely delicensed all industry. Moreover, the number of industries reserved for the exclusive operation of the public sector was drastically reduced, opening all industry areas to participation by private companies, except a few sectors vital to national interest, such as atomic energy. For thirty-five years, PSEs were used to operating without any competition and enjoyed monopoly benefits, although these were tempered by state regulations. Now, suddenly, they were subjected to the roiling forces of demand and supply in markets that shifted continuously.

In the steel industry, not only were private companies permitted to enter, but were actually encouraged to do so. Price controls imposed on steel products were removed and steel producers could now fix their own prices. The Steel Development Fund—created in 1978 for modernization and development of the steel industry and funded by extra levies on the ex-works prices—was withdrawn in 1994 since prices were no longer under control of the Joint Plant Committee. The Engineering Goods Export Assistance Fund was also disbanded.

While the competition from domestic private steel producers was low in the initial stages of reform, the real challenge was globalization and integration with the much more advanced global steel industry. Tariffs on most steel products and raw material imports were successively brought down. Overseas steel plants had had time to adjust gradually to newer technologies and to deal with the forces of globalization as early as the 1960s, working on re-engineering, cost-cutting, IT and logistics, among other ways to become competitive. By contrast, the Indian steel industry was beset with bureaucratic decision-making, inefficiency, delayed projects and other shackles. While the cost-plus pricing mechanism sheltered the plants from market vagaries, the new environment demanded high product quality, market-based pricing and complete customer orientation.

A public sector company was further subject to numerous controls and intervention from various government sources. It was answerable to the Parliament and liable to scrutiny from parliamentary committees. For any operational decision, it had to go to the relevant ministry. So for SAIL, the forces of change came from three different directions—from domestic companies, from globalization, and from the new demands placed on PSEs. Buffeted by this triple whammy, SAIL continued for a few years on the path of modernization that it had started on in the 1980s, but it was only a matter of time before it was hit by newer developments.

In addition, SAIL was one of the first PSEs to undergo the disinvestment process. In 1992, in a three-stage process, more than 10 per cent of the equity holding of the government was diluted and SAIL shares were listed in all the major stock exchanges of the country. Although further shares were offloaded in the next few years, the proportion was minuscule. In March 1996, SAIL took the bold step of issuing Global Depository Receipts (GDRs), again one of the first PSEs to do so. This brought down the government's stake further; nevertheless, to date, government ownership of the company is still as high as 86 per cent.

Modernization of the steel plants under SAIL commenced in the mid-1980s, as the Durgapur, Rourkela and Bokaro facilities were upgraded and expanded. Once again, the person tapped to lead this modernization drive was the legendary Dr V. Krishnamurthy. He was also chairman and CEO of Maruti Udyog Ltd at the time, but multitasking was a special characteristic of the dynamic and result-oriented PSE veteran. Dr Krishnamurthy was chairman of SAIL from 1985 to 1990, a period of high activity.

A number of initiatives were taken to raise the levels of productivity, yields and efficiency, while reducing costs and conserving energy. For example, at Durgapur, the new technologies included selective crushing of coal, base bedding and blending of raw sinter mix and continuous casting of billets. In Rourkela and Bokaro, hot strip mills were revamped and continuous casting of slabs was introduced, among other works. These activities continued until the end of the 1990s, by which time the steel capacities in these three plants went up to 8 million tons.

SAIL's position as a global steel producer improved; in 1985, it was ranked twentieth, and by 1997, it had become the ninth largest steel company in the world.

Recognizing that PSEs would need to be granted some measure of functional autonomy, the government introduced the concept of Navratnas in 1997. To be conferred the Navratna status, a PSE had to meet stringent criteria of performance and efficiency on the parameters of defined financial ratios. In return, it would be allowed 'to invest up to Rs 1,000 crore or 15 per cent of its net worth on a single project without seeking government approval', to establish financial joint ventures and wholly-owned subsidiaries in India or abroad. It could also spend Rs 1,000 crore or up to 30 per cent of its net worth in a year on such ventures. These steps were designed to provide the PSE 'greater autonomy to compete in the global market'.[1]

Despite these initiatives, the cumulative impact of liberalization began to take its toll on SAIL. This was further hastened by the Asian financial crisis in the second half of the 1990s, which led to a glut in the steel market. The Southeast Asian countries and China had emerged as major net importers of steel owing to their rapid growth since the 1980s. With the sudden and sharp contraction in their GDP growth, these countries turned surplus and became net steel exporters. Consequently, international prices dropped—by as much as 40–50 per cent—bankruptcies swept the industry and consolidation took place with numerous mergers and acquisitions. Advanced nations resorted to slapping an anti-dumping duty on imports to protect their steel industries, making 1997–2002 a crisis period for the global steel industry.

At home, matters were compounded by high interest rates, a halt in capital goods production, low demand for consumer durables and slowing project expenditure. Down the line, sectors that were heavy consumers of steel, like infrastructure and vehicles, decelerated. In addition, prices of raw materials like coal and power went up. All these factors resulted in high stocks for steel companies, leading to substantial discounts on the listed price and consequent pressure on profits.

Challenging Environment

The real transformation of SAIL thus took place during the global economic slowdown after 1996–97. Indian industry was severely affected by the financial crisis in Asia, with demand and investment sharply decelerating. Almost all the sectors were hit, but steel bore the brunt of the accumulated drop in demand and experienced a sharp plunge in the growth rate of consumption globally as well as domestically. Steel prices fell, but the cost of main inputs rose, so that profits were squeezed.

In the mid-1990s, SAIL accounted for about half of India's total production of saleable steel. But in 1996–97, its turnover dropped by 4 per cent and its profits plunged by 61 per cent. In 1998–99, SAIL profits went into negative territory. Year after year for the next four years, the PSE regularly reported losses and sales were depressed with only a marginal increase in this period.

According to Arvind Pande, then chairman of SAIL, 'The government had taken a view that it would not step up spending in infrastructure. This hit supplementary industries like steel and cement very hard. Then recession came at a time when a lot of new capacities had materialized, leading to a gross mismatch between demand and supply. At the same time, the lack of proper anti-dumping and safeguarding legislation is making the survival of domestic players more difficult.'[2]

The SAIL board of directors went into a huddle in the remote wilderness of a Sariska resort to figure out what factors were to blame for the poor performance and what could be done to remedy the situation. It was clear that there was no one single factor and that the troubles in the global economy could not solely account for all the ills of the company. If SAIL was to hold its own in the new era of competitiveness, it would need to look inwards for its sources of growth and retool its processes.

The major reasons identified by the company were:

- The drop in consumer demand in key sectors such as automotives and infrastructure, which were heavy steel consumers, hit steel production. The government's investment in infrastructure had fallen over the years, and while the private sector's investment had been robust following liberalization, it could not compensate for a lower steel demand from government.
- A huge mismatch arose between demand and supply due to capacity expansions by major players in the steel sector. This was not unique to the steel industry, since most large companies across the board had built up large capacities with the easier availability of funds and the anticipated surge in demand. It was estimated that by 2001–02, steel supply would outstrip its demand by as much as 33 million tons.
- Demand weakened throughout the emerging economies, particularly in the ASEAN countries and China, which had also invested greatly in building up their own steel sectors. The Asian financial crisis led to a sudden collapse of demand, turning the region from a net importer of steel to a net exporter. As a result, steel prices in the world fell sharply.
- At the same time, in the domestic market, prices of key inputs like coking coal and power, which continued to be regulated, went up. The pressure from both sales and costs sides squeezed bottomlines into net losses.
- Another factor identified for losses was the high cost of financing the sector. Modernization and capacity expansion of the previous years were estimated to have cost Rs 12,000 crore and had been funded through market borrowings, without budgetary support from the government. Both depreciation and interest costs increased between 1995–96 and 1997–98. In addition, the Steel Development Fund

levy, imposed only on integrated steel plants, added to their costs with respect to smaller producers.

- Finally, the burden of extra manpower was felt on the company's finances. While the pre-liberalization cost-plus pricing approach could take care of the bloated staff strength, the competitive era provided no such cushion. The company was also used to spending heavily on schools, hospitals and other amenities, and had several loss-making subsidiaries under its management.

Global conditions remained troubled for several years. The US hiked import duties on Japanese steel and approved a bailout package of $1 billion for its stressed domestic companies. In South-east Asia, the demand for steel lifted upwards only in 1999–2000, but the International Iron and Steel Institute estimated only a 2.3 per cent growth in steel consumption that year. In India, several projects were shelved completely while many small producers had to close shop. The focus was on consolidation rather than building new capacity.

Restructuring: Phase 1

Arvind Pande believed that 'the future will therefore belong to those who can discover, define and service opportunities well ahead of the competition'.[3] Realizing that only competitiveness would meet customer demands of higher quality products at lower cost, he planned to return SAIL into profitability by 2000–01 by structuring a financial turnaround. 'My prime objective is to change the entire orientation of the company and take a long-term view. The pressures of competition and globalization are here to stay. What is important is to get the organization prepared to meet the competition effectively on a sustained basis. For this, we have to unlearn many things of the past and take a fresh look at all the available options. If we cannot do it now, five years later, SAIL will be a totally unviable, sick, loss-making company.'[4]

A comprehensive plan was put in place. Over the short term, operational improvements were emphasized, while in the medium term, the focus was on enhancing technology, product and market capabilities. Finally, long-term measures were put in place for business restructuring. In addition, financial restructuring was required to improve the deteriorating financial ratios, which would involve the approval of the government. Although no additional cash infusion was necessary, the company would have to concentrate its resources on its core business of making carbon steel and exit from non-core and non-viable operations.

As Pande pointed out, 'The challenge of restructuring is at once a daunting and exciting task. At the same time, it involves a painful process as it means getting out of a traditional comfort zone and the SAIL family is gearing towards it.'[5]

The chairman set up seven expert groups headed by directors to examine areas such as marketing and production, asking them to come out with realistic solutions that could be implemented. The functioning and mindset of the company had to be turned around to begin with. Cross-functional teams and workforce motivation were seen as the key to success and strong emphasis was laid on cost-cutting, across each stage of the processing cycle. Workers, too, were part of the micro-planning that was required to reduce costs.

So what were the steps that the giant public sector company took to reconfigure itself?

Pande summed up, 'Since highly competitive markets restrict price increase, SAIL is focusing on exploiting its potential of being the lowest cost producer internationally. This is being done through a rigorous cost-cutting drive where all aspects of cost-operational costs, purchasing cost, working capital costs and social infrastructure costs are being targeted.'[6]

On top of the priority list was the costs profile. The cost before depreciation and interest and excluding salaries and wages was targeted. The two-pronged attack addressed both reducing the consumption of raw materials and other inputs, and streamlining the supply chains to minimize the landed cost at the plants.

Coking coal accounts for almost two-thirds of the total raw material costs for steel production. According to the SAIL calculations, reducing just one kilogram of coke for every ton of hot metal produced could add up to a saving of Rs 7 crore over the course of a year. The company went all out to ruthlessly trim the use of coke by measures such as increasing sinter proportions in the burden, higher charging of nut coke and the introduction of cold dust injections. At each stage, processes were examined to increase yields and lower diversion so that efficiency could be improved.

Reducing costs became a continuous endeavour for the PSE. Each year, specific performance targets are set for different areas and monitored. Reducing the consumption of power, stores and spares and bringing down administrative expenses were the operational processes that yielded promising results. Between 1997–98 and 2002–03, the company kept production costs at more or less the same level, despite hikes in the prices of raw materials, coal, and other goods.

SAIL also looked at its worker requirements, and took determined steps to reduce manpower. Voluntary retirement schemes were offered, and new recruitment was restricted. From 183,340 workers in 1996–97, manpower came down to less than 135,000 in 2003–04. With the cooperation of trade unions, employees agreed to suspend certain perks in order to ensure lower spending on manpower.

In tandem, the modernization and technological upgradation process continued. This in itself brought the benefits of greater efficiency, expansion of capacity and lower costs of production as well as more environment-friendly processes. For example, energy consumption and the coke rate came down by almost 10 per cent between 1997–98 and 2002–03.

Turnaround Strategy

While modernization, reduction in workforce and relentless cost-cutting stemmed the problems faced by the company for the time being, Pande realized that a long-term strategy would need to be put in place to completely transform it. IDBI was roped in to recommend a financial restructuring programme and SAIL itself devised an internal plan, engaging McKinsey & Co. to further advise on restructuring processes. A comprehensive financial and business restructuring proposal was then submitted to the government in 1998. It was approved in 2000, leading to a substantial improvement in the weak finances of the PSE. The measures included:

- Asset restructuring
- Operational improvements
- Organizational improvements
- Capital expenditure control
- Financial restructuring

Asset restructuring involved segregation of core and non-core activities so as to release resources for core competencies. The special steels' businesses were offloaded and power plants under the company's management were shifted to independent agencies, raising more resources. The fertilizer plant of the Rourkela Steel Plant was also sold to a joint venture partner. Locked up assets such as idle land, vacant houses in townships and some shops and units were all to be closed and sold to bring in cash.

The SAIL Power Supply Company was formed as a fifty-fifty joint venture with the PSE, National Thermal Power Corporation, to take over the 2 × 60 MW Power Plant-II at Rourkela and the 2 × 60 MW Power Plant-II at Durgapur. SAIL invested Rs 58.65 crore in the joint venture, but received a hefty Rs 391 crore from the sale of the power plants. Similarly, other power plants at Bhilai and Bokaro were transferred to various subsidiary companies or joint venture partners.

However, other non-core units such as Visvesvaraya Iron and Steel Ltd ran into problems or divestment was delayed.

Organizational improvements involved a shift in the marketing network to reduce the number of stockyards maintained all over the country by SAIL and more dealers were appointed. It also undertook several initiatives in common with the private sector company, Tata Steel. The marketing department was subdivided into flat and long product sections; key accounts were specially targeted to provide better customer interface; and production and sales teams came together for better support to customers. Capital expenditure was reviewed and further investments limited to essential activities such as competing in the market or maintaining equipment to the desired standards.

In the financial restructuring package, a key element was rejuvenating the Indian Iron and Steel Company (IISCO). It is worth recounting the history of this company since it pioneered the modern production of pig iron in India in 1874, at a time when Indian industry was barely beginning to stir in the colonial era. Its plant at Kulti, set up by Bengal Iron Works, was the first open-top blast furnace in the country, and it also started steel production through small open-hearth furnaces as early as 1904–06.

IISCO, promoted by one of the early engineering companies of India, Burn & Co, took over Bengal Iron Works and started steel manufacture in Burnpur, a town of legendary status in the steel industry until the 1960s. Being the first on the iron and steel industry scene, the company owned high-quality iron ore mines—its Chiria, Gua and Mandharpur iron ore mines are considered the best in the country—as well as collieries. IISCO was one of the first Indian companies whose shares were traded at the London Stock Exchange. But the departure of foreign participants after the new Foreign Exchange Regulation Act led to its decline, and IISCO was taken over by the government in 1972, by which time its production had dropped from over 1 million tons a year to 431,000 tons. It became a SAIL subsidiary in 1979.

The once-proud company limped along later since its outdated plant required large funds to bring it up to speed. The government was neither prepared to shut it down, which meant throwing its 25,000 employees out of work, nor invest in its modernization. In 1994, IISCO was finally referred to the Board for Industrial and Financial Reconstruction, which manages sick PSE companies. For a while, the company teetered between closure and revival, with the government unable to formulate strategies or find joint venture partners to assist the troubled plant. Its mines did attract interest from foreign companies keen to own the assets but they were not interested in reviving the plant.

With IISCO's production coming down to 30,000 tons and no investments taking place, its losses mounted and SAIL found it difficult to support its expenses, given its own negative profits. A series of loan waivers was undertaken by the PSE and by the government so that IISCO's balance sheet could be cleaned up. Finally, in 2006, when still no takers could be found, SAIL incorporated IISCO into its operations, renaming it IISCO Steel Plant. A revival package was instituted, costing about Rs 16,500 crore, to bring its capacity to 2.5 million tons annually.

Speaking at the foundation-stone-laying ceremony of the modernization and expansion programme, Prime Minister Manmohan Singh reiterated the importance of the plant for the steel industry in India. 'The IISCO plant is an example whereby we are exploiting its synergies with SAIL and investing in its future growth,' he stated, adding that the 'only way to stay consistently profitable is to ensure that the Indian steel industry is benchmarked with the most globally competitive producers.'[7]

Apart from writing off loans to IISCO amounting to Rs 2,454 crore, the government also waived loans to SAIL from the Steel Development Fund. Additionally, it provided guarantees to the PSE for raising loans from the market along with an interest subsidy for undertaking the voluntary retirement scheme and a similar facility for repaying previous loans. Another MoU was signed between the government and SAIL to monitor targets.

Financial and business restructuring led to gains for the company in the financial years of 2001 and 2002. Had these programmes not been initiated at the crucial time, SAIL would have suffered tremendously with its very survival at stake. At a time when many other steel companies were shutting down or turning bankrupt, SAIL managed to keep afloat with the help of government intervention. In 2002–03, it crossed the milestone of 10 million tons saleable steel production and the next year, the PSE stepped once more into positive profitability after five years.

SAIL's financial restructuring package, as well as supplementary efforts to reduce debts, led to a total cut in debts of Rs 8,000 crore, which marked the largest financial transformation in the history of corporate India at the time. During 2003–04, the debt–equity ratio of the company, a key indicator of financial strength, improved greatly from 6.5:1 to 1.86:1,[8] and each quarter, net profits soared. With the record profits, accumulated losses were wiped out and SAIL's turnaround was complete.

But this was only the first phase of the steel behemoth's directional change.

Restructuring: Phase II

The five years around the turn of the century were a difficult phase for the global economy. In addition, the Indian economy suffered from other numerous challenges, such as drought, which inhibited the growth of individual companies. It is to their immense credit that during the period of slowdown, Indian companies were not resting on their previous successes, but feverishly driving internal competencies and competitiveness, retooling their processes and shifting to a new level of productivity and performance.

From 2003–04, there was a distinct and sharp structural break in India's GDP and industrial growth. But this time, Indian companies were fully prepared to take advantage of the new growth forces and leverage them to their benefit. A new sentiment of confidence and cheer swept through industry as global growth conditions improved. Across the board, key sectors such as steel found themselves in a new growth phase. The steel sector, led by SAIL and ably supported by the private sector companies, moved up in global rankings of steel-producing nations—from the ninth position in 2004, it reached the fifth rank by 2006 with an output of 52 million tons.

SAIL's recovery phase was consolidated between 2003 and 2006. A corporate plan was put in place to meet new targets with a huge proposed investment of Rs 25,000 crore. This was to be financed by the internal generation of funds and more debt, while aiming to keep the crucial debt–equity ratio at 1:1. According to the plan, in 2012, SAIL's hot metal production would go up from 13 million tons to 23 million tons a year. It would also seek to incorporate a greater share of higher value added products to its offerings.

After a gap of six years, SAIL again started paying dividends in 2004–05 as net profits rocketed by 171 per cent. This was in spite of the pressure on costs due to rising input prices such as coal and iron ore. To ensure long-term supplies, SAIL inked agreements with gas PSE GAIL and took up the renewal of existing mining leases and new mining leases for iron ore with the government. The corporate plan also included new projects for modernization and technological upgradation at the Bhilai, Bokaro and Rourkela steel plants, and integration of the IISCO plant. Enterprise resource planning was initiated at Bhilai, to be extended to the entire organization in phases.

Amazingly, from 2006 onwards, the PSE entered a high-growth period that laid to rest all doubts about government-owned enterprises.

According to a study by the Hay Group, the period from 2006 to 2009 is a 'shining testimony of the resilience of SAIL'. In the three years up to to 2009, market capitalization went up more than three-fold, and the cumulative profit after tax was 60 per cent higher than the level between 1976–77 and 2005–06. In 2007–08, profits after tax were the third highest among all the companies in India. Its payments to the government coffers through taxes, royalties and other modes in the three years were almost equal to that in the previous ten years.

The study outlined the key areas of SAIL's 'remarkable journey of transformation and change'.

Customer-centricity was one of the strategies that SAIL espoused effectively. Its delivery and service levels were vastly improved, accompanied by excellent measures for meeting the demands of its customers. Communication became a key factor in this strategy. SAIL made determined efforts to make sure its products were easily available and the number of dealerships went up rapidly, so that the PSE had a presence in each one of the country's districts. Over 2,000 dealers were appointed in just two years, increasing sales from the network by ten times.

SAIL made huge improvements in understanding the customers' needs through regular interaction and responding to queries and complaints. It also made progress in supplying the required quantities of goods and meeting quality expectations.

The company set in place a Key Account Management process for a single point of contact and accountability for the 2 per cent of its customers who accounted for over half the sales. A key account manager was appointed for each major customer, accompanied by a plant account coordinator and plant information coordinator. This step helped the customer to work with the company for its demands, including forecasting its requirements, booking orders or addressing complaints. Regional managers themselves—in all four regions—closely monitored sales and services to the major customers, with regular meetings to look into any issues. Encouraging feedback through the Customer Satisfaction Index further helped identify and resolve problems.

Another part of the customer-centric strategy was the development of products for specific industries. Earlier, various items had to be imported for industries like defence and infrastructure, but SAIL ventured to supply these inputs itself by adding new designs to its product repertoire. For example, earthquake-resistant thermo-mechanically treated (TMT) rebars were developed, as also special structural items for the Bandra-Worli Sea Link project in Mumbai. The SAIL-Kavach HR Sheet was perfected to provide bullet-proof jackets for defence personnel. SAIL steel products were even used in the moon-mission Chandrayaan, and in the polar satellite launch vehicle series.

In the second set of strategies, changing mindsets internally was the key. The PSE worked on transitioning from the focus only on production to addressing a balanced set of performance measures in each part of the organization and at each level. Incentives became linked to certain performance measures to enhance an organization-wide buy-in.

The overall vision of the company is translated into defined indicators for each department and process. With the participation of the concerned employees, targets are set and broken down into monthly work plans and agreed upon internally by different departments in consultation with each other. Every employee then puts in efforts towards their implementation. Communication through direct interactions in a cross-functional manner is essential so that the entire organization is aware of and actively participating in departmental targets. For example, in the Bhilai Steel

Plant, which produces products for the Indian Railways, daily meetings are held to plan loading targets for wagon groups, taking into account material readiness, availability of wagons, the Railways' permission, and so on.

In the Hay Group survey, over 70 per cent of the top managers were happy with performance management, and 95 per cent of lower-level employees were absolutely clear on what was expected from them at their jobs.

Building employee talents was another vital factor in changing mindsets. Earlier, SAIL had become a top-heavy organization due to liberal promotions, and the fact that all incentives were based solely on production. 'Functional silos' led to little mutual understanding of goals and roles. To address this issue, SAIL started the multi-skilling programme to make work more meaningful for employees and to develop a new work culture. The Bhilai Steel Plant conceptualized the programme, identifying tasks and gaps. Workers were trained to multitask, so that there was less repetition and work stagnation. This helped enrich the working life of employees, giving them the encouragement to put in more effort in the workplace.

The modernization and expansion process carried several other elements. Ensuring raw material access was a vital component. The company estimated that its requirements of iron ore would go to 42 MT from the 26 MT in 2007–08, and set forth to renew its mining leases. SAIL finally won the mining lease for a 500-MT iron ore mine at Rowghat, a lease it had been attempting to obtain for as long as twenty-four years. One of the largest Chiria/Gua iron ore leases in Jharkhand was also renewed and two additional coal blocks were leased. Further, five PSEs came together to form a special purpose vehicle that would acquire coal mines overseas.

The Hay Group study also points to a new culture of 'inclusive decisions' for organizational transformation. 'The culture of empowerment has been the biggest change in SAIL in the last ten years,' stated a senior employee. 'Our systems have become much more flexible and delegation of decisions happens at the right levels.' Thus, senior people in the non-executive cadre were given the responsibility of coordinating production shifts. Suggestions and innovations received focused attention from whichever source they emanated from and 'calculated risk-taking' became a feature of the work culture. This strategy particularly helped the company to deal with the global economic crisis of 2008–09 by involving everyone in decision-making.

At the Bhilai Steel Plant, the programme 'Creating a Responsive Organization through People' (CROP) was instituted for a more seamless communication with 26,000 employees. 'SAIL's leadership was honest enough to confront reality at the peak of the crisis in the 1990s. They did not hide a single fact from us. We knew this would be a fight for survival. We were told in blunt terms that we need to become a more efficient organization if we are to survive,' commented a worker to the Hay Group analysts, who were impressed that the impact of the CROP workshops was remembered several years later by the workforce. The analysts reported several cases of employees whose parents or grandparents, too, had been SAIL employees.

In 2010, SAIL was one of the five PSEs to be granted the coveted Maharatna status by the government. This recognition arises from the large scale of SAIL as well as its potential to become an Indian multinational company.

Engaging with the Community

In August 2012, when Indian wrestler Sushil Kumar stood on the winners' podium at the London Olympics and was awarded the silver medal, few would have been as elated as SAIL chairman C.S. Verma.

As a PSE, the very ethos of SAIL embodied working effectively for the community right from inception. This could hardly be discarded just because liberalization and globalization demanded a new level of competitiveness.

Sports has been one of the successes of the company. Its large self-sufficient steel townships at Bhilai, Rourkela, Bokaro and Durgapur include sports academies that offer intensive training to identified sportspersons. Famed wrestlers Sushil Kumar and Yogeshwar Dutt were supported by SAIL for the Beijing Olympics and the Commonwealth Games. Sushil Kumar made the nation proud when he won the bronze at Beijing, followed up by the silver at London in 2012—the first Indian sportsperson to win individual medals at two Olympics—and Yogeshwar Dutt was the other wrestler funded by SAIL who collected a medal at London.

Apart from its sports initiative, the PSE has emerged as one of the largest operators of health and education facilities among corporates in India. In 2008, it greatly enlarged its commitment to the community by adopting seventy-nine villages in eight states to be developed as model villages. Health centres, schools, roads and sanitation as well as income-generation schemes were implemented. Its 2,400 medical camps, in a single year, helped almost 1.8 lakh people get access to healthcare.

The company has demarcated 2 per cent of its distributable surplus since 2006–07 towards CSR activities. Its infrastructure and outreach is truly impressive—fifty-four primary health centres, twelve reproductive and child health centres, seventeen hospitals, and seven super-specialty hospitals for more than 30 million people around its plants. For education, it operates some 150 schools in its townships and provides assistance to nearly 300 schools for tribal children. Seven special schools for children below the poverty line are operating with all facilities and school supplies completely free, while scholarships are provided for higher education. In addition, the company has adopted tribal children, including from the endangered Birhore tribe.

Sustainability with respect to the environment is a particular challenge for the steel industry, which contributes as much as 3–4 per cent of the total greenhouse gas emissions of the world. The Indian steel sector churns out about 1.5–2 times more of the toxic gases than the global best. 'Fortunately,' says Verma, 'the steel industry is alive to this issue and is putting in concerted efforts and adopting a multi-pronged strategy towards greater sustainable practices.'[9]

Over the years, SAIL has taken a range of initiatives to achieve greater efficiency and manage wastes and discharge. Air emission was brought down by 55 per cent in six years to 1.12 kg per ton of crude steel. Specific effluent discharges came down 16 per cent through painstaking efforts. The solid waste management initiatives, too, achieved a similar improvement. It has brought out a definite plan with specific targets under its Corporate Responsibility for Environment Protection agenda.

The Indian steel industry faces continuing challenges in its ambition to become the second largest steel-producing nation by 2015. 'One of the key challenges facing the steel industry is to ensure the desired quality and quantity of coking coal to meet its growing requirements, for which it is heavily dependent on imports,' notes Verma. 'This calls for reducing coal consumption (especially coking coal), developing indigenous coking coal blocks, acquiring coal assets abroad and also developing the necessary port and rail capacity to meet the enhanced requirement of imported coal.'

He continues, 'With the country's population of over a billion people, India could consume 500 million tonnes of steel per annum as it grows and develops. India's iron ore reserves would then last for twenty to thirty years, depending on how fast India grows, and we would all want India to grow faster. Thus conserving the iron ore reserves of the country is certainly one of the key issues.'

A Steely Resolve

When it comes to achievements, SAIL is hardly resting on its laurels. Verma observes, 'We need to take all the stakeholders along with us in the exciting journey of the steel industry to reach about 200 million tonnes by 2020.'

After 2002, the global steel industry underwent a complete shift. To a large extent, this was led by China's spectacular capacity creation, building up its production from 127 MT in 2000 to 684 MT in 2011. India, too, has scaled up its overall capacity to 78 MT in 2010–11 to become the fourth largest crude steel producer in the world. This was a big jump from the level of 51 MT just five years ago. But it is still just about 5 per cent of global crude steel production as compared to China's share of 44 per cent.

In terms of consumption, the per capita use of steel in India has gone up considerably as it has determinedly moved towards infrastructure construction in the past decade. While per capita consumption of steel was just 29 kilograms in 2000, in ten years, it went up to 55 kilograms.

It is interesting to note that following economic reforms and opening up of the steel sector, the private companies took the lead in expanding steel capacity. At the beginning of the 1990s, the private sector contributed less than half of finished steel production, but within the decade, their share shot up to more than two-thirds. In fact, in the second half of the decade of the 2000s, almost all of the increase in crude steel production in India took place in the private sector. Consequently, the share of public sector steel companies has declined from as much as 55 per cent in 1992–93 to less than a quarter after liberalization.[10]

Within this scenario, SAIL truly embodies the spirit of leadership that was envisaged by Pandit Nehru in the early years of nationhood. Traversing difficult circumstances, it has emerged as a $10-billion company with the ambition to ramp up its capacity to 60 MT by 2020. In 2009, SAIL emerged as the second highest net profit earning company in the world and in 2010, it was ranked second among world-class steelmakers by World Steel Dynamics, sealing its transformation journey from a loss-making entity to one of the best performers in the world.

Going ahead at full steam, it is implementing a modernization and expansion plan of $15 billion, or Rs 72,000 crore. A strategic plan, Lakshya 2020, has been set in motion to raise its market share to 30 per cent, a pet project of Verma.

Lakshya 2020 includes greater emphasis on R&D and globalization. The R&D master plan envisages reducing raw material and energy consumption as well as better use of inputs and reducing carbon emissions. Customer satisfaction by improving products is also on the agenda. Overall, the PSE aims at increasing R&D spending to 1 per cent of sales over the next few years.

Similarly, SAIL has started looking outward with determination. Bolstered by its Maharatna status, which permits it to make equity investments overseas up to 15 per cent of its net worth, it intends to leverage markets in Africa and South-east Asia that are implementing large infrastructure projects. 'SAIL is a domestic player and our first priority is to meet the growing domestic demand. However, we intend to keep a minimal international presence by exporting half a million tons every year. Going forward, when we scale up, we would like to increase this to 10 per cent to 15 per cent of our total sales [from the current 3 per cent to 4 per cent],' says Verma.

Prime Minister Manmohan Singh summed up the journey of SAIL in his speech while laying the foundation stone of the expansion project of Salem Steel Plant in Tamil Nadu in September 2008, 'The rising prominence of our steel industry on the world's steel landscape also mirrors the emergence of our country as a leading economic power in the world. From small beginnings, India has now become the fifth largest producer of steel in the world.... It is the dedicated service of each and every worker of SAIL that has made SAIL what it is today.'

And, as its tagline says, there's a little bit of SAIL in everyone's life.

9 JOURNEY TO 'WORLD-CLASS'

SONA GROUP

What does it take to start a business from scratch and go on to become a supplier of choice for companies worldwide? How does a medium-sized company with just one major customer move to global operations with plants in the US and Germany and a presence in six other countries? The simple answer is—unyielding determination to be the best.

The Sona Group's single-minded devotion to achieving world-class status led to its pre-eminent position as India's largest producer of steering systems for vehicles. To manage this feat in a manufacturing industry, and that too, in a sector dominated by huge multinational companies, is truly a stellar performance.

THE ENTREPRENEUR

At first glance, Surinder Kapur does not appear the restless entrepreneur that he is. His portly frame and measured soft-spoken manner hide a keen and dynamic brain that is always strategizing for the next opportunity. Belonging to a well-known family of jewellers from Delhi—the shop 'Kapur di Hatti' is part of the capital's beaten paths for jewellery patrons—Kapur was the first engineer among his siblings. In fact, the young Kapur went to the US for higher studies in the 1960s, when few Indians could manage it, and fewer still returned to India. He got admission in undergraduate courses at Stanford, New

York and Michigan universities, and chose the last as it was the cheapest. After eleven years in Michigan State University, Kapur returned to India armed with a doctorate in aerospace and fluid dynamics.

And then, of course, he went into automotives. His father-in-law, Raunaq Singh, himself a self-made entrepreneur, needed someone to look after his new venture, Bharat Gears, in Mumbai, and Kapur agreed to extend his professional support to this endeavour. He found success in tying up technology from overseas and setting up the plant, but fifteen years later, he felt he needed to set up his own venture.

'After leading Bharat Gears... for fifteen years, it was clear to me that (it) was not the company for me in the long term. I had no equity in the company and my brothers-in-law would soon take over; I had to start something of my own,' he said.[1] 'The urge to become an entrepreneur dawned with my idea of being the "boss of my own life" and also to create a culture that I aspired towards. My satisfaction came solely from creating a company based on my own vision and not duplicating anybody else's idea. I was driven by a desire to be independent; this, along with my passion to create something unique, catapulted my success.'

It was 1985, and Maruti Suzuki India Ltd (then called Maruti Udyog Ltd) was reshaping the automobile industry in India. Although a number of Japanese firms were present in the sector, it was still a challenging environment to operate in, given the need for licences and permits for setting up any manufacturing unit. But Kapur had zeroed in on the one company that had everything going for it. Maruti Suzuki was a government-owned company for which success was the paramount motivation and Kapur believed that a partnership with it would allow him parallel success. He had the experience, Maruti Suzuki was doing well, and steering system manufacturing faced a technology gap.

Kapur was introduced to the legendary first managing director of Maruti Udyog Ltd, Dr V. Krishnamurthy, who proposed a startling new business model—Maruti Suzuki would be a shareholder in the new company. It was not to be the usual supplier–customer relationship where both sides were at loggerheads with each other over business terms, but a partnership in which both companies would work together. The car company would mentor and work with the new ancillary for win-win outcomes.

Kapur named his new venture 'Sona Steering Systems Ltd' in keeping with his antecedents in gold and jewellery. He also laid down the Sona values:

a. Respect for the individual
b. Service to the customer
c. Excellence in the pursuit of goals

These values were the guiding force of the company right from the beginning and continue to be so. Bear in mind that at the time Kapur devised the values, the three points were not part of general Indian business practices. Right from the beginning, then, the chairman thought and acted differently, rooted in a strong ethical basis.

A steering system is visible to drivers only as a wheel. But behind the wheel is a complex set of interlocking parts that communicates the direction of the steering wheel to the steering arms connected to the tyres. A large number of precision-machined parts and sub-assemblies go into the system. It goes without saying that all of these have to work perfectly to ensure safety. Not a single faulty part can be tolerated.

The Japan Connection

Looking for technology tie-ups, Kapur headed for Japan, where companies were already excited about the potential of the Maruti Suzuki joint venture. Koyo Seiko (which merged with Toyoda Machine Works in 2006 to form JTEKT, the world's largest steering systems manufacturer) was based in Osaka and had just developed the world's first electronically controlled steering system. It also had a base in the US for the manufacture of bearings. In the 1980s, the company was not too keen on exploring a venture with a new Indian enterprise, as its earlier foray into India had not been promising. It took Kapur three trips before a technical agreement for manufacturing manual steering gears was firmed up.

During one such visit, Mr Futaba, then president of Koyo, taught Kapur some important lessons of doing business in Japan, valuable guidelines that have remained deeply etched in his mind since then. 'We have had a very painful experience in India,' Mr Futaba told him at a dinner. 'A bearing manufacturing company that we established as a partnership with an Indian state government never made any profits and never paid us any royalty. I had vowed that I will never do business in India. And here I am, sitting with you, discussing a technical agreement for manufacturing steering systems! Do you know why?' He then went on to answer his own question, 'We were very impressed with your persistence. Your behaviour told us that you are keen, serious and committed to this business. The Japanese always look at long-term possibilities, so we are looking at a long-term partnership with you.'

'I will tell you an important thing today,' he later said during that dinner meeting. 'We call it in Japanese *tatemae* and *honne*. Sometimes you say something to someone even if you do not actually believe it; even if actually you would not like it that way. You say so just because you respect the person and you do not wish to hurt him. This is *tatemae*. *Honne*, on the other hand, is your firm belief, your intention. In a sense, *honne* represents the kinship between friends and family where nothing is written down, yet it is generous and understood. If you want to do business in Japan, you should communicate with your partners the *honne* way.'

That evening was an eye-opener for Kapur. In those short three hours or so, he learned more about the Japanese way of business than any business school could ever have taught him.

He learned about the importance of informal, yet honest, communication. Above all, he learned about the long-term viewpoint of Japanese companies, and recognized that his actions today would yield results only after several years.

For Sona, the opening of the economy and the end of the industrial licensing regime was a huge boost. Revved up by the success of Maruti Suzuki, the passenger vehicle sector was one of the first to accelerate. The entry of car companies from all over the world meant that the demand for steering components surged. But at the same time, was Sona, newly entering the production scene, ready to face the challenges of competition from component manufacturers across the globe?

Kapur never had a doubt. He was already deep into planning his next move.

Japan was the destination of choice for Kapur. Although he never learned more than a few words in the Japanese language, he made it a point to understand the business culture of the country. It was very different from the culture of any other country, being based on an unwritten code of conduct that stressed trust and confidence rather than hard business facts. Kapur had to make efforts to ensure that the companies he contacted would support him wholeheartedly.

At the same time, the Japanese devotion to quality assurance as a manufacturing tool was completely alien to India, and a great source of learning for Indian companies. Kapur quickly zeroed in on this one major instrument as the foundation for the expansion of his own Group. He realized that the way to the hearts of Japanese businessmen was to inculcate the same passion for quality in his own operations. This worked. Over the next few years, Sona went in for several partnerships with Japanese companies, each of which brought the Group high accolades.

In 1992, Koyo signed up for an 8 per cent equity participation in the company, just five years after it had commenced production. By 1993–94, Sona had been awarded the title of Best Performing Vendor in the steering systems category by Maruti Suzuki. It had also successfully obtained the certification of ISO 9002 for quality assurance in production and servicing. The next year, it got Koyo's certification for exports and, remarkably, became the only company supplying steering components to a Japanese original equipment manufacturer.

From Strength to Strength

From then on, it was just an upward journey. Sales zoomed from Rs 44.6 crore in 1993 to Rs 226 crore in 1999–2000. Sona pushed up its steering gear capacity from 275,000 gears annually to 450,000 gears in 1996–97. Power steering was introduced and production for the new car categories of mid-size and luxury cars commenced. Sona Somic Components Ltd started production of ball joints after forging a technical collaboration with Somic Ishikawa of Japan, which would go into the steering and suspension systems. Sona Matsuda Cold Forgings Ltd was commissioned in the end of 1996 for cold forged components. A joint venture with Mitsubishi Material Corp Ltd called Sona Okegawa Precision Forgings came into being, yet another landmark for the company. This brought the latest technologies for precision-forging in manufacturing synchronizer rings and bevel gears to Sona.

But the journey was not always smooth. Sona faced a crisis in 1993. A worker noticed that the steel being used in a particular component appeared to be defective and when the steel was tested, it was found that it was mild steel rather than the higher quality required. Sona took immediate steps—first, it identified and weeded out the steel from the particular vendor who had supplied the defective raw material. Then Kapur approached Maruti and informed them about the problem. He recommended that Maruti recall the cars that had gone into the market with the lower-grade component.

Maruti agreed that the cars needed to be brought back and recalled 30,000 of them. This move created a huge media furore at the time, as this was probably the first time that an Indian company had resorted to recalls of defective products. In the event, only eighteen of the 30,000 cars were found to be defective and needed to be changed.

This proved to be a huge learning experience for Sona. It dealt with the setback in its characteristic innovative way—instead of cutting off supplies from the vendor that had created the entire problem, it worked with the company to improve its processes.

Kapur is sanguine about such failures, 'Sona Group's immediate reaction could have been to stop buying from the company that supplied the steel, but we realized that it had an internal problem. Our supplier needed to improve its processes, so we worked with the company to sort it out. We faced similar challenges with other component suppliers as well, but instead of immediately ending deals with them, we tried to solve their problems as we realized that setting up a new supplier would take nearly the same amount of energy and would not be congenial to the development of the industry.

'So, in my opinion, the best way to deal with vendors is not to repeatedly point out their mistakes, but to help them improve the quality of their supply while appreciating their contribution. Due to such mutual understanding, many of our smaller vendors have grown into massive suppliers today.'[2]

The fiasco cost the company Rs 30 lakh, but it gained immense credibility as a result. The fact that Koyo, the Japanese partner, stood by Sona during this period was a big support. In fact, in 1997, Koyo Seiko bought up an additional equity share in Sona, bringing its stake up to 20.47 per cent—and the company name was accordingly changed to Sona Koyo Steering Systems Ltd.

Soon thereafter, the company was selected as the only vendor for steering systems and columns of Maruti's proposed new car. It also expanded its customer base to include Hyundai, Mitsubishi and Toyota, among others, although Maruti continued to be its biggest customer. But the industrial slowdown and decline in auto sales at the turn of the millennium brought lower sales and profits. From the peak of Rs 226 crore in 1999–2000, sales slumped and could not recover for the next three years. The company hired consultancy firm A.T. Kearney to study its operations and suggest strategies. The consultancy advised Sona Koyo to leverage exports as a growth driver and improve its supply chain management.

In 2001–02, believing that recovery would take time, Sona set up a business development group. This would explore new markets and aggressively target new orders. Marketing, production, new product development and operations, all saw new initiatives. A key measure was setting up an R&D division for product development, truly a remarkable step for a company of its size, given that R&D was low priority even for bigger companies at the time. In its first year, Sona engineers developed a new lighter-weight collapsible steering column and the company received four Indian patents on this product.

The period of slowdown was utilized to accelerate productivity, set in place the quality systems of Total Productivity Maintenance (TPM) and Total Quality Management (TQM), institute better methods of planning and forecasting, and ramp up exports. In 2003, Sona competed for and wrested the highly sought-after Deming Prize of Quality, the culmination of its 'quality' journey. This amazing achievement is detailed in the next section of the chapter.

When the strong economic recovery finally began from 2003 onwards, the Sona Group was well-placed to take advantage of it. By 2006–07, sales went up by a multiple of 3.5. Exports soared more than ten times, from a low base.

In the middle of the decade, the company strategized to go in for an investment of Rs 400 crore up to 2010, which would include expansion and modernization of its operations. Scale and technology were both to be enhanced, to move from merely supplying parts to becoming an 'end-to-end steering solutions provider'. The company's three plants were at Gurgaon, Chennai and Dharuhera, all operating at high capacity, but more units were planned in Uttarakhand and West Bengal.

Among the company's many initiatives was the management of the supply chain since auto companies depended critically on timely and efficient procurement of all their parts. It was essential to lower costs of inputs while working with vendors for greater efficiency. Procurement was centralized for all Sona plants, and six commodity-sourcing groups were formed. A weekly monitoring system for managing stocks was set up, reducing turnover by a third. For all its vendors, Sona undertook a comprehensive review exercise and set measurable targets for cost control and reducing wastage.

Another major exercise was to embed IT in its operations. To begin with, Sona Koyo used Oracle to develop its own application for sales, maintenance, finance and other areas, but not extending to manufacturing and quality control. The dotcom boom and slowdown period helped bring new ideas where IT usage was concerned. In particular, new product development was taking too long, the management felt. Cost reduction, timely and accurate information, increase in productivity and a common platform for all the Group companies were the objectives identified for the IT system. The effort was spearheaded by the Group's chief financial officer, who also doubled as its chief information officer. In fact, the IT initiative was led by the functional departments, rather than the IT department itself.

A team was set up, including all departments, to study Enterprise Resource Planning (ERP) packages. It selected Oracle e-business suite, to be implemented with the help of PricewaterhouseCoopers, one of the most high-priced consultants. The quality systems of TQM and TPM made availability of information in real time critical, and this led the ERP effort. It took just five months for Sona Koyo to complete the pilot sessions, train users and roll out the ERP strategy. This helped it in reducing rejection levels by as much as 80 per cent, improving the inventory turnover ratio and finalization of accounts. It also added to the transparency of business operations. IT was then moved to the engineering operations. Two-dimensional Computer Aided Design (CAD) drawings were converted into three-dimensional drawings, which helped product design.[3]

As the India growth story took hold in the mid-2000s, the Sona Group joined the big Indian corporations in stepping out into the world, one of the amazing smaller companies to do so. Acquisitions and greenfield strategies were both part of its plan. It forged joint ventures for new plants at Bawal with JTEKT and Fuji and Sona AutoComp, a servicing company, came up in the US and Europe. Through a collaboration with Fuji Autotech France, the Group stamped footprints in France, the Czech Republic, Brazil and Sweden.

In January 2008, the Sona Group bought ThyssenKrupp Prazisionsschmiede, a leading German company, and renamed it Sona BLW Prazisionsschmiede. It now became the direct owner of the precision-forged technology, which it earlier got on a sub-licence from Mitsubishi. This was because Mitsubishi was also only the licensee of this technology by ThyssenKrupp Prazisionsschmiede. The new company has three plants in Germany and one in North Carolina in the US, accounting for 46 per cent of the Group turnover.

The Group's revenues have crossed $800 million, coming from the verticals of manufacturing auto components, services, mobility and global ventures. It has eighteen plants across India, including the automotive hotspots of Gurgaon,

Chennai, Nasik and Pune, as well as one in Sanand in Gujarat. The range of its products includes integrated steering systems, electronic power steering systems and bevel gears. It is India's largest steering systems producer, delivering millions of axle and transmission components to customers across the world. As an Original Equipment Manufacturer (OEM) supplier, it counts amongst its customers auto companies renowned for their quality and high performance—Daimler, Volkswagen, BMW, Audi, Caterpillar and many others. It occupies the top position in the manufacture of precision-forged bevel gears, the high-quality gears with two vertical shafts at an angle to each other.

From its humble beginnings, the Sona Group has truly raised the bar for smaller companies in the Indian entrepreneurial firmament. Much of this was due to its unrelenting commitment to quality.

Leveraging Quality

In my days as a bank officer in the early 1990s, I remember going to small factories for an inspection of our loan accounts. Invariably, the shopfloor was littered with raw material and waste products; machines, which appeared on the verge of constant breakdown, groaned and chugged; workmen seemed to be randomly moving around with no sense of purpose; tools were flung haphazardly on and around shelves; and the owners or managers seemed quite happy with the way things were run. In fact, there was a visible sense of pride—at having a factory producing stuff in the first place!

Of the panoply of strategies that Sona adopted for its growth, quality probably best defines its operations.

So what is quality? The American Society for Quality (ASQ) refers to quality assurance as 'the planned and systematic activities implemented in a quality system so that quality requirements for a product or service will be fulfilled'.[4]

So quality goes beyond just meeting specified standards for a particular item. It is a process that minimizes inefficiencies, wastage and defectives and then ensures that it maximizes productivity outcomes. Quality in operations can apply to each and every process in an organization, be it a single individual in her daily life, a household, a small enterprise, a school or a multinational conglomerate. In its evolved form, it extends to the concept of complete 'business excellence', including a range of processes such as planning and setting aspirational but doable targets, meeting the needs of customers, leadership and ethics, inculcating passion among employees, driving improvements at every stage through innovations and managing sustainability of communities and environments.

In the India of 1991, quality was an unknown concept. Most companies were comfortable operating in a protected environment, and averse to risks arising from competition. Competitiveness was not part of the businessman's glossary. It was the CII that pioneered the quality movement in India in the mid-1980s, but when it was setting up its Total Quality Management Division, members were sceptical and it took a lot of persuasion to get a few to sign up. Fortunately, Dr V. Krishnamurthy urged CII to continue its efforts and raise awareness about the need for quality. As late as 1991, the first Indian company, Sundram Fasteners, got ISO 9000 certification. The Quality Council of India was set up even later, in 1998, for laying out standards, providing accreditation and monitoring.

For Sona, quality was particularly remote as the car market was dominated by a single company, Maruti Suzuki, and there was little emphasis on cost and quality as long as Maruti's standards were met. Although the Sona plant was modeled on Koyo, marketing was still based on a cost plus approach. But sales were good and the company even obtained ISO 9002 certification in 1993.

Then, in 1994, the government announced a new automobile

policy that granted entry to global automotive component manufacturers into the Indian scene. Realizing that its survival depended on matching their standards, Sona set forth on its quality mission, 'to become a world-class quality company'.

A careful analysis of company affairs was carried out under the guidance of Kapur. The objective was to improve quality and reduce costs, simple enough. But the company decided to go in for the stringent quality control and assurance systems of the famous Toyota Production System (TPS). It also targeted upgradation of its vendors through a special cell and education and training of all personnel in the company. The assistance of Koyo was taken for this endeavour, which proved fruitful.

TPS stresses quick delivery of vehicles in the most efficient and waste-free manner. Its tenets are *jidoka*, or preventing defective products being produced, and just-in-time, or making only the right quantities. Under *jidoka*, a machine detects flaws itself and stops automatically, so that no more faulty goods are produced. This allows operators to rectify the errors and also simultaneously continue operations on other machines, enabling a single operator to be in charge of different machines.

The just-in-time philosophy means eliminating wastage of time and resources through continuous improvement. It includes 'mistake-proofing' and reducing parts positioned at each machine station, while at the same time supplying only those parts to the next machine that have been used up. All this has to be done with full adherence to quality control. Just-in-time expects complete commitment from all employees down the production chain.

TPS at Sona Koyo meant complete reorientation of the plant. In the original plant, raw material entered the factory premises through the doors, was moved to somewhere near the middle for the start of operations, then the goods-in-process meandered through the various stages of production in a convoluted pattern that required much to-and-fro movement.

Under TPS, the machines were placed in such a manner that the entry of raw material was from a designated entrance and the process chain was systematized in a single straight line in one direction and another straight line back in the other direction. The finished product finally ended up near the exit doors from where it was loaded. This drastically reduced the movement of materials within the plant and production per hour of the finished items went up from eighteen to forty-two with the number of operators coming down from five to two.

Sona also sent its engineers to Koyo for training in product and production technology. With the help of small Indian machine-makers, it developed its own Sona Special Purpose Machines.

But even deploying TPS was not enough to meet the growing sales requirements. Although efficiency improved, Sona began to experience problems in meeting delivery schedules and had to stop its production lines often. Its warranty failure rates increased and accidents, too, occurred more frequently. The company's financial performance fluctuated and the management was unable to cope with the rapid changes in the market. Soon, Sona's position as the monopoly supplier to Maruti was eroding.

More challenges were emerging as a result of the industrial slowdown and other factors. The fall in growth of the domestic market meant that exports had to be prioritized, which, in turn, placed pressure on the need to reduce costs and drastically improve quality. At the same time, car makers were quickly coming out with new models so that the time for developing new products had to be shortened. Sona Koyo analysed these developments and decided that it urgently needed to upgrade employee skills, leverage IT and develop cost-efficient technology.

Fortuitously, it was at this time that Maruti and CII got together for a quality training programme under the tutelage of renowned Japanese quality guru Dr Yoshikazu Tsuda of the Japanese Union of Scientists and Engineers. Aware of Surinder Kapur's ambitions to raise his company to world-class levels, Dr Krishan Kumar, chief engineer of Maruti, invited Sona Koyo to join the programme.

It was a unique programme, undertaken for the first time in India. The idea was to bring together a group of companies, not necessarily in the same manufacturing sector or even in the same location, to learn together and share experiences. CII called it 'cluster learning'.

And so, in the next phase of its quality journey, employees at Sona Koyo started to get familiar with new terms and new practices. Root cause analysis, daily work management, managing points and checking points, management for objectives, deep analysis, plan-do-check-act (PDCA), all entered the working lexicon. Then there was the plethora of Japanese words, which were not just terms, but entire philosophies—*pokayoke* for preventing mistakes; *kanban* for material identification, movement between machine lines and planning changes in the item supply line; *andon* for online production status; and finally, the mantra of *kaizen*, making small improvements on a continuous basis, relentlessly, across all processes with the overriding intention to make every single procedure more and more efficient.

The first concept that Professor Tsuda threw at his students was 'exactness'. In theory, this meant having full control over quantity, quality and delivery. But what exactly did 'exactness' mean in practice?

Kiran Deshmukh was in charge of quality at Sona Koyo, supported by Dinesh Sharma. Dinesh is an unassuming engineer who would not attract much attention outside the shopfloor—but he is a tenacious and passionate advocate of quality in Sona Koyo. Speak to him of quality, and he breaks into a stream of esoteric jargon which he is completely familiar with and has on the tips of his fingers. Kiran and Dinesh were responsible for developing complex charts and diagrams, analysing data, and identifying areas of improvement. Their relentless pursuit of quality in Sona Koyo is encapsulated in loaded shelves of thick, black folders that make the minds of ordinary persons spin in amazement.

Over a period of two years, Sona Koyo learned and inculcated exactness in its operations even as engineers and managers visited car dealers to understand end-user requirements. Manpower, machines, method, materials and the environment were the areas where exactness was infused to achieve daily targets in a consistent manner that brooked no disruptions. By rigorously examining each stage in its production chain, Sona broke down the processes to their simplest forms and then worked on them for improvement.

Some of these improvements were simple—issuing detailed work instructions for each operator; ensuring that components, tools and gauges were always kept in specific places and that they were close enough to the working area; monitoring machine conditions with charts and check sheets; and insisting that all materials went into the correct containers in the right locations in the correct quantities.

For example, the whole concept of monitoring machines changed under the new guidelines. Earlier, a machine would stop working, halting the entire line, which was when operators would examine the situation, diagnose why the machine had stopped and realize that it needed to be greased. Then the grease would be indentured from the store and applied. All this time, every machine in the entire line would be idle. Under the new method, the machine's working was studied to determine exactly when it needed to be greased. A schedule for greasing was instituted, and the grease placed at the stand in time. Before the machine broke down, the grease would be applied, and thus there was no stoppage of function.

Professor Tsuda was merciless during his visits to the cluster learning companies. Once, on seeing an open door of a raw material cabinet, he asked the invariable Japanese question, 'Why is this door open?' He was told that since the particular item was often needed, it saved time to keep the door open. His admonishment was immediate, 'Then remove the door,' he advised sternly. In a biscuit factory strewn with broken biscuit pieces, he asked, 'Why is there so much wastage?' The answer was that it didn't really matter since the company sold the waste biscuit as animal feed. Professor Tsuda's reply was scathing, 'You should be in the animal feed business then.'

In parallel, the concept of 'visualization' was also deployed, the premise being that the same information should be readily available to all who viewed it. Sona Koyo identified certain processes for visualization. Pictorial work instructions were put up, while tools and fixtures were colour-coded to distinguish the various models of production. Each cell had green boards put up nearby, which displayed their performance charts, and markings on machines indicated where a visual check of parts was necessary to avoid breakdowns. In this way, the manufacturing process was transparent and evident to all, so that each employee could align his operations with the whole system.

Exactness, visualization, *pokayoke* and QMS were part of the 'retainment' phase of work simplification for Sona Koyo, which lasted till 1998. Once these simple processes were stabilized and mistakes became fewer, the company shifted to the 'improvement' phase, which involved 'gap analysis' and setting up 'managing points and checking points'. This meant studying data to figure out where there were deficiencies or gaps in functioning, then keeping an eye on those points for potential mishaps.

The quality team came out with a unique chart that would clearly show the linkage between the company's vision, its medium-term plan and roadmap, its annual targets, its objectives for the current year and series of targets for the next few years. The chart broke down the activities that needed to be done in the present to achieve objectives of the future. This derived from the concept of policy management or Management for Objectives (MFO), which aligns the activities of people throughout the company so that key goals can be achieved and the company can react quickly to changing environments. Planning based on the previous year's achievements and the current business scenario, along with the vision roadmap, was stage one; deployment was the next stage, using the 'X-matrix' developed by the quality team; and finally, reviews for results and reviews for actions were carried out on a regular basis.

This phase of ensuring quality involved daily work management, a concept that derives from the PDCA cycle. Production targets were envisaged, and the actual results evaluated through measurements. Data was required on both inputs and outputs for determining the cause and effect relationship, with such a constant review process helping to improve cost, delivery, safety and employee morale. Daily work management meant that each manager had certain points that he had to manage and check regularly, for which he was accountable.

For 100 per cent employee involvement, a key factor in success, group 'kaizen' activities began in 2000. Every Wednesday, after the first shift ended and the next shift was to begin, all employees met in groups for 30 minutes. The sixty groups solved as many as 520 problems in three years. Every quarter, the six best groups were selected and rewarded, with the best group of the year getting to participate in the Koyo Kaizen Convention in Japan. Training on the use of quality tools and problem-solving techniques was also imparted to all employees.

The passion for quality reigned supreme in the Sona Group. 'Why-why analysis' was the overriding concern, with the ultimate objective of zero defects, zero waste, zero accidents. This was a deep examination of the root causes of any problems. For example, Sona Koyo took up a case where a part under warranty was returned as it was making an unusual sound. Peeling away the layers like in an onion, it found that the noise was due to some looseness and unnecessary movement in the assembly set. The reason for this was a hard steering feel. In turn, torque variation was found to be high. Digging even deeper, the poor accuracy of gear parts, which again arose from deformation in heat treatment, was identified. The corrective action was to establish a new straightening process, while the preventive action was to identify the raw material and heat treatment processes in order to improve them so that the defect did not occur again.

Competitiveness records, that is, of improvements in its own performance parameters fell like dominos. In-house rejections dropped from 23,000 parts per million to 876, while supplier rejections came down from 49,500 parts per million to less than a thousand. Customer returns, over 1,500, fell to just 112 parts per million. Manufacturing costs saw similar dramatic improvements, down-shifting from 8 per cent to just 4.9 per cent, while gross sales per employee went up from Rs 16 lakh to Rs 59 lakh.

New product development, instead of taking over a year, now took less than six months, while the number of Sona Koyo designed products rose from 11 per cent to 44 per cent of its total sales. Accidents and absenteeism were greatly reduced, indicating the rising morale of employees.

And finally, after its ruthless adherence to the concepts of quality, Sona Koyo received the Deming Application Prize, the Olympic gold medal for the quality effort, in 2003.

Breakthrough Management

'Do not forget that success is always the first step of failure,' said Professor Shoji Shiba, an international expert in TQM, visiting professor at MIT's Sloan School of Management, and a winner of the Deming Prize for Individuals, while addressing the group of 2003 Deming Prize-winning companies at the customary post-award-ceremony workshop in Tokyo. Elaborating on this advice, Professor Shiba added, 'You have won the Deming Prize because you excelled in your operations using the proven methods of TQM. However, these methods may not be sufficient for you to face the future. The world is experiencing the 10x changes. The incremental, continuous improvement methods of TQM alone cannot help you face these extraordinary changes. You need to unlearn your past and acquire the new methods of breakthrough management if you want to be successful in the coming decade.'

These harsh words, coming from an expert in TQM, just one day after the glory of receiving the coveted Deming Award made Kapur recognize what was approaching his way. He and his company had to unlearn the past and adopt new ways of doing business.

After 2004, the business environment once again shifted due to rapid growth in the economy and the manufacturing sector. Import duties were reduced and raw material prices and petroleum prices rose sharply. In the car industry, more global competition swept in, bringing ever faster introduction of new models and increase in customer expectations. For steering systems, there was a distinct shift to electric power steering.

Technology now became the strategy for Sona Koyo's next level of operations. The company had to attain more knowhow for electronic products and develop domestic products. It also wanted to anticipate and define customer needs. Its direction now moved from 'reactive quality' to 'proactive quality'.

Once again, policy deployment and the MFO system was leveraged, moving from stated objectives and defined action plans for the whole enterprise to breaking these down for each unit, each division and each department. A new list of acronyms—HVPT, QFD, QG 20—pervades the factories. Value engineering, reliability engineering, statistical TPM, customer voice, all these are the tools in use for the company. In recent years, the company has won many awards for its quality performance, including the TPM Excellence Award, and awards from its customers.

The Sona Group's global footprint, too, is a result of its quality journey. Being world-class means not just meeting global standards, but running operations overseas—being part of highly competitive global supply chains, and not just selling top-quality goods to the world, but also having a strong multi-location presence.

The acquisition of ThyssenKrupp's forgings business was a bold step. The German industrial Group had 180,000 workers in eighty countries with a turnover of about €45 billion. When it wanted to divest its precision-forging plants, enjoying a turnover of Euro 300 million, several Indian companies were reported to be interested, attracted by its markets in western Europe and its technology. Sona Okegawa, the joint venture with Mistubishi Metals, made the winning bid, and with this move, captured the top slot for precision-forgings in the world.

'Sona Okegawa developed a business strategy to have a global footprint to service customers and this acquisition fulfills that strategy. I am certain that the synergies we will bring about with low-cost development and engineering skills of India and high levels of productivity and leading technology from ThyssenKrupp will create value for global customers. We have also learned a great deal from Mitsubishi Materials regarding Japanese manufacturing excellence in production, which I am sure the German and US plants will want to learn from and implement,' said Kapur, announcing the deal.[5]

Atul Mittal, the Group financial officer, adds, 'Since our acquisition of Thyssen's precision-forging units in Germany and the US, Sona has been benefiting in the following areas: first, quality—Sona Okegawa has been making forging dies based on Mitsubishi technology. After the acquisition, we have adopted the German process for die-making, which has resulted in better quality dies and, consequently, the finished product. Our German units also help and guide us on selection of die material for improved life. We have also been benefited by adoption of many small techniques which contribute to quality.

'Second, technology—the acquisition has helped us adopt forging processes developed in Germany over the years, resulting in cost and quality improvement. Now we have access to a whole lot of process information of products which are manufactured in Germany. Many of these will be eventually produced in Sona Okegawa as new products. We have also introduced close die forgings based on the experience in Germany.

'Third, R&D—Germany has a lot of knowhow in the area of optimizing bevel gear design. Based on this, today Sona Okegawa can offer the solution of superior products to the customer. Sona Okegawa is also working closely with the German team on several new product development projects which will be first-time introduction in the market.'

Corporate social responsibility (CSR) ranks high on the quality mission and the Sona Group is no exception. Through its charitable trust, Sona engages in education and skill development, community development, healthcare and gender issues. It has adopted an Industrial Training Institute (ITI) in Haryana under the government's three-way partnership formula, which includes the central government, the state government and a company. This partnership is aimed at upgradation of the ITI in accordance with industry requirements so that graduates possess marketable skills. The trust has also taken up the holistic development of an entire village, as well as initiatives in the rural areas.

Taking Stock

The excellent growth of the Sona Group in the years after liberalization provides some lessons for aspiring entrepreneurs. First, leadership is the defining criterion for success, driven by passion and strong determination. Second, this passion has to be forged at all levels, from top managers to workers and vendors. Finally, the enterprise must be ahead of the curve in seeking out new opportunities and building on current forces for future growth.

As Kapur puts it, 'Financial limitations and technological drawbacks shouldn't thwart the entrepreneurial spirit of young business enthusiasts from reaching the heights of their potential.... Everyone has dreams, but do not let the results of your success be the goal. All entrepreneurs should create value and cater to a need.'[6]

10

THE PERENNIAL PIONEER

TATA STEEL

The Deming Grand Prize is the ultimate honour for a company striving to be the best in its field. Awarded by the Japanese Union of Scientists and Engineers, it is the highest recognition for excellence in quality operations. In 2012, Tata Steel achieved the rare honour of being the first integrated steel plant in the world and the largest company in two decades to receive this award. For a company over a hundred years old, which some world-renowned consultants once thought should exit the steel industry, winning the Deming Grand Prize represented a remarkable transformation.

It is difficult enough to survive as a company for over a hundred years. To do this under radically different environments, from an unhelpful colonial administration to the challenges of Independent India and the licence raj, is a major achievement. But to go on to attain best-in-class status globally is truly an astounding feat. Yet Tata Steel regenerated itself to do precisely that in the years after liberalization. The story of the venerable company after 1991 is a saga of superhuman effort, single-minded determination and innovation from leaders and workers alike.

In 1968, Jamshed J. Irani was a young doctoral fellow working at the British Iron and Steel Research Association at Sheffield, UK, when a letter from India winged its way to him. It was from J.R.D. Tata, iconic head of India's largest private sector conglomerate, the Tata Group, and it invited Dr Irani to work with the Tata Iron and Steel Company, the legendary TISCO. Giving up his 'comfortable'[1] stay in Britain, Dr Irani headed for a new life to Jamshedpur.

At around the same time as Irani received the letter from TISCO, B. Muthuraman, a fresh engineering product from IIT Madras, was completing his graduate traineeship in the company. Moving from iron-making and engineering development after ten years, Muthuraman then worked for almost two decades in sales and marketing. But when TISCO undertook a major expansion with its new cold rolling mill project in 1995, it was to Muthuraman that it turned, asking him to lead it. In just over two years, a record time and well before the scheduled date of completion, Muthuraman and his team had the mill up and running.

Widely credited as the mastermind of Tata Steel's makeover, Dr Irani, managing director of Tata Steel from 1992 to 2001, headed the team that led the transformation of India's largest private steel company in the liberalization era. Muthuraman, who took over the position from Irani and remained managing director till 2009, was the strategist for its global expansion. Together with a highly acclaimed management team and committed workforce, the two MDs steered the rapid progress of Tata Steel from an unwieldy behemoth to a limber and agile steelmaker near the top of the global chain. 'Continual improvement' is the credo that Tata Steel internalized to reach its goal of being the lowest-cost steel producer in the world.

Rich Legacy

The history of Tata Steel is indeed the history of Indian industry, tenaciously building its presence in a hostile colonial environment, turning uncompetitive within a controlled regime, then taking off unfettered after 1991. The famous words of Sir Frederick Upcott, chief commissioner for Great Peninsular Railways,[2] in the early 1900s, who derisively promised to eat every pound of steel rail that TISCO produced, are etched in our minds as the example of a heedless administration. When Jamsetji N. Tata, a pioneering genius, envisaged TISCO in 1900, it was considered a castle in the air. But his relentless passion despite all odds—and efforts by his sons after his death—led to this dream being realized when construction of the factory began in 1907. As the first steel ingots rolled out of the line in 1912, the entire nation cheered this demonstration of indigenous engineering and manufacturing capability. Since then, Tata Steel has been the leading light of India's private sector. A hundred years later, the nation cheered once again as Tata Steel successfully conducted the largest overseas acquisition in Indian corporate history.

Dorabji Tata, J.R.D. Tata, Russi Mody, Ratan Tata, and now, Cyrus Mistry—the names of Tata Steel's leaders are part of the lexicon of every household in India through the years after Independence. With their far-sighted vision and unique leadership, these giants of Indian industry forged the very foundations of the country's manufacturing sector, guiding the stately company through numerous cycles of prosperity and depression. But by the time industrial licensing finally came to an end, Tata Steel had suffered from lack of competition and limits to expansion to become, like many other companies, 'bloated and calcified'.[3] On taking over as chairman of Tata Sons soon after industrial delicensing, Ratan Tata set stretch targets for all the Group companies. For Tata Steel, the target was simple—to become a top global steel company with the lowest production cost in the world.

Within ten years, Tata Steel achieved this unimaginable landmark in a 'sunset' industry.

Steel Makeover

Tata Steel's expansion programme had begun in the mid-1980s. At that time, large-scale integrated capacity facilities of over 1 million tons were reserved for the public sector. Steel prices in India were decided by the government and railway freight was equalized for balanced regional growth so that distance was not part of the cost factor. Import duties were high enough to protect local industry, which, as in other sectors, saw no reason to be competitive if everything produced was sold. In fact, since the Joint Plant Committee, which fixed prices, did not cover seconds or poor quality products, these fetched higher prices in the market than the top-quality products.[4]

However, India's incipient liberalization commenced from 1980 onwards and this allowed Tata Steel to start a massive modernization programme. Its strategy derived from its strong prognosis for sectors such as automotives, packaging and consumer durables. This belief at the time was more the kind of business gut feeling that differentiates the outstanding from the ordinary. Although the auto sector had received a big boost from the advent of Maruti Udyog Ltd, there were only a very limited number of players in the passenger vehicle and commercial vehicle markets. The era of refrigerators and washing machines flooding the markets was still years away. Nevertheless, the company felt that hot-rolled flat products used by these sectors would be in high demand. Accordingly, it set in progress the first of four modernization and capacity expansion phases that would end in 1999.

Steelmaking has always been considered the foundation of other manufacturing industries, with a high prestige value attached to it. When Jamsetji Tata first envisaged a steel plant, it was not so much to actually produce steel as to show the world what India was capable of. Steel is an iron-based alloy, and steelmaking essentially involves converting pig iron into steel by removing impurities of sulphur, phosphorus and silicon. This is done through blasting pure oxygen at molten pig iron, which results in lowering carbon content and oxidization of impurities. The steel is then finished into usable shapes through different processes, primarily long products like bars, rods and wires, or flat products like plates, sheets and strips. Technology has greatly improved processes over the years, bringing in greater efficiency with fewer raw materials. An integrated steel plant begins with iron ore, and Tata Steel always had access to captive iron ore and coal mines, giving it a big advantage in terms of key resources at low costs.

As H.M. Nerurkar, MD of Tata Steel since October 2009, puts it, 'Steel has, arguably, a greater degree of complexity than many other industries. The reason is the nature of the business and the span of its operations. Mining, production, logistics and supply chain, technological complexity, safety and environment issues, regulatory norms, a huge workforce with varying degrees of education and skills, the cyclical nature of the industry, long payback periods, political sensitivity—you name it and we have to deal with it. The complexity level at Tata Steel is even higher due to its integrated operations and geographical spread.'[5]

Each of the factory's five modernization phases represented significant milestones for the steel industry in India. Two 130-ton LD converters (the L standing for Linz and the D for Donawitz, the Austrian towns where the process for making steel from pig iron was first used) using pure oxygen came up for the first time in an integrated steel plant in the country.[6] A bar and rod mill in the second phase was also the first of its kind in India. The centrepiece of the modernization programme was the G blast furnace, a state-of-the-art automated system that went on to churn out 2 metric tons (MT) of steel per annum in later years.

While these phases were in process, the scenario completely overturned in 1991 and 1992. Steel production was de-licensed in 1991. The next year, steel prices were decontrolled and the railway freight equalization was withdrawn. Import canalization of steel items ended and import duties were drastically reduced, with further cuts in subsequent years. Suddenly, Tata Steel found itself having to compete in a free, open domestic market amid a challenging economic environment.

Muthuraman explains, 'The first reaction was one of great elation. But as the news sank in, one realized that one was not ready for the open, market-oriented economy. Long years of government-led administrative controls and the socialistic pattern of governance had led to no competition in the marketplace, no innovative spirit, and no market- and customer-orientation. It was going to be a whole new environment facing us and we were unprepared to face it. We had a consultant at that time, Arthur D. Little, with whose help we started the journey of getting the organization ready to face the challenges of a market-oriented free economy.'

Dr Irani was president of the CII in 1992–93, and in that capacity, he led an industry delegation to meet then Prime Minister P.V. Narasimha Rao regarding the sudden policy changes. The industrialists were concerned about whether reforms were likely to be sustained. Prime Minister Rao assured them that reforms were not only there to stay but would have to be fast-tracked as there was little alternative for the Indian economy.

Ratan Tata took over the Tata Group just months before the Indian economy was unshackled. At his first meeting as chairman of Tata Steel in 1993, he was informed by the chief financial officer that the company could expect a $26 million loss for the year, resulting from the abolition of freight equalization. At dinner that evening, Tata directed that costs must be brought down by 8 per cent, leaving officials horrified.[7] A reputed consultancy firm was hired, and the company was advised in no uncertain terms that if it wanted to survive, it would have to drastically lower costs, improve marketing and upgrade processes.

Liberalization of the Indian economy in 1991 opened the doors to global competition but also ushered in a healthy GDP growth rate in the country. At the time, the global steel industry was passing through a phase of low growth rate, overcapacity and low prices. The quality of Tata Steel products was poor and the cost of production was high. But the top management was determined to enter the competitive area with new technology and processes in order to succeed against global competition.

When Muthuraman was asked about the challenges the company identified, his reply was expansive, 'There were several challenges, challenges in every function. Our high cost of manufacturing was one big issue. To address this we created a vision to become the lowest-cost producer of steel in the world and built strategies and action plans to achieve it. Our marketing- and customer-orientation was non-existent. We started a companywide campaign called "Customer First Har Haal Mein" (Customer First Always). We had too many people and the executive calibre, due to long years of a non-competitive environment, was not up to the mark. We started rationalizing our manpower, put in performance management systems and systematically matched the capability of individuals and the needs of the job.'

So the steel behemoth's reinvention covered every aspect of strategy management and daily functioning. 'All sources were tapped for working out solutions,' adds Muthuraman.

'Many ideas came from the people of the organization. The Arthur D. Little report, after studying the company for over a year, really showed us in a mirror. Although it was very critical of several functions of the organization, the report was shared among the executives of the organization and with the worker's union as well. The pride of the people was hurt. It was this pride that brought in many ideas for improvement.

'Of course, we looked around the world for ideas. Ideas came from consultants like McKinsey, BCG, Booz Allen and from other steel plants, notably from Nippon Steel, Thyssen and Hoogovens. Young executives were sent, on a regular basis, to a management programme at CEDEP [European Centre for Executive Development], France to get some global exposure. Hundreds of cross-functional task forces were formed in the company. We embraced TQM and other improvement techniques across the organization. All of these yielded results. By the year 2000, we had become the lowest-cost producer of steel in the world. We had brought down our employee force from 78,000 in 1992 to about 40,000 in 2000, with the support and understanding of the union and the employees. We became a far more customer-oriented company. A culture of constant and continuous improvement had set in.'

The years from 1991 to 2000 were a period of self-renewal for Tata Steel—it enhanced its capacity to 4 million tons per annum (MTPA) with fully modernized world-class technology, scrapping obsolete equipment and technology and bringing in new technology and equipment, initiating severe cost-control measures, and sowing the seeds of changing mindsets. To support the change process, many Total Quality Management (TQM) tools and processes were introduced during this period. Tata Steel followed the approach of the Management by Objectives (MBO) framework to plan and monitor the performance vis-à-vis the targets.

Tata Steel's objective during this period was to improve the overall efficiency, including cost-competitiveness, and become a supplier of choice through focus on customer needs. Additionally, it sought to become technologically up-to-date and a knowledge-based organization with a positive outlook.

Strategy Planning and New Projects

In phase III of the modernization programme, the new one-million-ton capacity G blast furnace was commissioned in November 1992. With the completion of the third phase, the added infrastructure led to a rise in saleable steel output to 2.39 million tons with a total capacity of 2.7 million tons. In all, the long process of modernization absorbed Rs 7,000 crore worth of investment.[8]

India's per capita consumption of steel in the early 1990s was just 20 kilograms, compared to 60 kilograms in China and 610 kilograms in Germany.[9] Thus, the potential for growth was huge. Moreover, the company had its own mines for iron ore and coal and was well positioned to meet its ambitious objectives.

Tata Steel now strategized for a multipronged drive towards competitiveness. The main elements included greater attention to market requirements and what customers actually needed, a shift to modern steelmaking, and focusing on flat products for key sectors such as automobiles and consumer durables. Constant paring of costs was the idea, accompanied by cutting down on non-core activities to keep steelmaking at the heart of all operations. Finally, the steel company would benchmark itself against global best practices.

'We realized early that the key to the transformation process was to fix our processes and make them world-class; if the processes were in place, the results would automatically follow. These include processes for business, market development, human development, social responsibility, risk management and so on. We identified eight key processes and set about re-engineering them. To get the entire company behind the change process, we created a powerful vision and shared it continuously with everyone across the organization,' explained Muthuraman.[10]

Not resting on its laurels of record levels of production, sales and profits, Tata Steel embarked on phase IV of its modernization programme to double the capacity of hot rolled coils and triple the production of bars and rods, both high-value-added products. The goal was nothing less than being the lowest-cost producer of steel in the world. Jamshedpur was going to become the pride of the Indian steel industry, with the steel infrastructure transformed into a modern integrated steel plant.

But difficult times were ahead. Changes in the government hampered decision-making and infrastructure projects were delayed, with a concomitant impact on the steel industry. At the turn of the century, conditions in global markets remained depressed with the dotcom slowdown, followed by recessionary conditions as a result of 9/11. In India, too, a period of marked economic deceleration took hold, with a contraction in investments, declining sales of automobiles and consumer durables, and stagnation in key infrastructure projects, all of which affected the demand for steel.

The highlight of the modernization process during this difficult time was the cold rolling mill (CRM) to produce sheets for consumer durables and automotives. The TISCO board decided on the project in November 1997, to be led by Muthuraman. It was to set high standards in project implementation and use the most modern techniques. Although the approved time was thirty-six months, R.P. Singh, in charge of project implementation, set a target of twenty-eight months, which would be a world record. It was a 'battle of the mind' for the baffled team and suppliers: 'From January 1998 to June 1998, the reactions of the group ranged from polite amusement to outright disagreement,' noted a management case study.[11]

The project was handled on a war footing. A stringent process for the selection of vendors was instituted, with hard bidding and monthly reports. Decisions were made quickly and monitoring was intense, creating a complete buy-in from all stakeholders. The results were evident when Tata Steel faced a cash crunch and contemplated delaying payments—suppliers then were willing to take ownership and continued to provide inputs in spite of late payments. The success of the project changed the attitudes of all those associated with it, reflecting the mindset shift that all of Indian industry was undergoing at the time. Dr Irani described the process as 'yanking' people out of their comfort zones.[12]

The story of the Merchant Mill 2 plant is especially interesting. With lack of funds to revive it and a demotivated staff, it was slated for closure. But in an unprecedented show of leadership and optimism, improvements were carried out in maintenance and operations as well as attitudes so that the mill became economical once again. This was yet another example of the determination and teamwork that the Tata Steel management and workers internalized to bring the company to world-class levels.

'The people of the mill are proving that capacity is not on a nameplate but it is in one's mind,' said Muthuraman in a congratulatory message after visiting the Merchant Mill.

And in 2001, Tata Steel quietly achieved its long-standing dream of becoming the lowest-cost steel producer in the world. Production of hot rolled coils at $150–160 per ton beat the operating cost of POSCO, the Korean steel giant. World Steel Dynamics ranked Tata Steel as the best amongst the twelve identified world-class steelmakers in the world.[13]

New Challenges

The slowdown from 1998 to 2002 had a major impact on performance for the steel industry, whose fortunes were dependent on downstream sectors. The condition of the steel industry was even worse. People started seeing steel as a sunset industry. Worldwide, value was eroding for most steel plants and all other Indian steel plants were making heavy losses. Tata Steel, though profitable, was not able to create value for its shareholders. Even the Tata Group was in doubt about continuing with the steel business!

A new set of strategies was required as the country headed into the new millennium. The options were to look at opportunities outside of metals, to consider metals other than steel, or to make the core steel business sustainable and attractive.

The company chose to remain in steel. This came from its strong internal belief in the ability of its managers to create value, even though the global steel industry was haemorrhaging value. A clear and powerful vision was co-created by the senior management and employees with the focus on becoming Economic Value Added or EVA-positive and of continuing to improve the quality of life of employees and the communities served.

Although the demand at home as well as overseas was weak, Tata Steel continued to drive its expansion plans, realizing that the low per capita steel consumption of the country inevitably would lead to better conditions at a future date. The new instrument deployed in phase V of the modernization programme was knowledge management and instituting IT-enabled Enterprise Resource Planning (ERP) systems. The application, System Application and Products (SAP), was used for keeping tabs on stocks and managing finances. E-commerce became a marketing device, which quickly reached the top of its class globally, and Metaljunction.com, a website for serving steel industry customers, was launched by the Steel Authority of India, Kalyani Steel and Tata Steel.

To strengthen the strategy and planning process, Tata Steel followed a process of alignment of the organization towards overall company objectives and linking targets with activities.

The years 2002 to 2005 were those of intense strategic thinking about the company's future, formulating and initiating plans for the company's organic growth in Jamshedpur and initiation of green-field projects in India. Business processes were further strengthened, continuous improvements became embedded in the day-to-day work style, and marketing initiatives were taken further in terms of branding of products and customer reach. As a step towards globalization, in 2004, Tata Steel took up the first overseas acquisition, that of NatSteel based in Singapore, and also undertook the first overseas joint venture for coking coal in Australia.

Consultancy firm McKinsey was roped in to help the company reinvent itself. It suggested a 'Performance Ethic Plan' to transform the human capital of the company towards even greater commitment to excellence. Key positions were identified along with the people to man them after a comprehensive exercise to match the right person to the right job with a view to create a team of motivated and high-performing managers. Governance was high on the agenda with all employees signing on to the Tata Code of Conduct.[14]

This was also the time when Tata Steel was heading into the final years before its centenary in 2007. In 2002, the company presented its Vision 2007 statement, led by Muthuraman and prepared with the help of inputs from employees.

The Vision
To seize the opportunities of tomorrow and create a future that will make it an EVA-positive company
To continue to improve the quality of life of our employees and the communities we serve
Uphold the spirit and values of TATAs towards nation-building

Strategic Goals
Move from commodities to brands
EVA-positive core business
Continue to be lowest-cost producer of steel
Value-creating partnerships with customers and suppliers
Enthused and happy employees
Sustainable growth

Strategy
Manage knowledge
Outsource strategically
Encourage innovation and allow the freedom to fail
Excel at the Tata Business Excellence Model
Unleash people's potential and create leaders who will build the future
Invest in attractive new businesses
Ensure safety and environmental sustainability
Divest, merge, acquire

The key idea in the vision was to emerge as an EVA-positive company within three years. EVA was defined as the return on net assets minus the weighted average of the cost of capital multiplied by the invested capital. It was a performance monitoring instrument designed to create value for shareholders and manage investments. Stern, Stewart and Co. was hired to provide training to forty officers who would further hand it down to each employee.

Quality

In the late 1980s, Tata Steel had embarked on a venture that Indian companies barely recognized—striving towards quality as the keystone of its business. Dr Irani travelled as part of a CII delegation to Japan, where he was impressed by the attention to quality, and systems and processes that strengthened quality.[15] TQM was not a concept that Indian companies particularly worried about, since in the licensing regime, not only could any product find a market, but there were long queues for certain items like scooters.

The journey of the company towards the attainment of quality was long and arduous, depending on a continuously changing environment and different business needs. Tata Steel was a humongous operation, across different stages of steelmaking and selling a diverse range of steel products. Moreover, it had a large employee base and plants, units and mines in different locations. The challenge was to get all the processes working together, from a functional organization to business unit structure, towards a common corporate objective. The complex value chain meant that each division required a specific TQM approach and specific training, making 'People vitality' a key tool.

In an interview with ASQ, Dr Irani said, 'Twenty years back, India opened out internationally. We realized that there was much more to quality than what we were experiencing before that, and that for our economic success and for our continuing presence in a competitive world, we would have to have a system that was not something that the chief executive or individuals would practise; it had to be institutionalized.... We finally adopted the Malcolm Baldridge model [of quality].... Big Q is quality in everything we do, in dealing with each other, in trust.... The quality of the product we can always change... at short notice. The quality of the management systems, which is the DNA of the organization, is far more difficult and far more time-consuming to change.'[16]

The first phase, which commenced in 1988, related to standardization, a process which involved being ISO-compliant, starting IT systems and engaging employees in improvement through quality circles or groups. The next phase was, as Dr Irani mentioned, 'modernization of the mind', in which TQM was initiated along with total productivity maintenance systems. Training and education and value engineering for improving productivity were key parts of this endeavour, which lasted from 1992 to 1996.

Cost-competitiveness was the third stage of the journey, lasting till 2004. In this period, basic TQM tools began to be deployed. The vision was revisited and the EVA mission began. The Tata Business Excellence Model, a groupwide effort to inculcate total quality, led by Dr Irani from 1996, was the framework for achieving excellence through what was known as FACT—facilitation, assessment, consulting and training. From 2005, Tata Steel went in for expanding its global outlook and growth, integrating the TQM framework in the complete value chain and focusing on customer 'delight'. As TQM became institutionalized in the system, the company started the process of applying for the prestigious Deming Award in 2005.

Efficiency and a relentless drive for greater competitiveness was ingrained in the staff of Tata Steel through a sustained campaign to inculcate awareness. Change-management was the mantra. Over the years, Tata Steel adopted the value-engineering technique, ISO 9000 for good-quality management practices and standards, ISO 14000 for environmental management practices, QS 9000 for automotive industry quality, Six Sigma for data-driven perfection standards and the in-house Tata JRD Quality Value (JRD QV) systems. The idea was to reach for global standards and practices across all areas, such as operations, processes and marketing.

Here is just one example of the improvements made. The 8.0 mm rebars (reinforced bars) are produced by rolling, and in this process, the roll grooves get worn down due to friction between the groove surface and the hot bar. The wear is compensated by adjusting the roll gap. The operators were closely monitoring the process and adjusting it according to the prescribed 'standard operating procedure', but there were still many mistakes that slowed down the whole production chain.

Closely examining the situation, the quality team found that operators were making the adjustments based on their experience gained in previous practice. But wouldn't it be better if they knew exactly how much to adjust rather than guess each time? So a series of tests was done under controlled conditions to understand the relationship between the required weight of the roll grooves and how it was to be determined. Statistical data was taken and analysed and the relationship scientifically defined. The team then formulated the calculations and advised operators to calibrate the machines accordingly. So where earlier the operation relied on human judgement, it was now standardized with hard facts and aligned with rigorous benchmarks. This greatly cut down on abnormalities.

By the mid-1990s, the company was regularly shortlisted for the CII-Exim Bank Business Excellence Award, which it won in 2000. In the same year, it was the first Tata company to bag the JRD QV Award and then came the Prime Minister's Award for the Best Integrated Steel Plant. By 2008, the quest for excellence and continued passion for TQM made it the first integrated steel plant outside of Japan to be awarded the medal of quality—the

Deming Prize, presented by the Japanese Union of Scientists and Engineers, the body spearheading the quality movement.

The journey is still ongoing. The latest phase of the quality effort is termed as 'seeking world class'. Improvement savings kept going up year by year, touching Rs 6,875 crore for 2011–12. The number of improvement projects is also steadily going up. Tata Steel is working on a codification of the improvement initiatives to come out with the 'Tata Steel Way' so that a positive workplace culture is promoted and employees of diverse backgrounds can work together as a single entity through continual improvement. This is again part of the change in mindset that Dr J.J. Irani talks about.

Resizing

The most challenging task in the restructuring process was managing employment to fit the company's requirements. As a socially responsible company, Tata Steel had liberally hired people from the surrounding communities over the years. At almost 80,000 workers in the 1990s, the company was hugely overstaffed—as pointed out by potential investors. Why, they said, would they put money into a system that was underperforming and unproductive to begin with? It was necessary to both reduce the staff strength and to improve workforce productivity. But this was a challenge, given the company's welfare commitments and excellent relations with the trade union.

To begin with, the need for productivity was discussed with the workers' union through an intense dialogue that continued patiently over a couple of years. The process was transparent and honest, with the emphasis being on the continuation of the company. Existing joint department councils, which consisted of members from the senior management and workers, met regularly to drive home the message, not an easy one to understand in a culture where job security was taken for granted. For example, when Tata Steel employees retired, it was a matter of routine to offer a job to a close family member and workers were used to this system. It was difficult for them to accept that if productivity remained low, their own jobs were at stake.

To pave the path to resizing, the Early Separation Scheme was instituted, a programme that offered to pay a monthly salary to employees who retired early till such age as they would normally have retired. The scheme began in 1995–96, with the company identifying workers whose contributions were not as high as expected. Workers were also assisted in finding jobs elsewhere. The trust employees had and the credibility of the management, built over decades, were instrumental in the success of the scheme. Even then, heartrending stories were heard from workers and the company did all it could to help out.

At the same time, to increase productivity, the management had to demonstrate it was serious. In the mid-1990s, some departments, such as the Tubes Division and Collieries, went in for go-slow tactics. Dr Irani warned them to improve their performance and lower costs within a reasonable period of two years. After three years, when there was little progress, he shut down one of the tube units and two of the collieries, the first time such an action was taken in the company's history. This unprecedented step sent out strong signals about the importance of productivity and competitiveness in each unit.

'I always give an example of a bowl,' says Dr Irani. 'Every department has to come and put something into the bowl so that the kitty grows.'[17]

Despite regular hiring, the strength of the company declined gradually over the next decade to less than half of what it was at the beginning of the scheme. This situation was not always easy, but there was no protest from the workers, who felt that they were given a fair deal. By the end of the scheme, Tata Steel had a staff strength of less than 47,000, and the average age had declined from forty-six to thirty-nine years.[18]

Throughout the restructuring process, Tata Steel maintained good industrial relations, always stressing on the team work and efforts made by each and every one of its employees. The Domestic Management Programme was instituted with the help of Dr Irani's wife so that the company's excellence model was carried over to the spouses and children of employees.

Productivity improvements followed as a natural consequence of a smaller workforce and higher output. In 1994–95, the worker output was 93 tons per man-year of crude steel and 79 tons per man-year of saleable steel. By 2002–03, the respective figures had gone up to 245 and 227, almost three times higher.[19]

Marketing

It was not enough to just produce more steel. Marketing and Customer Value Management (CVM) was another area in which the company innovated. Steel companies were accustomed to focusing on volumes and prices with little regard for quality. Specific products for different customers were not considered a priority since this was done by ancillaries or other manufacturing units. But in 2001, Tata Steel decided to restructure into two centres, one for flat products and the other for long products, which included production as well as marketing. The focus would be on providing retail customers the products that they wanted, to be determined through hard data rather than relying on the instincts of the sales team. The company did not have the expertise to deal with complexities of retail, but that was hardly a consideration for a team that had proved its new thinking and drive to succeed.

As Muthuraman wrote in a paper for Harvard Business School, the company went in for the strategy of 'selling more to existing customers' through customer retention and growth.[20] For this plan, it was essential to choose the right customers, companies that were winners in their markets, that had a culture of long-term thinking rather than short-term value creation, that were reasonably mature, and shared a desire for 'co-destiny' or working together for the success of all parties in the value chain. A process was initiated to be rolled out over twelve weeks of intense activity. Tata Steel's CVM team would study the customer's use of steel and entire chain of processes. Cross-functional teams from Tata Steel and the customers would then work on ideas together and shortlist about fifteen ideas. These would be studied and an implementation plan would be drawn up.

As Dr Irani pointed out, 'Tata Steel was earlier operating in a sellers' market, but since 1991 we are operating in a buyers' market where competition is very severe. Earlier, it was the customer who came to us for steel because it was in short supply; now, we have to go out and convince him that he will get the best value for money by purchasing from us. We do not sell the cheapest steel; in fact, our products are one of the most expensive, but we guarantee quality. Today, it is a customer–supplier relationship that we have to build, which was not there earlier—that is the main change. The other change is in our marketing orientation: we have had to change from being mere distributors to marketing people.'[21]

Tata Steel also made a shift towards a definite brand strategy to differentiate its products and leverage the Tata name. Reinforced bars became 'Tata Tiscon' and galvanized corrugated sheets were sold under the brand name 'Tata Shakti'. The company intensified its activities in rural markets, believing that this was where the next growth spurt would emerge.

Innovation as a Creed

Tata Steel early on demonstrated its passion for innovation by becoming the first corporate entity to set up an R&D centre in India in 1937. Right from the beginning, the centre established its credentials in developing new steel products and processes. In recent times, the Research and Development and Scientific Services (R&D and SS) division has led the global competitiveness of the company. This relates not only to steel products and innovation in processes, but also environmental sustainability, testing, quality and energy efficiency. The division consists of various units dealing with specific areas such as raw materials, refractory technology and iron and ferro alloys. A Global Research, Development and Technology centre is under way, combining the five research units in the Netherlands, the UK and India, which integrates the Indian operations with Tata Steel Europe as one seamless entity, sharing technologies and knowhow and developing new technologies jointly.

Innovation was always a part of Tata Steel's intrinsic culture, deriving as it did from Jamsetji's genius. But in the new liberalization era, the company set itself challenging targets for coming out with new products and cost-efficient systems. For example, the iron ore in its mines had a phosphorus content of 0.08 per cent, which considerably weakens the steel produced, but buyers in the key automobile and consumer goods industries needed nothing more than a level of 0.025 per cent. Purchasing iron ore of this grade from other sources was an easy option. Instead, Tata Steel went in for research to see how its own ores could match this requirement. Through a series of steps—changing the converter blowing regime, bottom injection and lance geometry—the phosphorus content was brought down to 0.012 per cent.[22]

In its fiscal year 2012, Tata Steel made fifty-six patent filings, the second highest ever, with seventy-three papers in twenty peer-reviewed journals and thirty-five other papers. 'These are very high numbers, reflecting innovation and novelty [of Tata Steel],' says Mark Denys, the then chief of the R&D and SS division. 'Key achievements were the commissioning and start-up of a new coal organo-refining pilot plant that demonstrated the production of 8 per cent ash coal with 55 per cent yield from local 30 per cent ash coal. This would double the fraction of usable coal from our mines once successfully commercialized by 2018, and will have a high impact on conservation of natural resources.'

Tata Steel has been awarded the government citation for the highest number of granted patents in the five years to April 2011 amongst all Indian private companies. As Denys puts it, 'Who says only Infosys or Wipro is innovative!'[23]

The research journey helped Tata Steel become one of the lowest-cost steel producers worldwide. The company now has a target of 30 MT capacity globally by 2015.

The Minnow and the Whale: Era of Globalization

While domestic facilities were to be expanded, acquisitions and divestments were integral to the new approach. After years of benchmarking itself against global standards, Tata Steel now wanted to go global. Globalization and 'de-integration' was the new strategy.

Exports had always been a part of the steel major's operations. In 2003–04, its exports were close to Rs 1,500 crore of a total turnover of over Rs 12,000 crore. While earlier, policy restrictions had been imposed on overseas investments by Indian companies, in 2000, foreign exchange capital transactions out of India became significantly liberalized, allowing corporates to think about strategies for a global presence. At a time when the worldwide steel industry was expanding outwards for trade and investment, Tata Steel had the natural advantage of access to resources like iron ore.

'A truly global company is one where global thinking prevails and decides every aspect of business—where to manufacture, where to research, what type of people to employ and where and how to market the products and services,' believes Muthuraman.[24]

Markets were reviving across the world, including China,

East Europe and the US. In March 2004, China accounted for as much as a quarter of the global steel consumption at over 200 million tons, North America at 100 MT, and South-east and East Asia about 200 MT. Key questions had to be considered—what were the customer requirements in different parts of the world? Which locations could best serve which markets, taking into account costs of production and transport?

To begin with, Tata Steel decided to opt for acquisitions rather than setting up new ventures from scratch. This approach would not only bring in assets but also technologies, markets and brands. But there was just one consideration, normally not part of strategies adopted by other companies. As Dr Irani explained, 'By the way, before we start talking to any company for mergers or acquisitions or even joint ventures, we try to do a due diligence on their value systems and even if it is a very profitable proposition, if the value systems don't match, we try to keep away from them.'[25]

According to Muthuraman, 'It is very important to understand where value gets added in a marketplace. If I manufacture in India because it is easier to dominate the Chinese market by being here, I would consider myself global because I have applied a global mindset to take that decision.'[26]

In August 2004, Muthuraman announced the first acquisition overseas by India's steel giant. In a video link from Singapore, he informed journalists in Mumbai about the takeover of NatSteel Asia, headquartered in Singapore. The deal was valued at $486.4 million, or Rs 1,313 crore, in an all-cash transaction, and it gave Tata Steel access to almost 1.8 MT finishing capacity and a presence in seven countries around the booming Asian region. Apart from providing a foothold in the Chinese market for long products, the acquisition also added 3,000 employees to the Indian firm as well as R&D, logistics, procurement, engineering consultancy and other services that NatSteel Singapore supplied to its branches and joint ventures in the other countries. One of the largest overseas FDI from India at the time, Tata Steel's decisive entry into the Asian region was marked by universal acclaim.

But the best was yet to come. The real story in Tata Steel's global march was the acquisition of Corus, a daring initiative that catapulted the Indian steel company into the global league.

Anglo-Dutch steel company Corus came into being when British Steel merged with Hoogovens in the Netherlands in 1999.[27] It was the ninth largest steel producer in the world in 2005. Tata Steel was just fifty-sixth in the ranking but this was a minor consideration for the perennial pioneer.

The company carefully kept its plans under wraps, although talks had been in progress since 2005. In September 2006, the Tata Group announced the purchase of the premium Ritz Carlton Hotel in Boston and a stake in Joekels, a tea company in South Africa. When Tata Sons executive director R. Gopalakrishnan was asked about the rumours regarding Corus, he offered cryptically, 'We are looking for opportunities in all areas where we are present.'[28]

Fervid speculation preceded any announcement. It was believed that the Tata Group was willing to spend several billions on acquiring Corus and that it had all the finances in place. The Arcelor–Mittal deal earlier in the year fuelled further interest in another Indian company bidding for a much larger global enterprise. 'With an estimated steelmaking capacity of 18 million tons [Corus]—more than three times Tata Steel's—it would be a case of a minnow swallowing a whale,' observed an Indian journalist.[29]

But the company had it all figured out. Domestic expansion was primarily financed by internal accruals and debt. Tata Sons had increased its stakes in Tata Steel and banks were prepared to lend to the prestigious Group. However, the mere rumours circulating around the deal had led to Corus shares going up substantially, raising the cost of the proposed purchase.

Towards the end of October 2006, the Anglo-Dutch steel

major laid rest to all speculation by confirming that it had indeed received a takeover proposal from Tata Steel for about $7.7 billion.[30] The logic behind the offer was simple—Corus would gain access to low-cost iron and coal resources of Tata Steel in exchange for its markets in Europe, providing the Indian firm a foothold in a new market. The European company operated three high-end integrated plants in the UK and one in the Netherlands, along with others across Europe. It laid strong emphasis on R&D with over 900 employees engaged in research. Corus products targeted the growing sectors of construction, automotives and packaging, among others, providing not just a range of innovative products but also on-time service and technical advice. It was the third largest supplier to the robust and advanced automotive sector in Europe, and was busy exploring new high-growth markets. Among all these considerations, a key factor for Tata Steel was also the fact that Corus accorded high importance to environment sustainability and working with the community, in line with Tata's own ethos.

From the beginning, this was a difficult deal. Corus shares had dropped to 18 pence in 2003 after four consecutive years of losses. But by 2006, it had recovered following the substantial restructuring and sale of its aluminum business and was looking for a partner. Russian steel company Evraz had already considered Corus and found it overpriced.[31] Tata offered as much as 455 pence per share, and valuations kept climbing. Shareholders of Corus felt that the initial offer was below the company's value. Moreover, Corus employees, over 41,000 in number, had to be kept in mind.[32] Although by no means was the deal final, India was already celebrating.

And then at the end of November came the rival bid—Companhia Siderúrgica Nacional (CSN), one of the largest steelmakers of Brazil, announced that it would launch a bid for Corus before the Anglo-Dutch company's shareholders met to consider the Tata offer on 4 December.

Tata Steel responded by upping its offer to 500 pence a share. CSN retaliated within hours with a bid of 515 pence per share for a total of 4.9 billion pounds. Now it was a question of whether the Indian company would beat this price. Already, Tata Steel shares in Mumbai were falling, as shareholders felt the company may be going in over its capacity. The British regulator for mergers and acquisitions, the Takeover Panel, suggested an auction and the date for this was finalized for 30 January 2007, a nail-biting finish to the most challenging goal the company had ever set for itself.

Before the auction began, the Tata Steel board of directors met for almost three hours at Bombay House, while journalists waited with bated breath for an announcement of a gameplan. But after all that suspense, only the third quarter results were mentioned and the spokesperson remained silent on the Corus auction later that day.

Arun Gandhi, director, Tata Sons, along with a formidable team of bankers, represented Tata Steel at the auction. In Bombay House, luminaries of the Tata Group gathered in a show of strength to offer advice and the Tata Steel management stayed awake to match Britain's working hours. Over nine rounds of the auction lasting ten hours, the deal went down to the wire.

Excitement rippled across the Indian media as the results were announced—Tata Steel emerged as the victor! The largest overseas acquisition by an Indian company at 608 pence per share totalling 6.7 billion pounds, it was universally hailed as not just a win for the Indian steel company and industry, but a major leap for the Indian economy. It was viewed as the ultimate vanquishing of colonialism. 'Much of India erupted with jubilation...,' said the *New York Times*.[33]

Completing the acquisition of Corus on 2 April 2007, Tata Steel now emerged as the seventh largest steel manufacturer in the world with a crude steelmaking capacity of 28 MTPA and a visible presence across continents. From 2010 onwards, the rebranding exercise commenced, so that the name Tata Steel is now imprinted on all aspects of the Corus identity, from email addresses and staff uniforms to chess tournaments in the Netherlands and the British Triathlon Federation. Today, Tata Steel Europe, the continent's second largest steelmaker, is at the forefront as the manufacturer of innovative products, supplying low-noise railway tracks at Blackfriars station in London, pipes for crude oil export in the Gulf of Mexico, steel plates for wind towers, and many other major projects.

The acquisition of Millennium Steel in Thailand was another step in that journey of growth and globalization. So was the setting up of Tata BlueScope Steel Ltd to go into construction solutions and the formation of the joint venture with Nippon Yusen Kaisha (NYK) for ocean logistics. And at the end of it all, the small steel plant morphed into a world-class conglomerate, in a phenomenal process of growth and change that was made possible by well-laid-out strategies and plans by its remarkable leaders.

In her centenary year, the venerable old lady of the Indian private sector had once again demonstrated that she was still nimble on her feet and head and shoulders above others.

Quality of Life

One of the most laudable aspects of Tata Steel's operations from inception has been its pioneering role in community affairs. This derives directly from the values that Jamsetji Tata brought to his entrepreneurial ventures, going far ahead of his times to envision a strong commitment to employee welfare and community engagement. As an institution-builder, Jamsetji had personally brought in funds to set up the Indian Institute of Science and to finance budding scholars. He directed his son Dorabji Tata to set up a town, 'Be sure to lay wide streets planted with shady trees, every other of a quick-growing variety. Be sure that there is plenty of space for lawns and gardens. Reserve large areas for football, hockey and parks. Earmark areas for Hindu temples, Mohammedan mosques and Christian churches.' Tata Trusts, devoted to social development and institutional capacity-building, control two-thirds of the shares of Tata Sons, the Group holding company.

In fact, corporate philanthropy and corporate governance are at the heart of the confidence that the Tata brand universally enjoys.

Jamshedpur, the city envisaged by Jamsetji Tata, is today one of the most progressive cities of India, with a well-planned structure taking into account the presence of factories of various Tata companies. A green city, it embodies sensible environmental practices and living conditions in its operations. Greenery, parks and playgrounds, recycling plants and excellent infrastructure make it a model industrial township. It was selected as one of the cities for the UN's Global Compact Cities Pilot Programme, the only one in South Asia under the initiative. Tata Steel was one of the founder-members of the UN Global Compact, an initiative that enhances the role of companies in human rights, labour, environment and anti-corruption.

As the plant started coming up in the 1900s, Jamshedpur witnessed waves of migration, with unskilled workers from surrounding areas and tribal villagers pouring in. Crowding and lack of amenities led to poor hygiene and occurrence of diseases such as cholera and malaria. The company intervened to set up cooperative societies to provide missing public services. When it shifted focus to rural areas, it decided to establish a community-based NGO that would meet the specific requirements of socio-economic change among underprivileged communities. This was a unique initiative as most companies in those days preferred working with NGOs rather than setting up their own.

The Tata Steel Rural Development Society came up in 1979 to work for social and economic empowerment in rural areas around the steel factory and mines. This is a comprehensive venture that includes health, sanitation, income-generation, education and skill development, agriculture and other aspects of village life. Starting with thirty-two villages, TSRDS embraced some of the poorest and most underprivileged areas of the country, introducing new ideas for water management, multiple crop farming, animal husbandry and reforestation. Its strategy was to build capacity among the communities so that they could manage the new programmes themselves. It also worked with state governments and district administrations to facilitate delivery of welfare services and public goods. TSRDS now has a positive impact on about 600 villages, some of them in remote and inaccessible areas, working through decentralized units across Bihar, Odisha, Chhattisgarh, Jharkhand and Madhya Pradesh.

Apart from TSRDS, the Tribal Cultural Society, the Tata Steel Family Initiatives Foundation, Urban Services and Tata Steel Parivar also run various schemes for rural services in mines, collieries and project-affected areas. Self-help groups have been facilitated by the company, bringing together women for microfinance in more than 650 groups. Training for various livelihood opportunities is being provided along with linkages to banks for credit. The Tata Steel Parivar is dedicated to resettlement and rehabilitation for improving the quality of life of families displaced due to projects. It tracks each family for at least five years, and offers training for new livelihoods. The Community Development and Social Welfare Department of the company runs centres and subcentres in the basti areas to provide infrastructure, civic amenities, vocational training and medical care.

The plethora of awards won by Tata Steel for just one year's activities in social and community work, according to its annual report of 2010–11, is nothing short of impressive. Among others, it got the Safety and Health Excellence Recognition Award 2010 by the World Steel Association.

Conclusion

From a bloated steel company in a restricted industrial environment to the fifth-largest steel company in the world, Tata Steel has come a long way in the liberalization era. The journey was full of pain and adjustment, but every bit was worth it as success after success was achieved. Every manager, every worker, and indeed every family in the larger Tata Steel community contributed singular passion and commitment, and went far beyond the call of duty to make the company the leading steel producer of the world.

What next for a century-old company that has gone beyond each milestone it set for itself?

Growth plans in India are robust, with the company's proposed expansion in Odisha, Chhattisgarh, Jharkhand and Karnataka. Greenfield projects are progressing, though somewhat slower than planned. New projects deploy the best technologies to facilitate high-quality, cost-effective and environment-friendly processes. The new facilities are targeted at high-end products to complete the company's strategy of moving up the value chain.

Continuous improvement projects are being given focus in all sites and businesses. To sustain the world benchmark in its Earnings Before Interest, Taxes, Depreciation and Amortization (EBITDA) performance, the company embarked on another improvement journey in March 2010, known as 'Kar Vijay Har Shikhar' (KVHS), which means 'Conquer every peak'. The initiative intends to challenge the previous best achieved and is giving tremendous results in terms of improving operation efficiency, cost saving and throughput enhancement.

Going forward, to achieve the vision 'To be the global steel industry benchmark in Value Creation and Corporate Citizenship', Tata Steel would move towards adding to its portfolio of captive raw materials, such as mines. The company wants to move ahead even faster to achieve a larger scale in the growing global steel industry, and catalyse cash flows. At the same time, safety, health and environmental performance remain uppermost in its agenda, while it will continue to support and improve the lives of people in surrounding communities.

A sense of quiet satisfaction is evident as Muthuraman concludes the story of the transformation of Tata Steel. 'Over the last twenty years, there have been more reforms in India. The world economy has gone through a severe economic downturn from which it has not fully recovered. Adaptability to the external environment is a key to success. Actions to "adapt" continuously are the DNA of any organization. It comes from leadership at all levels. A leadership that can enthuse, energize, empower and make people envision their organizations. A leadership that can ignite the passion and create an aspirational thinking in the people of the organization. This is the key.'

The 2012 Deming Grand Prize for Tata Steel's India operations was just another milestone in the grand passage of the company, as the perennial pioneer steps into the next century of its leadership of the nation.

NOTES

Introduction

1. Kantha, Sharmila and Subhajyoti Ray, *Building India with Partnership: The Story of CII 1895–2005*, Penguin India, 2006.
2. Acharya, Shankar, 'India's Growth: Past and Future', paper for presentation at the Eighth Annual Global Development Conference of the Global Development Network, 14–16 January 2007, Beijing; http://depot.gdnet.org/cms/conference/papers/acharya_plenary1.pdf
3. Godrej, Nadir, 'Innovation' quoted in Naushad Forbes, 'Doing Business in India: What has Liberalisation Changed?' February 2001, Center for Research on Economic Development and Policy Reform, Stanford University, Working Paper 93.
4. Bulent, Unel, 'Productivity Trends in India's Manufacturing Sector in the Last Two Decades', IMF Working Paper, January 2003; http://www.imf.org/external/pubs/ft/wp/2003/wp0322.pdf B.
5. Acharya, Shankar, 'India's Growth: Past and Future'.
6. Rodrik, Dani and Arvind Subramanian, 'From Hindu Growth to Productivity Surge: The Mystery of the Indian Growth Transition', IMF Working Paper, May 2004; http://www.imf.org/external/pubs/ft/wp/2004/wp0477.pdf
7. Acharya, Shankar, 'India's Growth: Past and Future'.
8. Forbes, Naushad, 'Doing Business in India: What has Liberalisation Changed?' February 2001, Center for Research on Economic Development and Policy Reform, Stanford University, Working Paper 93.
9. Cappelli, Peter, Harbir Singh, Jitender Singh and Michael Useem, 'The India Way of Doing Business', *Forbes*, 14 April 2010; http://

www.forbes.com/2010/04/14/india-business-way-leadership-citizenship-useem_2.html

CHAPTER 1

1. Karanjia, B.K., *Godrej: A Hundred Years 1897–1997*, Volumes I and II, Viking Penguin India, 1997.
2. 'How the Godrej Group is Creating a New Culture that Remains True to Its Core Values', *Corporate Dossier, Economic Times*, 21 September 2012.
3. 'The New Godrej', *Corporate Dossier, Economic Times*, 21 September 2012.
4. Ibid.
5. 'Indian Firms Abroad: Under the Radar', *Economist*, 1 August 2011.
6. Salokhe, Ujwal, 'Are the Children Ambitious Enough to Take Over?' *Society*, 2 September 2010.
7. CII website; http://www.cii.in/
8. Morais, Richard C., 'Who Needs P&G?' *Forbes*, 23 March 1998; http://www.forbes.com/forbes/1998/0323/6106130a.html, accessed on 7 May 2012.
9. Godrej, Adi, 'You Need Continuous Introspection to Improve', *Outlook Business*, April 2012; http://www.godrej.com/godrej/GodrejIndustries/Pdf/ThinkBeyondStayAhead_300312.pdf

CHAPTER 2

1. *The Reserve Bank of India*, vol. 2, 1951–67, chapter 13.
2. ADB Project Completion Report on a Loan to the Industrial Credit and Investment Corporation of India Ltd, December, 1992; http://www2.adb.org/Documents/PCRs/IND/17130-IND-PCR.pdf
3. Shirai, Sayuri, 'Assessment of India's Banking Sector Reforms from the Perspective of the Governance of the Banking System', November 2001; http://www.unescap.org/drpad/publication/fin_2206/part4.pdf, accessed on 27 June 2012.

   Mohan, Rakesh, 'Financial Sector Reforms in India: Policies and Performance Analysis', *RBI Bulletin*, October 2004; http://www.rakeshmohan.com/docs/RBIBulletinOct2004-2.pdf
4. *RBI Handbook of Banking Statistics*.

5. Kamath, K.V., 'Challenging the Status Quo', *Businessworld*, 20 November 2011; http://www.businessworld.in/businessworld/businessworld/content/Challenging-Status-Quo.html?print=yes
6. *McKinsey Quarterly* interview with K.V. Kamath, reprinted in *Mint*, 2 April 2007.
7. 'India's Banks: Living Dead', *Economist*, 4 January 2001; http://www.economist.com/node/466612, accessed on 5 July 2012.
8. Kamath, K.V., 'How ICICI Changed', 8 February 2005; http://www.rediff.com/money/2005/feb/09bspec.htm
9. Ibid.
10. Trivedi, Gunjan, 'ICICI Banking on IT: K.V. Kamath'; http://www.cio.in/view-top/icici-bank-banking-it
11. Kamath, K.V., 'How ICICI Changed'.
12. Ibid.
13. 'How Kamath Built ICICI into a Global Giant', Moneycontrol.com, 9 June 2007; http://www.rediff.co.in/money/2007/jun/09icici.htm.
14. Kamath, K.V., 'How ICICI Changed'.
15. *McKinsey Quarterly* interview with K.V. Kamath, reprinted in *Mint*, 2 April 2007.

CHAPTER 3

1. Singh, Ajay, and Shirish Nadkarni, 'Watch that Ashtray: Can Deveshwar Handle ITC—and the Tax Man?' *AsiaNow Asiaweek*, 1 March 1996; http://edition.cnn.com/ASIANOW/asiaweek/96/0301/biz5.html, accessed on 2 October 2012.
2. Deveshwar, Y.C. 'Sometimes, Not Taking a Risk is the Biggest Risk', *Outlook Business*, 18 February 2012.
3. Gooptu, Pradeep, 'How Yogi Deveshwar Changed ITC', *Business Standard*, 9 April 2005; http://www.business-standard.com/india/news/newsmaker-y-c-deveshwar/205727/
4. Deveshwar, Y.C., 'Sometimes, Not Taking a Risk is the Biggest Risk'.
5. Deveshwar, Y.C., 'Triple Bottom Line Approach', *Outlook Business*, 3 May 2008, business.outlookindia.com/printarticle-aspx? 100947
6. Ibid.
7. ITC Annual Report, 2001; http://itcportal.com/about-itc/shareholder-value/annual-reports/itc-annual-report-2001/content.aspx?

8. Deveshwar, Y.C., Chairman, ITC Ltd, Q&A, *Business Standard*, 30 June 2011.
9. Deveshwar, Y.C., speech at AGM 2001.
10. Prahalad, C.K., *The Fortune at the Bottom of the Pyramid: Eradicating Poverty Through Profits*, Wharton School Publishing, Pearson Education, 2010; http://books.google.lk/books?id=RPSG4JxAZzYC&pg=PA333&lpg=PA333&dq=e-choupal&source=bl&ots=TUnRDnc2Nh&sig=lj6dugLC-W1nj4foiKg7hYbAutY&hl=en&sa=X&ei=VQpoUOSTEoj5rQe7hIGYDg&redir_esc=y#v=onepage&q=e-choupal&f=false
11. Dasgupta, Somnath, 'Leading a Focussed Conglomerate', *Financial Express*, 5 April 2002; http://www.itcportal.com/about-itc/newsroom/press-reports/PressReport; aspx?id=802&type=C&news=leading-focussed-conglomerate
12. Deveshwar, Y.C., Q&A, *Business Standard*, 30 June 2011.
13. Segal, David, 'Restaurants' Best Press: "Bill Clinton Ate Here"', *New York Times*, 25 October 2010; http://www.nytimes.com/2010/10/27/dining/27clinton.html?pagewanted=all, accessed on 12 May 2013.
14. Sinha, Chinky, 'Bukhara Ready with a Very Meaty Platter for Obamas', *Indian Express*, 7 November 2010; http://www.indianexpress.com/news/bukhara-ready-with-a-very-meaty-platter-for-obamas/707715/0
15. 'Creating a Future-ready Conglomerate', India Knowledge @ Wharton interview with Yogi Deveshwar, 13 January 2011, accessed on 12 May 2013.
16. Deveshwar, Y.C., 'Innovation for a Sustainable Future', *Economic Times*, 28 June 2010; http://m.economictimes.com/opinion/guest-writer/innovation-for-a-sustainable-future-yc-deveshwar-chairman-itc-ltd/articleshow/msid-6099713.cms

Chapter 4

1. 'Jubilant Lifenet Jumps to Rs 152 Crore in Q2', Pharmabiz.com, 7 November 2012; http://pharmabiz.com/NewsDetails.aspx?aid=72053&sid=2
2. Shyam Bhartia, Awaaz, 9.50 pm, 30 August 2012, published on 6 September 2012; http://www.youtube.com/watch?v=8tauoWnxo8Y

3. Rai, Saritha, 'India's 100 Richest: the Bhartia Brothers: Doughnuts to Dollars', *Forbes Asia*, November 2012.
4. Shmavovian, Karl, 'Pharma and Fast Food Fuel the Jubilant Bhartia Group', *Forbes Asia*; 5 November 2012; http://www.forbes.com/sites/forbesasia/2012/10/24/pharma-and-fast-food-fuel-the-jubilant-bhartia-group/2/
5. Ibid.
6. 'Jubilant Organosys to Make Jivanjor Umbrella Brand', *Business Standard*, 3 December 2001; http://www.business-standard.com/india/news/jubilant-organosys-to-make-jivanjor-umbrella-brand/103672/
7. Ibid.
8. Mishra, Richa, interview with Shyam S. Bhartia 'Rechristened Vam Organic "Jubilant" of its Gains', *Hindu BusinessLine*, 27 January 2002; http://thehindubusinessline.in/2002/01/28/stories/2002012800680500.htm
9. 'Eli Lilly, Jubilant Organosys for R&D Joint Venture', *Economic Times*, 4 October 2008; http://articles.economictimes.indiatimes.com/2008-10-04/news/28487998_1_jubilant-organosys-drug-discovery-global-drug
10. Jubilant press release, 1 October 2010; http://www.jubl.com/mycgi/jubl-com/mediacenter.pl?id=218, accessed on 12 May 2010.
11. International Finance Corporation and Sustainability, 'Market Movers: Lessons from a Frontier of Innovation', December 2007 Case Study: Jubilant Organosys 'Sweet Solutions'; http://www1.ifc.org/wps/wcm/connect/84c8b780488551b4a94cfb6a6515bb18/MarketMovers_CS_Jubilant.pdf?MOD=AJPERES&CACHEID=84c8b780488551b4a94cfb6a6515bb18

CHAPTER 5

1. Bhargava, R.C. with Seetha, *The Maruti Story: How a Public Sector Company Put India on Wheels*, HarperCollins India, 2011.
2. Ibid.
3. Ibid. p. x.
4. 'Small Car, Big Heart', *Outlook Business*, 16 May 2009; http://business.outlookindia.com/article.aspx?102116, accessed on 11 July 2012.

5. Elliott, John, 'Riding the Elephant', blogpost on 14 December 2008, '25th Anniversary of Maruti Suzuki Car that Transformed India's Motor Industry'; http://ridingtheelephant.wordpress.com/2008/12/14/today-is-the-25th-anniversary-of-the-maruti-suzuki-car-that-changed-india%E2%80%99s-motor-industry/, accessed on 11 July 2012.
6. Bhargava, R.C., *Business Standard*, Q&A, 3 September 2008; http://www.business-standard.com/india/news/people-advised-me-against-joining-maruti/333307/, accessed on 11 July 2012.
7. 'Maruti Faced Problems Introducing the Japanese Culture', *Rediff Business*, 3 September 1997; http://www.rediff.com/business/sep/03mul.htm
8. Press release, Maruti Suzuki India Limited, 4 January 2012.
9. Auto Expo 2010, 5 January; http://marutistorage.blob.core.windows.net/marutisuzukipdf/MD-Speech-at-the-Auto-Expo-2010.pdf

Chapter 6

1. Report of the Expert Committee on Small Enterprises, 27 January 1997; http://dcmsme.gov.in/publications/comitterep/abid.htm
2. Annual Report 2011–12, Ministry of MSME.
3. Report of the Expert Committee on Small Enterprises.
4. Ibid.
5. Report of the Working Group on Micro, Small and Medium Enterprises for the Twelfth Plan (2012–17), Foreword by Chairman R.K. Mathur; http://www.dcmsme.gov.in/working_group2012.pdf

Chapter 7

1. Dasgupta, Somnath, 'Shining in His Own Light', *Business Today*, 21 August 2011; http://businesstoday.intoday.in/story/sanjiv-goenkas-business-empires/1/17556.html
2. Agarwal, Nirati, 'A Man of Contrasts', *Marwar India*, November–December 2011.
3. Bajaj, Harbans L. and Deepak Sharma, 'Power Sector Reforms in India'; http://www.google.com/url?sa=t&rct=j&q=&esrc=s&source=web&cd=15&ved=0CEgQFjAEOA0&url=http%3A%2F%2Fwww.worldenergy.org%2Fdocuments%2Fp001438.

doc&ei=W2_IUIqtD5CnrAeMoIGYDA&usg=AFQjCNHRoShh9Aq_nqEpzV4PfWcjiURiBQ

4. Invest India website, Power; http://www.investindia.gov.in/?q=power-sector
5. Economic Survey 2011–12.
6. 'Power Grid Failure: CESC's Smart Move Saves Kolkata', *Economic Times*, 1 August 2012; http://articles.economictimes.indiatimes.com/2012-08-01/news/32981551_1_grid-failure-cesc-vice-chairman-rp-sanjiv-goenka
7. 'Sanjiv Goenka Unveils New Identity for RP–Sanjiv Goenka Group Companies', *Economic Times*, 14 July 2011; http://articles.economictimes.indiatimes.com/2011-07-14/news/29773414_1_sanjiv-goenka-corporate-identity-new-group
8. 'Man Who Switched Off Power Cuts in Kolkata', Times News Network, 12 March 2011.
9. 'Goenkas Take Full Control of Spencer's', *Telegraph*, 12 August 2004.
10. 'Looking to Enter Different Biz Segment: Sanjiv Goenka', *Business Standard*, 26 October 2012.
11. Agarwal, Nirati, 'A Man of Contrasts'.
12. 'Shining in His Own Light: Sanjiv Goenka Prefers to Build Companies', *Business Today*, 21 August 2011.

Chapter 8

1. National Portal of India, Public Sector Undertakings in India, india.gov.in/spotlight/public_sector.undertakings.india
2. 'Sail or Sink, It's a Titanic Job', Arindam Mukherjee, *Outlook*, 6 April 1998; http://m.outlookindia.com/story.aspx?sid=4&aid=205316
3. India Infoline, interview with Arvind Pande, 1 November 1999; http://www.indiainfoline.com/Research/LeaderSpeak/Arvind-Pande-Chairman-Steel-Authority-of-India-Ltd./11292204
4. 'Sail or Sink...', *Outlook*.
5. India Infoline interview.
6. Ibid.
7. 'Govt Committed to Growth, Viability of Public Sector: PM', *Hindu BusinessLine*, 25 December 2006;http://www.thehindubusinessline.in/2006/12/25/stories/2006122502890100.htm
8. SAIL chairman's speech, 2004.

9. Speech on 8 April 2011 on 'Achieving Sustainable Corporate Growth: Exploring New Frontiers in Technology and Management'.
10. Steel Ministry Annual Reports, 2000–01 and 2011–12.

Chapter 9

1. Kapur, Surinder, 'There's a Lot to Learn from Failure'; http://entrepreneurindia.in/opinion/insights/%E2%80%9Cthere%E2%80%99s-a-lot-to-learn-from-failure%E2%80%9D/6350/ 21 January 2011.
2. Kapur, Surinder, *Entrepreneur India*, 21 January 2011; http://entrepreneurindia.in/opinion/insights/%E2%80%9Cthere%E2%80%99s-a-lot-to-learn-from-failure%E2%80%9D/6350/
3. Arora, Shipra, 'Sona Leverages IT to Bring about Functional Efficiency', 2 June 2003; http://www.expresscomputeronline.com/20030602/ebiz1.shtml, accessed on 1 August 2012.
4. ASQ, http://asq.org/learn-about-quality/quality-assurance-quality-control/overview/overview.html
5. 'Sona Okegawa Precision Forgings to Buy Thyssenkrupp Tech', 21 January 2008. http://www.moneycontrol.com/news/business/sona-okegawa-precision-forgings-to-buy-thyssenkrupp-tech-322285.html
6. Kapur, Surinder, 1 Aug.com/money/2006/nov/21spec3.htm21spec3.; http://entrepreneurindia.in/opinion/insights/%E2%80%9Cthere%E2%80%99s-a-lot-to-learn-from-failure%E2%80%9D/6350/

Chapter 10

1. Noronha, Christabelle, 'Doctor Steelheart', tata.com, January 2000.
2. Tata Steel 100, Pioneers; http://www.tatasteel100.com/people/index.asp
3. Perry, Alex, 'How Ratan Tata Turned the Country's Oldest Conglomerate into a Global Force', *Time Asia Magazine*, 19 June 2006, accessed on 18 April 2012.
4. Roy, Subir, *Made in India: A Study of Emerging Competitiveness*, Tata McGraw-Hill, 2005.
5. Chacko, Philip, interview with H.M. Nerurkar, tata.steel.com, December 2009.

6. Annual Report 2006–07.
7. Meredith, Robyn, 'Tempest in a Teacup', Forbes.com, 1 October 2005; http://www.forbes.com/global/2005/0110/024_2.html, retrieved on 20 April 2012.
8. Koovapaddy, Ananth, 'Tata Steel PEPs It Up', tata.com, July 2001.
9. Annual Report 1993–94.
10. Koovappady, Ananth, 'Stepping into a Giant's Shoes', tata.com, July 2001.
11. Seshadri, D.V.R., IIM Bangalore, and Tripathy, Arabinda, IIM Ahmedabad, 'Reinventing Project Management at Tata Steel (A): Implementation of Cold Rolling Mill', 2004.
12. Noronha, Christabelle, 'Doctor Steelheart', tata.com, January 2000.
13. Steel Ministry Annual Report 2001–02.
14. Annual Report 1999–2000.
15. Koovappady, Ananth, 'Tata Steel PEPs It Up', tata.com, July 2001.
16. ASQ interview with Dr J.J. Irani, uploaded on 12 July 2011; http://www.youtube.com/watch?v=wZ7jZlgNEow
17. Seshadri, D.V.R., IIM Bangalore, and Tripathy, Arabinda, IIM Ahmedabad, 'Reinventing Tata Steel (B): The Company Embarks on Consolidation', 2003.
18. Sinha, Rabindra Nath, 'Tata Steel's "Rightsizing" may Continue', *Hindu BusinessLine*, 11 May 2002.
19. Roy, Subir, *Made in India*.
20. Muthuraman, B. et al., 'Understanding the Process of Transitioning to Customer Value Management', paper presented at ISBM (Institute for Study of Business Markets) at Harvard Business School, August 2004.
21. Interview with Dr Irani, tata.com, March 2001.
22. Meghani, Saloni, 'Take That', tata.com, September 2004.
23. Handwritten note by Dr Denys on material sent to the author.
24. Noronha, Christabelle and Saloni Meghani, 'Stealing the Show', tata.com, March 2004.
25. ASQ interview with Dr J.J. Irani, http://www.youtube.com/watch?v=wZ7jZlgNEow, uploaded 12 July 2011.
26. Meghani, Saloni, 'Take That'.
27. 'Tata Poised for 5 bn Corus Offer', BBC News, 9 October 2006; http://

news.bbc.co.uk/2/hi/business/6031509.stm, accessed on 27 April 2012.

28. 'Tatas Seek Big Play in S. Africa', *DNA*, 6 October 2006; http://www.dnaindia.com/money/report_tatas-seek-big-play-in-s-africa_1057165, accessed on 27 April 2012.
29. John, Satish, 'Can Tata Steel Handle Mother of All Buys?' *DNA*, 5 October 2006; http://www.dnaindia.com/money/report_can-tata-steel-handle-mother-of-all-buys_1056969, accessed on 27 April 2012.
30. 'Corus Confirms 4bn Tata Proposal', BBC News, 17 October 2006; http://news.bbc.co.uk/2/hi/business/6058746.stm, accessed on 27 April 2012.
31. David, Ruth, 'Tight-Lipped Tata Circles Corus', *Forbes*, 14 October 2006; http://www.forbes.com/2006/10/14/ratan-tata-corus-face-cx_rd_1013autofacescan04.html, accessed on 27 April 2012.
32. Carpenter, Claudia and Ravil Shirodkar, 'Tata Steel of India Offers 4 Billion Pounds for Corus (Update 3)', Bloomberg, 17 October 2006; http://www.bloomberg.com/apps/news?pid=newsarchive&sid=a6pDVBzoIDHU&refer=uk, accessed on 27 April 2012.
33. Giridhardas, Anand, 'India is Reveling in Being the Buyer', *New York Times*, 5 February 2007; http://www.nytimes.com/2007/02/06/business/worldbusiness/06rupee.html?_r=1, accessed on 30 April 2012.

ACKNOWLEDGEMENTS

This book has been made possible by the unstinting support and cooperation of each of the companies covered. I am very grateful to each of their leaders for participating in this project and for sharing their stories. I am also grateful to all those who coordinated from the companies. They provided inputs, guided on content and thoroughly went over the facts. I thank the following people for their patience and assistance: Usha Iyer from Godrej Industries; Anindya Banerjee at ICICI Bank; Nazeeb Arif, vice-president, Corporate Communications, ITC Ltd, and Nandini Basu, senior manager, Corporate Communications, ITC Ltd; Ajay Khanna and Sudhakar Safaya at Jubilant Life Sciences Ltd.; R.C. Bhargava for permitting me to take inputs from his book on Maruti and adding new insights; Gopal Rathi from RP-SG; Arti Luniya, Saurabh Pandey and Sanjay Sinha at SAIL; Atul Mittal and Anand Seth from Sona Koyo; and Rajiv Soni at Tata Steel. At CII, Gurpal Singh, Sarita Nagpal, Rajesh Menon and Marut Sen Gupta helped out in different ways. Above all, I thank Chandrajit Banerjee, director-general, CII, for accepting my proposal to explore the fascinating journey of these exemplary companies. It has been a voyage of discovery for me.

INDEX

acquisitions by, Godrej, 11, 13, 17
  Goenkas, 146, 147, 155, 159, 165
  ICICI, 35, 36
  Jubilee Bhartia Group, 92, 93
  SAIL, 172
  Sona, 201, 212–13
  Tatas, 217, 226, 236, 237–38, 240, 241
active pharmaceutical ingredient (API), 91–92
Ahluwalia, Dr Montek Singh, 97
Allison, Richard, 99
American Society for Quality (ASQ), 202, 228
Anand, Bharat, 12
Anand, Nakul, 74
Asian Development Bank (ADB), 29, 31, 153, 154
Asian financial crisis, 67, 87, 172, 174
ATMs, 37, 39, 40, 41, 42, 43, 50, 52, 55
Axis Bank, 30

Bank of Madura, 35, 36, 39
Bharat Gears, 193
Bhargava, R.C., 105, 107, 108, 109–10, 112, 113, 114, 115, 116, 121, 122
  The Maruti Story: How a Public Sector Company Put India on Wheels, 105
Bhartia, Hari S., 84, 85, 86, 88, 91, 100
Bhartia, Kavita, 85
Bhartia, Shobhana, 85
Bhartia, Shyam S., 84, 85, 86, 88, 89, 90, 91, 92, 95, 100
Birla, Ghanshyam Das, 85

CEDEP [European Centre for Executive Development], France, 221
Chugh, K.L., 61
corporate philanthropy, 242
Credit Rating Information Services of India Ltd (CRISIL), 27, 30
Custom Research and Manufacturing Services (CRAMS), 83

Denys, Mark, 235–36
Department of Company Affairs, 35

Deshmukh, Kiran, 206–07
Deveshwar, Yogesh Chander (Yogi), AGM speech of, 63–64, 65, 66
  established three-tier structure for management, 73–74
  Padma Bhushan, honoured with, 58
  philosophy of, 57, 59
  sustainability is a passion for, 77
Dhobale, P.V., 74
Doyle, Patrick, 99
Drug Discovery and Development Solutions (DDDS), 83
Dubash, Tanya, 3
Dutt, Yogeshwar, 187

Financial Information Network and Operations Ltd (FINO), 50
Foreign Exchange Regulation Act, 58, 60, 180
Foreign Investment Promotion Board, 35
Futaba, Mr, 195

Gambhir, Vivek, 7
Gandhi, Arun, 240
Gandhi, Indira, 104, 108
Gandhi, Mahatma, 7, 85, 107
Gandhi, Sanjay, 104
Global Depository Receipt (GDR), 33, 61, 148, 150, 154, 171
Godrej & Boyce companies, 2, 6, 7–8, 16, 22
Godrej Industries Ltd and Associate Companies (GILAC), 360-degree feedback, 4–5
  and 1991 economic liberalization, 14
  and CII, 14, 21
  CREATE, 20
  diversification of industries, 2, 3
  Economic Value Added, 5
  environmentally conscious, 20–22
  family members highly qualified, 10
  focus of, 3, 6–8
  international business interests, 13–14
  joint ventures with large multinationals, 15, 18
  legacy of, 1, 2
  new initiatives taken by, 10–13
  on social responsibility, 20
  overseas acquisitions of, 11, 13, 17
  restructuring of, 17–20
  Vision 2020, 5–6, 22–24
  zeroed in on four areas, 19
Godrej, Adi, agenda for Indian economy, 14
  early jobs of, 4
  invites feedback, 5
  on joint ventures, 18
  personality of, 3–5

Godrej, Ardeshir, 2, 7
Godrej, Jamshyd, 8, 14, 21
Godrej, Nadir, 23
Godrej, Navroze, 8, 10, 11
Godrej, Nisaba, 3, 10, 11
Godrej, Pirojsha, 9, 10, 11, 21
Goenka, Badridas, 146
Goenka, Hariram, 146
Goenka, Harsh Vardhan, 144, 146
Goenka, Keshav Prasad, 146
Goenka, Rama Prasad, 144, 146
Goenka, Ramdutt, 146
Goenka, Sanjiv, 144–50, 152–65
 advice to entrepreneurs, 165
 business philosophy of, 164
 leadership qualities, 164–65
Goenka, Shashwat, 165
Good Manufacturing Practices (GMP), 91
Grant, Kurush N., 74
Gupta, D.S., 105

Haksar, A.N., 60, 63
Harvard Business Review, 8
Harvard Business School, 10, 12, 233
Haryana, 118, 124, 213
Housing Development and Finance Corporation, 30
Hussain, Abid, 140

ICICI Bank, anywhere banking, 41, 42, 43
 approval of new banks, 29, 31
 bank nationalization (1969 & 1980), 28, 48
 computerization programme, 27, 30
 diversified financing activities, 27, 32–33, 38, 45
 factors contributing to bank's success, 55–56
 Four-Cs strategy, 53–54
 growth was driven by a strategy, 46
 inclusive rural banking strategy, 49
 Information technology distinguished, 40–41
 innovation in credit, 44
 interest rate deregulation, 28–29, 35, 36
 international best practices adopted by, 29, 40
 key challenges faced by the new bank, 32–33
 microfinance, 50
 new customer interface, 47–48
 openness to learning, 36–37
 overseas expansion, 37
 reverse merger by, 36
 second generation of reforms, 29
 slogan of, 39
 structuring of its operations, 35
 technology-intensive model, 39
 three-pronged strategy for growth, 37
ICICI Securities and Finance Co. Ltd, 30
India GDP deceleration, 34

Indian Institute of Management (IIM), 30, 105, 127
Indian Iron and Steel Company (IISCO), 179–81, 182
Industrial Credit and Investment Corporation of India Ltd (ICICI), 26
Industrial Development Bank of India (IDBI), 26, 178
Industrial Finance Corporation of India (IFCI), 26
Industrial Policy Resolution (IPR), 150, 166
Integrated Services Digital Network (ISDN), 42
Irani, Jamshed J., 215–16, 220, 224, 228, 229, 231, 232, 233, 234, 237
ITC Ltd, awards & recognitions to, 58, 72, 79, 80–81
  and British American Tobacco (BAT) Industries, history of, 59–62
  BAT tried to regain control of, 58
  board delineated core businesses for, 64, 66
  Bukhara cuisine, 61, 68, 76–77
  creates new drivers of growth, 59, 62
  diversification by, 57, 60, 61, 68, 73, 81
  e-choupal, initiative, 63, 68, 69, 70, 71, 72
    model has received international acclaim, 72
    Choupal Saagar, 72
    soya choupal, 70
  edible oils and financial services, 61, 62, 67
  FMCG (fast moving consumer goods), 62–63, 67, 68, 72, 73, 75, 77
    expansion strategy in, 62–63, 67, 68, 72, 73, 75, 77
  hotel sector, 75, 76, 77
    platters named after Clintons and Obama, 77
  information technology, 69, 71
  ITC Bhadrachalam Paperboards, 61
  ITC Classic Finance, 61, 62, 67
  leader in sustainable business practices, 63, 77
  paperboard business, 60–62, 64, 65, 73, 74, 78–79
  phase of rationalizing, restructuring and repositioning the company, 62
  state-of-the-art, cigarette plant, 65
    life sciences research centre, 81
  strategies identified, 59, 61, 63, 64–65, 67–68, 71, 72–73, 75
    hotel sector, 76
    marketing, 75
  trials and tribulations of, 57, 58

Triple Bottom Line approach of, 57, 59, 63, 81–82
water management by, 80
wind energy, 80

Jamshedpur, 216, 223, 226, 242
Jubilant Bhartia Foundation, 102
Jubilant Bhartia Group, 83, 84, 85, 87, 96, 100, 102
Abbreviated New Drug Applications (ANDAs), 83, 96
86, 92, 93
aligns itself with the MDG of UN, 102
approach to sustainability, 100, 101
awards & recognitions, 85–86, 90, 97, 100
company names changed, 88, 90, 95
corporate social responsibility (CSR), 96, 102
diversification and restructuring, 87, 88, 89, 95
joint ventures of, 93, 94
objective of, 89–90
restructured operations into three Strategic Business Units (SBUs), 89
set up special economic zone (SEZ), 96
sustainability a mission for, 100, 101
tie-ups, 85, 87, 98
Triple Bottom Line, 96, 101
Jubilant Biosys, 93
Jubilant First Trust Healthcare Ltd, 94
Jubilant FoodWorks, 84, 86, 97, 98, 100
Jubilant Industries Ltd, 95
Jubilant Kalpataru Hospital, 94
Jubilant Life Sciences, 83, 88, 93, 95, 96

Kamath, K.V., 29, 30, 32, 34, 36, 37, 39, 40, 41, 42, 45, 49, 52, 54, 55
Kapur, Surinder, 192–96, 197, 198, 204, 206, 211, 212, 214
Khanna, Ajay, 85
Khattar, Jagdish, 113
Kochhar, Chanda, 29, 31, 33, 36, 45–46, 51, 52, 53, 56
Krishnamurthy, Dr V., 105, 109, 116, 171, 194, 203
Kumar, Dr Krishan, 120, 206
Kumar, Ritu, 76
Kumar, Sushil, 186–87

Lehman Brothers, 51, 52
liberalization of 1991 and its impact on SMEs, 127, 129, 130, 135

Maruti Suzuki India Ltd (MSIL), 114, 121–24
AVANTHA Centre of Excellence for Competitiveness of SME, 121

created new ecosystem for the automotive industry, 121
delicensing of industry by GOI, 114
driving training facilities (IDTR) established by, 123
elements of ISO, 120
GOI from equal partnership with Suzuki Motor Corporation (SMC) to exit, 112–13
India, economic slowdown in, 109, 114–15
Japanese institutions provided help to, 120, 121
Maruti Udyog Ltd (MUL), 104–14, 118–21
MSIL, Association of Overseas Technical Scholarships, 115
MUL, found suitable partner in SMC, 106
new work culture developed at, 116, 125
shared learning programme for vendors, 120
state-of-art facility to design, develop and launch cars, 124
Suzuki Motor Corporation (SMC), 106–07, 109, 112, 113, 116, 124
team spirit developed, 117
workers' strike, 117–18
Micro, Small & Medium Enterprise (MSME), 139–40, 141–43
Micro, Small & Medium Enterprise Development (MSMED) Act, 139
Ministry of Iron and Steel, 166
Mittal, Atul, 212
Modi, Narendra, 96
Modigliani, Franco, 4
Mody, Russi, 217
Monopolies and Restrictive Trade Practices Act, 60
Moolgaokar, Sumant, 105
Mukherjee, Pranab, 86, 95
Mumbai, 1, 21, 76, 127, 146, 184, 193, 237, 240
Muthuraman, B., 216, 220, 221, 223, 224, 225, 227, 233, 236, 237, 245

Nakanishi, Shinzo, 113, 125, 126
Narasimham Committee, 29
National Board for MSME, 141
Nehru, Jawaharlal, 110, 144, 166, 167, 189
Nerurkar, H.M., 219
New York Stock Exchange, 34
NGO, 20, 22, 49, 242
Nivo Controls, 127, 131, 138
CII's supporting role, 135
dependent on imports, 128
import licences a hurdle until liberalization, 128
import of technology, 129
industrial licence had strict conditions, 129
invested in R&D set-up, 131
products redesigned, 132

Restrictions of Hazardous Substances (RoHS), 134
short-term Returns on Investment (ROI) not the target, 138
standards to be met for European and US markets, 133–34
Non-performing assets (NPAs), 28

Over the Counter Exchange of India (OTCEI), 27

Pande, Arvind, 173, 175–76, 178
POSCO, the Korean steel giant, 225
Prahalad, C.K., 63, 71
The Fortune at the Bottom of the Pyramid: Eradicating Poverty through Profits, 71
Public Sector Enterprises (PSEs), 30, 105, 107, 108, 110–12, 115, 116, 167–68, 169, 170–72, 173, 177–78, 180–81, 182–83, 184, 185, 186, 187, 190
and liberalization, 168, 169
Indian Telephone Industries Ltd, 167
Public Sector Iron & Steel Companies (Restructuring) and Miscellaneous Provisions Act, 167

Rafi, Mohammad, 161
Rahman, A.R., 161
Rao, P.V. Narasimha, 220
Reserve Bank of India (RBI), 26, 27, 29, 31, 32, 35, 41, 45, 47, 51, 53, 129, 146
RP–Sanjiv Goenka Group, 145, 146, 147, 155, 158, 159, 164, 165
collaborations with, 155, 159
debt-restructuring exercise, 153, 155
McKinsey as consultant, 145, 147, 164
new tariff system led to problems, 153
PCBL, 145, 146, 158, 159–60, 164
post-1991, companies were sold off, 148
power sector reforms, 151
Saregama brand, 145, 146, 160–61, 164
Spencer's Retail, 145, 146, 161–63, 164
takeovers, 146, 148
voluntary retirement scheme (VRS), 156

Sapru, J.N., 61
Securities and Exchange Board of India, 35
Seiko, Koyo, 194, 198
Shankar, Pandit Ravi, 161
Sharma, Dinesh, 206–07
Shinohara, A., 110
Shipping Credit and Investment Corporation of India (SCICI), 30, 35
Shrivastava, Nirmal Chandra, 167
Shroff, A.D., 26

Singh, Prime Minister Manmohan, 100, 180, 190
Singh, R.P., 224
Singh, Raunaq, 193
Sivakumar, S., 69, 70
Small and Medium Enterprises (SME) sector, 127, 131–39, 142
  and 1991 liberalization, 127, 129, 130, 135
  important for large industries, 138–39, 143
Small Enterprises, Expert Committee on, 140
Small Industries Development Bank of India (SIDBI), 141
Society for Worldwide Interbank Financial Telecommunication (SWIFT) system, 41
Sona Group, acquisitions, collaborations and joint ventures of, 197, 201, 212–13
  business development group set up to explore new markets, 199
  bought Sona BLW Prazisionsschmiede, 201
  consultancy firms hired, 199, 201
  corporate social responsibility (CSR), 213
  Enterprise Resource Planning (ERP) packages, 200–01
  help vendors to improve, 198, 200, 204
  in a crisis, 197
  Japanese devotion to quality assurance, 196–97, 202
  Japanese words denoted entire philosophies, 206
  lessons for aspiring entrepreneurs, 213–14
  name changed to Sona Koyo Steering Systems Ltd, 198
  Oracle e-business suite, 200
  quality systems of TQM and TPM, 199, 201, 212
  Sona Okegawa Precision Forging, 197, 212–13
  Sona values, 194
  steering system manufacturing faced a technology gap, 193
  Toyota Production System (TPS), 204–05
Steel Authority of India Ltd (SAIL), 172
  and liberalization, 168, 169–72, 174, 175, 187, 189
  challenges facing the steel industry, 188
  Corporate Responsibility for Environment Protection agenda, 188
  Creating a Responsive Organization through People (CROP), 186
  CSR activities, 187
  customer-centricity strategies, 183–84
  disinvestment process, 171
  factors for the poor performance of, 173–75
  financial and business

restructuring by, 176, 178, 181
Hay Group study, 185
Hindustan Steel Private Ltd (HSP), 166–67
instituted strategy 'Priorities for Action', 169
issuing Global Depository Receipts (GDRs), 171
Lakshya 2020, 190
largest operators of health and education facilities, 187
Maharatna status granted to, 186, 190
modernization and expansion process, 180, 185, 190
SAIL Steel Development Fund, 170, 174, 181
steps took to reconfigure itself, 176–77
sustainability with respect to the environment, 188
takes a long-term view, 175
Subbulakshmi, M.S., 161
Suzuki, Osamu, 107, 113

Tata, Dorabji, 217, 241
Tata, J.R.D., 215, 217
Tata, Jamsetji N., 210, 217, 218, 235, 241, 242
Tata, Ratan, 217, 220
Tata Iron and Steel Company (TISCO), 217, 226, 236, 237–38, 240, 241
Arthur D. Little as consultant, 220, 221
awards, 215, 229, 230, 236, 243
community based NGO, 242
corporate philanthropy, 242
Deming Grand Prize, 21, 245
difficult times for, 223–24
Domestic Management Programme, 233
Early Separation Scheme, 232
excellence through FACT, 229
first phase of, 229
followed Management by Objectives (MBO) framework, 222
ideas came from consultants, 221
innovations, 215, 227, 234–35
joint ventures, 226, 237, 241
management programme for executives, 222
Marketing and Customer Value Management (CVM), 233–34
modernization and capacity expansion phases, 218
modernization programme, 218, 219, 222, 223, 226
new strategy, 236
R&D and SS division, 235
restructuring process, 231, 233
set itself challenging targets, 235
steel production de-licensed, 219
Tata Code of Conduct, 227
training by Stern, Stewart and Co, 228

Vision 2007 statement, 227–28
Tata Steel Rural Development Society, 242
Technology Development and Information Company of India Ltd (TDICI), 30
Toshniwal, Praveen, 127, 138
Tsuda, Dr Yoshikazu, 120, 206, 208

Unit Trust of India (UTI), 30
US Food and Drugs Administration (USFDA), 83, 92

Vaghul, Narayanan, 26, 30, 31, 36, 52
Vam Organic Chemicals Ltd, 84, 86, 87, 88
venture capital, 30, 74, 141
Verma, C.S., 186, 188–89, 190
Very Small Aperture Terminals (VSAT), 41, 42
Vinyl acetate monomer (VAM), 85, 89

Wadhwa, Hitendra, 12

Y2K fears, 43